Paddling Montana

Help Us Keep This Guide Up to Date

Every effort has been made by the authors and editors to make this guide as accurate and useful as possible. However, many things can change after a guide is published—trails are rerouted, regulations change, techniques evolve, facilities come under new management, etc.

We welcome your comments concerning your experiences with this guide and how you feel it could be improved and kept up to date. While we may not be able to respond to all comments and suggestions, we'll take them to heart, and we'll also make certain to share them with the authors. Please send your comments and suggestions to the following address:

FalconGuides
Reader Response/Editorial Department
P.O. Box 480
Guilford, CT 06437

Or you may e-mail us at:

editorial@GlobePequot.com

Thanks for your input, and happy trails!

Outfit Your Mind
falcon.com

Paddling Montana

Second Edition

Hank and Carol Fischer
with updates by Kit Fischer

FALCONGUIDES ®

GUILFORD, CONNECTICUT
HELENA, MONTANA
AN IMPRINT OF THE GLOBE PEQUOT PRESS

FALCONGUIDES®

Falcon and FalconGuides are registered trademarks of Morris Book Publishing, LLC.
Text design by Nancy Freeborn
Maps © Morris Book Publishing, LLC
Photos by Hank and Carol Fischer, except where noted

Library of Congress Cataloging-in-Publication Data
Fischer, Hank.
    Paddling Montana / Hank and Carol Fischer. – 2nd ed.
        p. cm.
    Includes index.
ISBN-13: 978-0-7627-4352-0
 1. Canoes and Canoeing–Montana–Guidebooks. 2. Rafting (Sports)–Montana– Guidebooks. 3. Fishing–Montana–Guidebooks. 4. Rivers–Recreational use–Montana-Guidebooks. 5. Montana–Guidebooks. I.Fischer, Carol. II. Title.
    GV776. M9F57 2008
    797.12209786–dc22

Printed in the United States of America
10 9 8 7 6 5 4 3 2 1

To buy books in quantity for corporate use or incentives, call **(800) 962–0973** or e-mail **premiums@GlobePequot.com.**

This book is dedicated to all those people who not only enjoy Montana's rivers but also work to conserve them.

Contents

River Trips

◀ *The spectacular cliffs of the Dearborn River.*

Overview Map

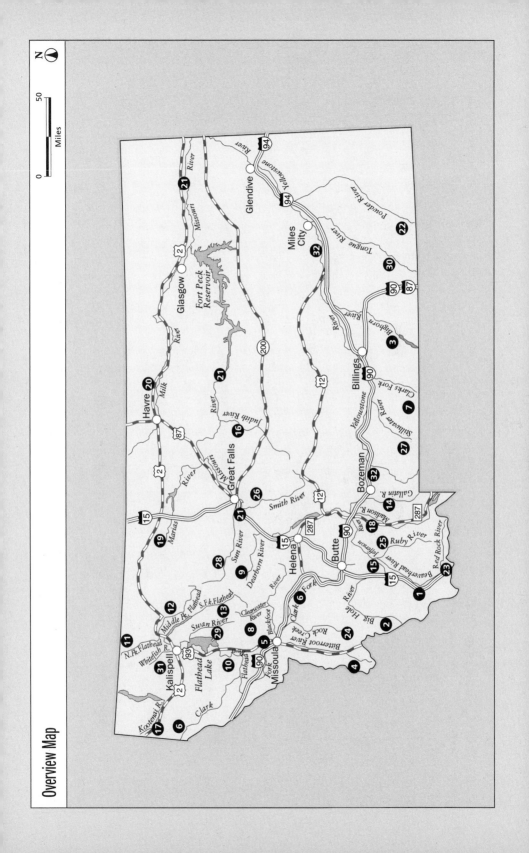

N

0   50

Miles

Lewis and Clark's Montana River Routes

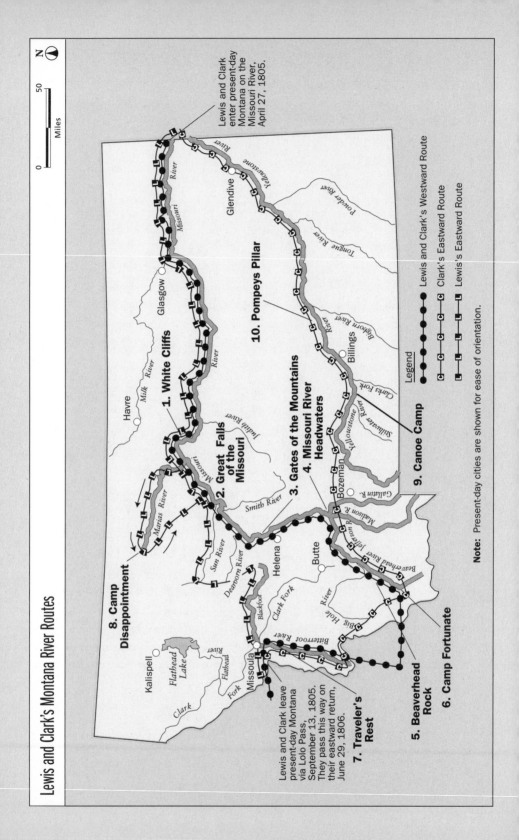

8. Camp Disappointment

1. White Cliffs

2. Great Falls of the Missouri

3. Gates of the Mountains

4. Missouri River Headwaters

10. Pompeys Pillar

9. Canoe Camp

5. Beaverhead Rock

6. Camp Fortunate

7. Traveler's Rest

Lewis and Clark enter present-day Montana on the Missouri River, April 27, 1805.

Lewis and Clark leave present-day Montana via Lolo Pass, September 13, 1805. They pass this way on their eastward return, June 29, 1806.

Havre

Glasgow

Kalispell

Flathead Lake

Missoula

Helena

Butte

Bozeman

Billings

Glendive

Missouri River

Milk River

Judith River

Smith River

Marias River

Sun River

Dearborn River

Blackfoot

Clark Fork

Bitterroot River

Flathead River

Flathead Fork

Clark

Big Hole River

Beaverhead River

Jefferson River

Madison R.

Gallatin R.

Stillwater River

Yellowstone River

Clarks Fork

Bighorn River

Yellowstone River

Tongue River

Powder River

Legend

C—C—C—C Lewis and Clark's Westward Route

C—C—C—C Clark's Eastward Route

L—L—L—L Lewis's Eastward Route

Note: Present-day cities are shown for ease of orientation.

N

0   50

Miles

Lewis and Clark: Paddling Montana, 1805–1806

These dates and events correspond to the labeled sites on the map on the preceding page. The map shows the routes Lewis and Clark followed on several Montana rivers on their way west and their eastward return.

1. White Cliffs, May 31, 1805—A spectacular 35-mile section of the Missouri River, described by Captain Lewis in a journal entry as resembling "a thousand grotesque figures."

2. Great Falls of the Missouri, June 21–July 15, 1805—Termed a "sublimely grand spectacle" by Lewis; it took the Corps of Discovery nearly a month to make the 18-mile portage.

3. Gates of the Mountains, July 18, 1805—Lewis said this place had the most remarkable cliffs the expedition had seen to that point. "These clifts rise from the waters edge on either side perpendicularly to the height of 1200 feet. Every object here wears a dark and gloomy aspect. The tow(er)ing and projecting rocks in many places seem ready to tumble on us." A boat tour excursion carries modern-day visitors to the site.

4. Missouri River Headwaters, July 27–29, 1805—Lewis described the place where the Jefferson, Madison, and, a short distance upstream, the Gallatin Rivers merge as "an essential point in the geography of the western world."

5. Beaverhead Rock, August 8, 1805—Sacagawea recognized this landmark, which resembles a swimming beaver, and knew her tribe, the Shoshones, would not be far away.

6. Camp Fortunate, August 17, 1805—Sacagawea found the Shoshones here, and they provided horses for the Corps' trip over the mountains.

7. Traveler's Rest, September 9–10, 1805; June 30–July 2, 1806—The Corps of Discovery rested here in preparation for what turned out to be their arduous passage over the mountains. On their return trip, the expedition camped here again and separated into two parties. Lewis headed for the Blackfoot River; Clark led his party down the Bitterroot River.

8. Camp Disappointment, July 22–25, 1806—The northernmost point reached by Lewis on an exploration of the Marias River; this is close to the spot where Lewis and his party had a hostile encounter with Blackfeet Indians. Two braves were killed.

9. Canoe Camp, July 19–23, 1806—Clark and his men built two canoes at this site for their return down the Yellowstone River.

10. Pompeys Pillar, July 25, 1806—Named for Sacagawea's son, this sandstone pillar holds the only physical evidence of Lewis and Clark's passage through Montana: Clark's name and the date carved into the rock.

Legend

Interstate Highway	(00)	Mileage Marker	26
U.S. Highway	(00)	Gate	
State or County Road	(00) (000)	Ranger Station	
Bureau of Indian Affairs (BIA) Road	(00)	City or Town	Craig ○ or Craig
Interstate Highway	⟹	Campground	△
Paved Road	⟹	Cabin or Building	■
Gravel/Unimproved Road	⟹	Railroad	┼┼┼┼┼┼┼┼┼┼┼
State Boundary		Indian Reservation Boundary	– – – – –
Wilderness Boundary	– – – – –	Mine Site	✕
Access Site	◢ Access here	Overlook/Point of Interest	◻
Dam	╱	National or State Forest/Park Boundary	
Diversion Dam	∿		
Lake, River/Creek, Rapids/Waterfall		Map Orientation	N
Tributary		Scale	0 0.5 1 Miles
Bridge			

Acknowledgments

We'd like to thank the following people from the USDA Forest Service, the Montana Department of Fish, Wildlife and Parks, the U.S. Geological Survey, the Bureau of Land Management, the Army Corps of Engineers, and others for their contribution of information and advice for this book:

Mike Backes, FWP, Miles City
Woody Baxter, FWP, Seeley Lake
Dave Blackburn, Kootenai Angler, Libby
Dave Briar, USGS, Helena
Buck Damone, BLM, Lewistown
Jim Darling, FWP, Billings
Mark Deleray, FWP, Kalispell
Wayne Fairchild, Lewis & Clark Trail Adventures, Missoula
Bruce Farling, Trout Unlimited, Missoula
Ken Frazer, FWP, Billings
Tom Greason, FWP, Bozeman
Doug Habermann, FWP, Great Falls
Dick Harlow, USFS, Libby
Matt Holtz, Absaroka River Adventures, Absarokee
Brian Hopkins, BLM, Dillon
Craig Lange, USFS, Hungry Horse
George Liknes, FWP, Great Falls
Jim and Dianne McDermand, Medicine River Canoe Club, Great Falls
Four Rivers Fishing Company, Twin Bridges
Fred Nelson, FWP, Bozeman
Dick Oswald, FWP, Dillon
Don Peterson, Portage Route Chapter, Great Falls
Tom Reilly, FWP, Helena
Marek Rosin, Adventure Whitewater, Red Lodge
Scott Rumsey, FWP, Kalispell
Angie Schmidt, FWP, Kalispell
Phil Stewart, FWP, Miles City
Ryan Trenka, Bozeman
Jim Vashro, FWP, Kalispell
Dick Wernham, ACE, Libby Dam
Mel White, USGS, Helena
Steve Woodruff, Missoula

Introduction

"If there is something magic on this planet, it is contained in water."
—Loren Eiseley

Montana's Rivers

Most people carry an "escape" dream, an idyllic plan for the time when life becomes too harried or complicated. For some the dream takes them on a long wilderness trek. Others hope to sail off to sea. For many the fantasy is simpler: Put a canoe, kayak, or raft in the nearest river, lie back, let the sun warm the body, trail a hand in the water, and drift away.

It's a dream that started with the excursions of early river explorers like Lewis and Clark and John Wesley Powell. It has been kept alive by writers like Mark Twain, Ernest Hemingway, and Bernard DeVoto; and now it is being relived by modern river runners.

Montana's rivers have a special kind of historical significance, as the waterways played a key role in the Treasure State's early development. In early times the rivers carried only Indians and intrepid explorers. Later they brought miners, cowboys, sodbusters, soldiers, and shopkeepers. Indian bullboats and French pirogues were gradually replaced by flatboats and even steamships. It was only with the coming of the railroads in the late 1800s that Montana's rivers faded in importance.

One reason the rivers were so important is that they are easily navigated. Despite the cold waters and rapid flow, most Montana rivers can be floated by people with only moderate river skills. Those who have seen Montana's towering mountains often find this hard to believe, as did Meriwether Lewis of the Lewis and Clark Expedition. He noted in his journal of 1805:

> "I can scarcely form an idea of a river running to great extent through such a rough mountainous country without having it's stream intersepted by some difficult and dangerous rappids or falls, we daily pass a great number of small rappids or riffles which descend one to or 3 feet in 150 yards but we are rarely incommoded with fixed or standing rocks and altho' strong rapid water are nevertheless quite practicable & by no means dangerous."

The majority of Montana's rivers lie in the mountainous western portion of the state, where they flow down broad valleys between mountain ranges. In arid eastern Montana, where only a few major rivers flow, the streams are generally broad and flat as they cut through open grassland and sagebrush country. While the sparkling

◄ *The lower Madison River boasts good fishing and exceptional wildlife viewing.*

western streams may be more spectacular, the eastern rivers have a quiet beauty and offer better opportunities for solitude.

On most Montana rivers, whitewater sections occur primarily in narrow canyons and last only a few miles. While much of the whitewater is extremely challenging, most runs can be covered in a day. Unlike some western states, Montana has few rivers suitable for extended whitewater trips.

Montana rivers have a distinctly different appeal. They offer a deep sense of history and adventure still easily felt. In many instances, floaters can follow the river routes of early explorers and, if diligent enough, can seek out the same campsites that were used long ago. The countryside surrounding some rivers has changed only slightly since the days of westward expansion; floaters may travel for a week and see only a few bridges and farmhouses.

As the rivers wind through secluded canyons, heavily timbered bottomlands, or isolated marshes, one can observe eagles, deer, bighorn sheep, osprey, bear, and waterfowl. More than anything else, wildlife sightings define Montana float trips. Watching an osprey catch a fish, floating past a great blue heron rookery, or seeing a deer with newborn fawns creates memories long remembered. Quiet floaters often won't disturb wildlife as they drift by, allowing excellent opportunities for observation and photography.

Outstanding trout fishing lures many people to Montana rivers. Fisheries biologists report that some streams contain more than a ton of trout for each mile of stream; other rivers hold a trout two pounds or larger for every 10 feet of streambank and a four-pounder or larger for every 20 feet. Montana has about 450 miles of blue-ribbon trout water, and most of it can be floated.

Canoes, kayaks, and rafts allow a quiet approach and can take anglers to secluded portions of rivers not often visited on foot. Float anglers often become addicted to this style of angling.

We write this book in hopes that everyone who experiences Montana's rivers will become addicted to them. Anyone who has floated a free river, relished its natural beauty, fished for its wild trout, or challenged its whitewater should become an advocate for its protection. Hopefully, getting to know Montana's sparkling streams will give people a personal stake in the rivers' future.

Zero Impact

If floaters are careful, rivers can be floated again and again without showing signs of us. Your attentiveness to caring for the river could prevent the need for permit systems that limit use. Floaters on overnight trips should be especially mindful of their activities. Here are a few suggestions.

Plan Ahead and Prepare

- Know and respect the regulations for the river you plan to visit.
- Prepare for extreme weather conditions and emergencies.

The rocks lying beneath these pillars on the Missouri River formed a geologic treasure, a sandstone arch, before vandals destroyed the work of eons on a sad day in 1997. PHOTO BY WAYNE FAIRCHILD

- Float in small groups to reduce social conflicts and impacts.

- Plan river trips that are compatible with the skill level of everyone in the group.

Camp on Durable Surfaces

- Durable surfaces include designated campsites, rock, gravel, and dry grasses.

- Concentrate use on existing campsites; avoid places where impacts are just beginning.

- Water-saturated soil and wet vegetation are particularly vulnerable to impact from recreational users.

Dispose of Waste Properly

- Littering degrades Montana's rivers. Police your campsite before leaving, and pack out all litter.

- Deposit solid human waste in a "cat hole" 6 to 8 inches deep at least 200 feet from water sources, campsites, and trails. Fill in and disguise the cat hole when finished.

- Strain and scatter dish washing and cooking water.

Leave What You Find

- Preserve the past: Examine but do not touch or remove archaeological, historical, or paleontological resources.

- Leave rocks and plants and other natural objects as your find them.

- Avoid introducing or transporting nonnative species.

- Do not build structures or furniture or dig trenches around campsites.

Minimize Campfire Impacts

- Campfires cause long-lasting impacts on our rivers. Consider using a portable stove for cooking and a lantern for light.

- If you must have a campfire, contain all fires in established rock fire rings, metal fire grates, or your own portable fire pan.

- Do not construct new rock fire rings—they blacken rocks, sterilize the soil, and leave lasting impacts.

- Collect down and dead firewood only that can be broken by hand, or pack in your own firewood.

- Keep fires small, and burn all wood down to white ash. Ensure that fires are completely extinguished before leaving.

Respect Wildlife

- Observe wildlife from a distance. Do not follow or intentionally approach them.

- Feeding wildlife is harmful to their health, alters natural behavior, and exposes them to predators and other dangers. It is also unsafe and unlawful.

- Protect wildlife and your food by securing rations and trash properly.

Floating and the Law

Montana has one of the West's most progressive stream access laws. This legislation was precipitated by lawsuits involving access disputes on the Beaverhead and Dearborn Rivers. In 1984 the Montana Supreme Court ruled the public has a right to recreational use of the state's waters up to the high-water mark.

In 1985 the Montana Legislature further defined stream access rules. The law provides that rivers and streams capable of recreational use may be used by the public, up to the high-water mark, regardless of streambed ownership. The law does require, however, that certain activities require landowner permission and that camping and other recreational activities must take place specific distances away from occupied dwellings.

The law defines "recreational use" as floating, fishing, hunting, swimming, and other water-related pleasure activities. It defines the ordinary high-water mark as the

Serenity and solitude can be found on the lower Flathead River.

line the water impresses on land by covering it for a sufficient time to cause different characteristics below the line, such as deprivation of the soil of substantially all its terrestrial vegetation and destruction of its value for agricultural vegetation.

The law divides the state's rivers and streams into two categories, Class I and Class II. These classes are not to be confused with the international system of rating rivers and streams according to difficulty and recommended skill level. That system is thoroughly explained in **How to Use This Guide.**

Class I streams are capable of recreational use and have been declared navigable or are capable of certain kinds of commercial activity, including commercial outfitting. All other Montana rivers are Class II. For the most part, the rivers discussed in this book are Class I streams, with the exception of the Clarks Fork of the Yellowstone, Clearwater, Judith, Milk, Powder, Red Rock, Ruby, Stillwater, and Whitefish. Review appendix D for further details on the classifications and the regulations regarding each.

Recreationists should also be aware of trespass law passed by the Montana Legislature in 1985. This law states that lands can be closed to the public either by verbal communication or by actual posting. Do not trespass on posted land. When in doubt, ask permission. A special brochure is available from Montana Fish, Wildlife and Parks that explains important provisions of the stream access law.

One aspect of stream access remains controversial. Private landowners on the

Be sure to match your safety equipment to the river you are floating.

Blackfoot and Ruby Rivers have challenged whether rights-of-way associated with county bridges constitute legal access to streams and rivers. The State of Montana has argued that they do, and floaters typically use county bridges without seeking permission. In fact, the Montana Department of Transportation has started to construct access for floaters on new and repaired bridges. Boaters should be vigilant to ensure this happens when bridge repairs take place on local streams of interest.

Have a Safe Trip

Although few people like to talk about it, floating in Montana can be dangerous. Not only are many streams powerful and fast, but they are also quite cold, even in summer. Hypothermia can be as serious a danger as drowning. With proper caution and appropriate clothing, however, these problems can be overcome.

Several persons die in Montana each year due to floating-related accidents. Statistics show that the overwhelming number of floating deaths occur in May and June, when rivers are running at three to four times their normal flow. Beginners should be extremely wary about taking trips during the high-water period or in cold weather. Know your limitations, and respect the rivers.

In addition, make sure you leave for every paddling trip with the proper equipment. The following checklist suggests the essentials and some optional items. You'll want to add items if you're planning an overnight or extended trip.

Paddling Checklist

Basics

- [ ] spare paddles
- [ ] life jacket (personal flotation device, PFD)
- [ ] ropes for bowline and for securing gear
- [ ] drinking water or water filter
- [ ] waterproof storage bags with extra dry clothes
- [ ] flotation bags (optional)
- [ ] maps in a watertight map case (or a Ziploc bag)
- [ ] repair kit for boats

Emergency Equipment

- [ ] knife
- [ ] whistle
- [ ] waterproof matches, lighter, fire starter
- [ ] multipurpose tool (Leatherman-type)
- [ ] throw bag (optional)
- [ ] duct tape
- [ ] extra rope

First-aid Kit

- [ ] first-aid book
- [ ] adhesive bandages
- [ ] butterfly closures
- [ ] sterile compresses
- [ ] gauze roll
- [ ] adhesive tape
- [ ] Ace bandage
- [ ] triangular bandage
- [ ] first-aid and burn ointment
- [ ] skin lotion
- [ ] Vaseline
- [ ] safety pins
- [ ] aspirin and pain pills
- [ ] tweezers
- [ ] needle
- [ ] moleskin and blister kit

Clothing

- [ ] shorts (fast drying)
- [ ] short-sleeve polypropylene shirt
- [ ] long-sleeve polypropylene shirt
- [ ] wind parka
- [ ] rain parka and pants
- [ ] baseball cap
- [ ] waterproof sandals and/or aqua socks

Miscellaneous

- [ ] sunglasses with strap
- [ ] water bottles
- [ ] sunblock
- [ ] lip balm/block
- [ ] insect repellent
- [ ] fishing license
- [ ] food and beverages
- [ ] trash bag
- [ ] camera
- [ ] binoculars

How to Use This Guide

This book's intent isn't to provide a mile-by-mile guide to Montana's rivers. To the contrary, our purpose is to tell the minimum amount necessary for a safe, enjoyable trip. Knowing everything in advance is like having someone tell you how a movie ends. Discovery and exploration are essential components of any river trip.

Additionally, this book only includes what we regard as the major Montana rivers for floating. Other small streams in the state have boating potential, although usually only for short stretches or during high-water periods.

Every river trip begins with a brief summary of the river and its unique features. Basic information for each river can then be found in the at-a-glance section. The information includes several headings.

Vital statistics: The total length of the river, where it begins, and where it ends.

Level of difficulty: The difficulty of the river according to the international system of river rating described on pages 9 and 10.

Flow: Provides average annual flow in cubic feet per second (cfs), explains whether the river is generally floatable year-round, estimates the minimum flow for floating (below which continual hauling over shallow spots is required), and the maximum flow for safety (the flow over which only experts should be on the river). (**Caution:** The maximum and minimum flows can vary significantly based on your craft and skill level.)

Hazards: The specific hazards for each river. Pay special attention to these.

Where the crowd goes: The most popular stretch on each river.

Avoiding the scene: The most isolated spots on each river.

Inside tip: Special information gleaned from our experience.

Maps: A listing of maps that are more detailed than the ones in this book. The book's maps are only meant to provide a general idea of the course of the rivers, the most challenging rapids, dams or other hazards, and the points of access that can help you plan a trip. These maps are not intended to be used as navigational tools. Please refer to **About the Maps** to learn where you can get more detailed maps to help you navigate these rivers.

River rules: Regulations to be followed while traveling on the river. Most are enforced by Montana Fish, Wildlife and Parks (FWP) or, for rivers that flow through Indian reservations, tribal law enforcement organizations.

For more information: Lists the names of agencies or offices that can provide additional help to readers planning a river trip. Addresses, phone numbers, and Internet addresses for these organizations can be found in appendix A.

The paddling: A narrative description of the river.

We use the international scale of river difficulty (which rates rivers on a I to VI scale) in the **vital statistics** and in some of the whitewater descriptions. In the general text, however, we use three grades of ability level to help readers determine if the river is suitable for their skills: beginner, intermediate, or expert.

It's wise to check flow conditions before starting out on any river trip.

This approach has limitations. First, it doesn't account for drastic changes in river conditions caused by spring runoff. Cold water, heavy current, and potential river debris characterize peak stream flows. During May and June, beginners and even intermediates should be extremely cautious about taking river trips and should pay close attention to flow levels. Probably nine out of ten river deaths occur at this time of year. Second, beginning rafters can negotiate some rivers that beginning canoeists cannot, simply because of the inherent stability and buoyancy of good inflatable crafts. On the other hand, rafters might want to avoid some of the small, winding streams where canoeists do fine. We try to suggest what style of boat works best for each river, but it's often personal choice.

Here's how we rate the different levels of paddling skill:

Beginner—Knows the basic strokes (for canoeists: front paddle, back paddle, draw stroke, and pry stroke) and can handle the craft competently in smooth water. Knows how to bring the boat to shore safely in fast current, can negotiate sharp turns in fast current, can avoid logjams, and understands the difficulty of the stream he or she intends to float. A beginner is not a person who is picking up a paddle for the first time. Novices should get some practice on a lake or with an experienced floater before taking the first trip alone.

Intermediate—Knows basic strokes and uses them effectively. Can read water well and can negotiate fairly difficult rapids with confidence (knows how to safely catch an eddy). Won't panic and knows what to do in the event of an upset. For canoeists, knows how to coordinate strokes between bow and stern and can paddle at either end. Can come to shore quickly to inspect dangerous spots, and knows when to portage.

Expert—Has mastered all strokes and uses them instinctively. Confident of own ability even in very difficult situations. Skillful in heavy water or complex rapids. Knows when a rapid is unrunnable and has a deep respect for all safety precautions. Doesn't need to read guidebooks but does anyway.

Remember, this guide only contains the minimum information needed for a safe trip. Rivers are living, dynamic systems that change constantly. A channel free of barriers one year may contain a dangerous logjam the next, or there may be a diversion dam or a new barbed-wire fence. Thoroughly check out the stretch of river you plan to float *before* launching your craft.

Carefully check water conditions before starting any trip. U.S. Geological Survey (USGS), Montana Fish, Wildlife and Parks, and USDA Forest Service offices are usually good sources of information. Sporting goods stores can often provide information as well.

While the river adventurer won't face the perils of Odysseus—Sirens, Cyclops, or giant whirlpools—floaters should be aware of the hazards that await them. These include diversion dams; fallen trees; and logs, weirs, and fast water studded with rocks. Know in advance how to deal with each hazard, and know what to do in the event of an upset. Consult a kayaking and canoeing manual for recommended rescue techniques, and practice them in a safe setting—perhaps a pool or pond where the water is warmer and slower than what you'll find on many Montana streams.

INTERNATIONAL SCALE OF RIVER DIFFICULTY

This is the American version of a rating system used to compare river difficulty throughout the world. This system is not exact; rivers do not always fit easily into one category, and regional or individual interpretations may cause misunderstanding. It is no substitute for a guidebook or accurate firsthand descriptions of a run.

Paddlers attempting difficult runs in an unfamiliar area should act cautiously until they get a feel for the way the scale is interpreted locally. River difficulty may change each year due to fluctuations in water level, downed trees, recent floods, geological disturbances, or bad weather. Stay alert for unexpected problems!

As river difficulty increases, the danger to swimming paddlers becomes more severe. As rapids become longer and more continuous, the challenge increases. There is a difference between running an occasional Class IV rapid and dealing with an entire river of this category. Allow an extra margin of safety between skills and river ratings when the water is cold or if the river itself is remote and inaccessible.

The six difficulty classes:

Class I: Easy. Fast-moving water with riffles and small waves. Few obstructions, all obvious and easily missed with little training. Risk to swimmers is slight; self-rescue is easy.

Class II: Novice. Straightforward rapids with wide, clear channels that are evident without scouting. Occasional maneuvering may be required, but rocks and medium-size waves are easily missed by trained paddlers. Swimmers are seldom injured, and group assistance, while helpful, is seldom needed. Rapids that are at the upper end of this difficulty range are designated "Class II+."

Class III: Intermediate. Rapids with moderate, irregular waves that may be difficult to avoid and that can swamp an open canoe. Complex maneuvers in fast current and good boat control in tight passages or around ledges are often required; large waves or strainers may be present but are easily avoided. Strong eddies and powerful current effects can be found, particularly on large-volume rivers. Scouting is advisable for inexperienced parties. Injuries while swimming are rare; self-rescue is usually easy, but group assistance may be required to avoid long swims. Rapids that are at the lower or upper end of this difficulty range are designated "Class III-" or "Class III+," respectively.

Class IV: Advanced. Intense, powerful but predictable rapids requiring precise boat handling in turbulent water. Depending on the character of the river, it may feature large, unavoidable waves and holes or constricted passages demanding fast maneuvers under pressure. A fast, reliable eddy turn may be needed to initiate maneuvers, scout rapids, or rest. Rapids may require "must" moves above dangerous hazards. Scouting is necessary the first time down. Risk of injury to swimmers is moderate to high, and water conditions may make self-rescue difficult. Group assistance for rescue is often essential but requires practiced skills. A strong Eskimo roll is highly recommended. Rapids that are at the lower or upper end of this difficulty range are designated "Class IV-" or "Class IV+," respectively.

Class V: Expert. Extremely long, obstructed, or very violent rapids that expose a paddler to above-average danger. Drops may contain large, unavoidable waves and holes or steep, congested chutes with complex, demanding routes. Rapids may continue for long distances between pools, demanding a high level of fitness. What eddies exist may be small, turbulent, or difficult to reach. At the high end of the scale, several of these factors may be combined. Scouting is recommended but difficult. Swims are dangerous, and rescue is difficult even for experts. A very reliable Eskimo roll, proper equipment, extensive experience, and practiced rescue skills are essential. Because of the large range of difficulty that exists beyond Class IV, Class V is an open-ended, multiple-level scale designated by Class 5.0, 5.1, 5.2, etc. Each of these levels is an order of magnitude more difficult than the last. Example: Increasing difficulty from Class 5.0 to Class 5.1 is a similar order of magnitude as increasing from Class IV to Class V.

Class VI: Extreme and Exploratory. These runs have almost never been attempted and often exemplify the extremes of difficulty, unpredictability, and danger. The consequences of errors are very severe, and rescue may be impossible. For teams of experts only, at favorable water levels, after close personal inspection, and taking all precautions. After a Class VI rapid has been run many times, its rating may be changed to an appropriate Class 5.x rating.

Reprinted by permission of the American Whitewater Affiliation

About the Maps

The maps that accompany the text provide a general picture of the location of access points. We suggest you use them in combination with our charts of access points to plan trips. Under the **Maps** heading, which precedes each narrative, we suggest the best maps to use if you want detail and the ability to chart mile-by-mile progress. In appendix A we've included contact addresses and phone numbers for acquiring these maps.

When using the maps in this guide, pay careful attention to the scales, as they vary considerably. A map of an 80-mile river gives more detail than one of a 200-mile river.

We've included most bridges and all official public access points on the maps. A triangle marks all public access points—Forest Service; Bureau of Land Management; Montana Fish, Wildlife and Parks; county; and municipality.

Some county bridges that are poor accesses have not been included. Some access points where roads run next to the river or where old roads and trails lead to the river also haven't been included. Many of these "local" access points are privately owned, so ask permission before launching. Again, consult the appendix A for maps that show all roads and land ownership.

Finding Detailed Maps

There are five basic sources for floaters who want detailed maps of rivers and the surrounding lands: the Montana Afloat series; Bureau of Land Management (BLM); USDA Forest Service (USFS); Montana Fish, Wildlife and Parks (FWP); and U.S. Geological Survey (USGS). While the USGS provides the most detailed maps, you could go broke buying all the maps for a long river trip. The standard BLM and USFS maps have an advantage over USGS maps because of their smaller scale and their well-defined land ownership patterns, roads, trails, and access points. The most useful maps for strictly river floating are the privately produced Montana Afloat maps that show access points, river miles, bridges, and interesting historical information. You will find the maps you need for a particular river under the **Maps** heading at the beginning of each river description.

The Montana Afloat series covers sixteen rivers with large foldout maps. Although these maps don't necessarily include the entire river, they do include the sections most often floated, with excellent information on history, topography, and fishing. The maps clearly show access points, bridges, roads, and river hazards. The rivers included in this series are the Beaverhead, Big Hole, Bighorn, Bitterroot, Blackfoot, Clark Fork, Gallatin, Jefferson, Madison, Middle Fork of the Flathead, Missouri, North Fork of the Flathead, Rock Creek, Smith, and Yellowstone Rivers. Maps are available at most outdoor stores; from Montana Fish, Wildlife and Parks; and from FalconGuides.

The BLM's "1:100,000 series" maps can also be quite useful. These 128 maps cover most of Montana and are especially functional because they block up to one another. They currently cost $4 each and are available at most BLM offices or by writing to the BLM state office at the address listed in appendix C. The scale is 1 centimeter to 1 kilometer (about 0.5 inch per mile), and the maps show roads, trails, streams, rivers, lakes, and recreation sites.

The excellent BLM Recreation Access Guide (RAG) map (1:100,000) is printed on heavy, water-resistant paper and contains information about recreational opportunities. It differentiates between public and private roads and shows topographic features. Unfortunately only one map in this series covers Montana rivers. RAG 36 partially covers the Yellowstone and Clarks Fork of the Yellowstone.

The Forest Service's Forest Visitors Series maps each cover one national forest or a part of a national forest (some large forests have more than one map) and have essentially the same features as BLM maps. These maps cost $6 apiece and are available at most Forest Service offices or by writing to the USDA Forest Service in Missoula (see address in appendix C). Make your check for the amount of purchase only; it's not necessary to include postage. The Forest Service has maps of wilderness areas available for $6 as well. The Forest Service maps are on a scale of 0.5 inch per mile. The only bad part about these maps is that the forests don't block up to one another, which can result in annoying gaps in coverage.

Montana Fish, Wildlife and Parks publishes a free Montana Recreation Map that shows all state fishing access sites (usually good launch sites), recreation areas, and state parks. Pick one up at any regional office or write to Montana Fish, Wildlife and Parks at the address listed in appendix C. Throughout this book, and especially on our maps, we have used the abbreviation "FAS" to indicate fishing access sites.

For those who want more detail than the Forest Service or BLM maps provide, or for those sections of rivers that just can't be found elsewhere, USGS topographic maps (7.5-minute series) are the best bet. An index for these maps is printed on FS maps. You can send your request and $12.95 for each map, plus $5 for shipping, to the U.S. Geological Survey at the address listed in appendix C. The scale of these maps is 1:24,000, so they can be a bit bulky if you're planning a long trip—it may take four or five maps to cover a 30-mile section of river. Be prepared to cut and paste. Such maps are usually available locally from drafting or blueprint offices or from sporting goods stores. USGS also has a 1 x 2 degree series (1:250,000). Twenty-five of these maps cover all of Montana, but you obviously lose a lot of detail. These are the maps we have listed under USGS for each river. In between these two series is the 3 x 60 series (1:100,000), similar to the BLM series.

Perhaps the best tool for researching floating trips can be found online through Montana's Natural Resource Information System (NRIS). This online database provides up-to-date GIS mapping of land ownership and watersheds statewide. The NRIS Web site is http://nris.state.mt.us/. Interactive USGS topographical maps can also be bought on CD at most sporting good and bookstores.

For Lewis and Clark buffs, an excellent map is available that shows the route and campsites of the explorers in Montana. To purchase this map, write or e-mail the Portage Route Chapter of the Lewis & Clark Trail Heritage Foundation, Inc., at the address listed in appendix C. There are also excellent pullout maps of Lewis and Clark campsites along the Beaverhead, Jefferson, and upper Missouri Rivers in the book *Lewis and Clark in the Three Rivers Valley* (see appendix C).

River Trips

Paddlers take a swimming break on the South Fork of the Flathead.

1 Beaverhead River

Sinuous and serpentine with a jungle of vegetation, the Beaverhead meanders through rock canyons and broad valleys. High interest for Lewis and Clark aficionados.

Vital statistics: 80 miles long from Clark Canyon Dam to the Jefferson River.

Level of difficulty: Almost all Class I water. Suitable for intermediates south of Dillon, practiced beginners north of town.

Flow: Annual mean flow: 408 cfs near Twin Bridges. Above Barrett's Dam flows usually adequate all year. Below Barrett's (especially north of Dillon) may be too low in dry years. Flows of 75 cfs are a bare minimum, with flows above 300 cfs being optimum.

Hazards: Bends, narrow channels, and swift current in the upper 20 miles. Numerous irrigation jetties, diversions, low bridges, fences, and logjams. Low bridge (Hildreth Bridge) about 2 miles below High Bridge. Three diversion dams require caution: Barrett's, Dillon Diversion Dam, and a diversion dam 1 mile below Twin Bridges.

Where the crowd goes: High Bridge to Henneberry.

Avoiding the scene: Downstream from Dillon.

Inside tip: Excellent bird-watching or waterfowl hunting in season north of Dillon.

Maps: BLM: #33 (Butte South), #34 (Dillon) USFS: Beaverhead Interagency Travel Plan (East and West)
USGS: Dillon, MT
Montana Afloat: #7, The Beaverhead River

River rules: Complex fishing and floating regulations are in place to alleviate crowding and overfishing. Check with Montana Fish, Wildlife and Parks for current regulations.

For more information: Frontier Anglers, Dillon; Four Rivers Fishing Company, Twin Bridges; Montana Fish, Wildlife and Parks, Bozeman.

The Paddling

The Beaverhead River flows for only 43 air miles, but if the Army Corps of Engineers ever decided to straighten it (and we're certainly not recommending it), the Beaverhead probably would stretch halfway across Montana. Sinuous and serpentine, from the air it looks like a swimming snake. The Beaverhead today is much the same as Meriwether Lewis described it in 1805: "from 35 to 40 yards wide very crooked many short bends constituting large and general bends; insomuch that altho' we travel briskly and a considerable distance yet it takes us only a few miles on our general course or rout." Expect to travel about 3 river miles for every air mile.

Not only does the Beaverhead meander a great deal, it also supports a jungle of vegetation along its banks. The combination of deeply undercut banks and thick brush provides the habitat that makes the Beaverhead one of the very best trout streams in the country. Biologists estimate that some sections of the river contain more than 400 two- to four-pound trout per mile and another 100 over five pounds.

The sinuous Beaverhead offers great fishing and wildlife viewing. ▶

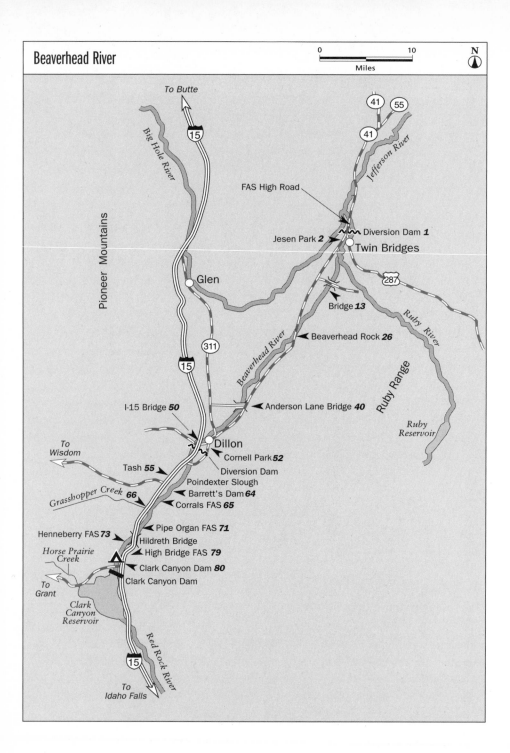

Beaverhead River

0   10
Miles

N

To Butte

15

41 55

41

Jefferson River

Big Hole River

Pioneer Mountains

FAS High Road

Jesen Park **2**

Diversion Dam **1**

Twin Bridges

Glen

287

Bridge **13**

Beaverhead Rock **26**

Ruby River

Beaverhead River

311

15

Ruby Range

Anderson Lane Bridge **40**

I-15 Bridge **50**

Ruby Reservoir

To Wisdom

Dillon

Cornell Park **52**

Tash **55**

Diversion Dam

Poindexter Slough

Grasshopper Creek **66**

Barrett's Dam **64**

Corrals FAS **65**

Pipe Organ FAS **71**

Henneberry FAS **73**

Hildreth Bridge

Horse Prairie Creek

High Bridge FAS **79**

Clark Canyon Dam **80**

To Grant

Clark Canyon Dam

Clark Canyon Reservoir

Red Rock River

15

To Idaho Falls

Key Access Points along the Beaverhead River

Access Point (River Mile)	Next Access Point	Access Point (River Mile)	Next Access Point
Clark Canyon Dam (80)	1 mile	Tash (55)	3 miles
High Bridge FAS (79)	6 miles	Cornell Park (52)	12 miles
Henneberry FAS (73)	2 miles	Anderson Lane Bridge (40)	14 miles
Pipe Organ FAS (71)	5 miles	Beaverhead Rock (26)	13 miles
Grasshopper FAS (66)	1 mile	Bridge (13)	11 miles
Corrals FAS (65)	1 mile	Jesen Park (2)	none
Barrett's Dam (64)	9 miles		

The Beaverhead originates at the confluence of the Red Rock River and Horse Prairie Creek, at the present site of Clark Canyon Dam (about 20 miles south of Dillon). The upper section of the river flows through a highly scenic but arid canyon edged by house-size boulders and surrounded by hills carpeted with sagebrush. By the time the river reaches Dillon, the valley opens up and the Pioneer and Ruby ranges provide a scenic backdrop.

Floaters north of Dillon can orient themselves the same way that Lewis and Clark did—by looking for Beaverhead Rock. This notable landmark, located just upstream from the Highway 41 bridge, juts about 150 feet above the river. It's the place where Sacagawea first recognized her homeland while guiding Lewis and Clark through the Rockies. Viewed from many angles in the large valley—particularly from near Sheridan—the rock resembles a swimming beaver. The land around Beaverhead Rock is publicly owned, so feel free to explore.

Beaverhead floaters shouldn't expect to find crystal-clear water. Often it's downright murky, due to a combination of irrigation returns, heavy livestock grazing, and natural siltation. Nevertheless, the river's rich load of nutrients produces the insects that make trout fat and trout anglers happy.

Clark Canyon Dam regulates the flow of the Beaverhead, and it can create unusual water conditions. Early in the floating season (May, June, and July), flows can be moderate, particularly in dry years. When most rivers are blown out with spring runoff, the Beaverhead may have excellent floating conditions. But then during the fall, when floating conditions are normally ideal on most Montana rivers, the Beaverhead may have high flows if it has been a wet year and water is being released from the reservoir. Heavy irrigation demands can result in extremely low flows in dry years, and floating may not be possible north of Dillon. It's always smart to call a local source or to check water levels on the Internet. (Check the USGS Web site for flows near Twin Bridges and the Bureau of Reclamation Web site for Clark Canyon Dam releases.)

The upper section of the Beaverhead offers the easiest access and the best fishing. Predictably, it receives the heaviest floating pressure, including many outfitters. In summer it isn't a place for solitude.

If fishing is secondary, however, the river between Dillon and Twin Bridges may be more to your liking, since it receives much less floating pressure. Access is limited but adequate. This is an excellent stretch for wildlife viewing. Expect to see white-tailed deer, great blue herons, beaver, and waterfowl. Sandhill cranes are very common here, particularly at migration times. In spring these ungainly birds perform their unique courtship rituals in open meadows. Tundra swans can be another Beaverhead migratory treat, and great horned owls like the willow bottoms.

Floaters can camp near the actual campsites, numbering more than a dozen, that Lewis and Clark used on the Beaverhead. It's fun to read the journals and then try to locate the precise campsites. One historic spot you can try to find is a place Lewis and Clark named Three Thousand Mile Island. Located a few miles downstream from Anderson Bridge, it's the place where the Corps of Discovery estimated they were exactly 3,000 miles from the mouth of the Missouri River.

Floaters on the Beaverhead south of Dillon must be able to negotiate sharp turns and maneuver down narrow channels, particularly above Pipe Organ Rock. The current is quite swift in the upper 20 miles of the river and frequently runs right into the brushy banks. This isn't a place for beginners in a raft or canoe.

Intermediate rafters and canoeists shouldn't have any trouble with the upper 20 miles of the river. Canoeists must be sure not to overload their boats on winding rivers like the Beaverhead. Three people in a canoe or too much gear can result in lost maneuverability, which translates into dangerous situations and possible upsets.

Floating gets easier north of Dillon. The river still meanders repeatedly, but the current isn't as swift. When the water is low, beginners can handle this part of the Beaverhead all the way to Twin Bridges. At low water, keep your eyes peeled for occasional barbed wire across the stream, as well as the occasional diversion dam. At higher flows, watch for low bridges.

Float fishing is extremely popular on the Beaverhead, as the deep runs and brushy banks make wading difficult. According to biologists, some sections of the Beaverhead support a trout weighing four pounds or better for every 20 feet of bank. But before you rush off to strap your boat on your car, read a little more. The Beaverhead offers some of the most frustrating and expensive fishing imaginable. The roots and bushes that extend into the water act like a safety screen for the fish and like a magnet for flies and lures. Anyone with plans to fish the Beaverhead should have a full tackle box, a fat wallet, and a cheerful disposition.

The tackle box should contain a few Girdle Bugs, one of the most successful creations for catching canny Beaverhead trout. Developed by a Dillon angler particularly for the Beaverhead, this strange fly looks like it might be more at home on a lazy, Southern bass pond. Consisting of a black or brown chenille body with trembling rubber legs, it reputedly was originally tied with the materials from a woman's girdle. While some purists view this bundle of fuzz and rubber with disdain, it does resemble the crane fly, a long-legged insect that hatches on the Beaverhead in late summer. Knowledgeable locals tie this fly onto stout leaders and cast into the bushes with impunity. While there are enough fake flies on the bushes to confuse the real insects, they do catch trout.

2 Big Hole River

Amber waters flowing over cobbled bottoms and through scenic valleys create one of Montana's most famous fishing rivers.

Vital statistics: 156 miles long from Skinner Lake near Jackson (Montana) to the Jefferson River.

Level of difficulty: Mostly Class I water except for the canyon between Wise River and Divide, which is Class II and even Class III at high flows. Swift flows, numerous snags, and obstructions make this river too difficult for beginners except between Wisdom and Wise River.

Flow: Annual mean flow: 1,121 cfs near Melrose. Upper sections may be unfloatable in August and early September in dry years. Flows of 75 cfs are minimum on the upper river. The lower sections below Melrose are floatable down to 300 cfs. Stay away if flows exceed 8,000 cfs.

Hazards: Fences, sharp bends, and overhanging branches in the upper river. Logjams and numerous channels in the last 25 miles of the lower river. Dangerous diversions at Divide and Pennington.

Where the crowd goes: Divide to Melrose.
Avoiding the scene: Glen to the Big Hole's confluence with the Beaverhead.
Inside tip: Try fishing in late March or April—before runoff—to avoid crowds. Try birding from a raft or canoe between Wisdom and Wise River during spring migration.
Maps: BLM: #23 (Wisdom), #24 (Salmon), #33 (Butte South), #34 (Dillon)
USFS: Beaverhead Interagency Travel Plan (East and West)
USGS: Dillon, MT
Montana Afloat: #8 (Big Hole River)
River rules: No motors allowed. Complex fishing and floating regulations. Check with Montana Fish, Wildlife and Parks for current regulations.
For more information: Montana Fish, Wildlife and Parks, Bozeman; Four Rivers Fishing Company, Twin Bridges; The Montana Fly Company, Melrose; Big Hole River Outfitters, Wise River.

The Paddling

When Oliver Wendell Holmes said, "A river is more than an amenity, it is a treasure," he could have been speaking about Montana's highly popular and nationally famous Big Hole River. The Big Hole's amber waters and picturesque scenery are dear to everyone who has floated or fished this river.

The Big Hole received its name from early trappers, who called all valleys "holes." Since this one was substantial, it earned the name Big Hole. The valley has had many other names. The Shoshone Indians called it Ground Squirrel Valley. Lewis and Clark labeled it Hot Springs Valley, due to nearby thermal features. More recently, travel brochures have dubbed the Big Hole "the Valley of 10,000 Haystacks," as this is one of the biggest hay-producing areas in the nation. Some ranchers still use the picturesque wooden "beaver slides" to stack hay.

Big Hole River

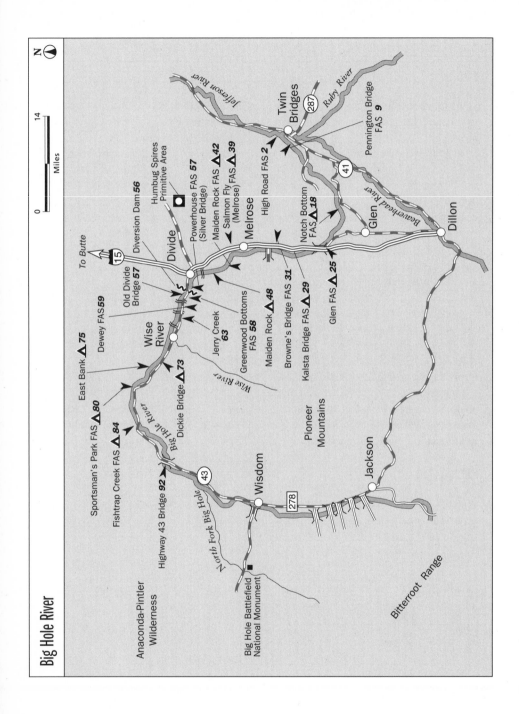

Key Points along the Big Hole River

Access Point (River Mile)	Next Access Point	Access Point (River Mile)	Next Access Point
Highway 43 bridge (92)	8 miles	Maiden Rock (48)	6 miles
Fishtrap Creek FAS (84)	4 miles	Maiden Rock FAS (42)	3 miles
Sportsman's Park FAS (80)	5 miles	Salmon Fly FAS (39)	8 miles
East Bank (75)	2 miles	Browne's Bridge FAS (31)	2 miles
Dickie Bridge (73)	10 miles	Kalsta Bridge FAS (29)	4 miles
Jerry Creek (63)	4 miles	Glen FAS (25)	7 miles
Dewey FAS (59)	1 mile	Notch Bottom FAS (18)	9 miles
Greenwood Bottoms FAS (58)	1 mile	Pennington Bridge FAS (9)	7 miles
Old Divide Bridge (57)	1 mile	High Road FAS (2)	none
Powerhouse FAS (57)	9 miles		

Few Montana rivers have as many enthusiastic devotees as the Big Hole. This delightful river has a cult of followers that make Reverend Moon's disciples look downright apathetic. George Grant, lifelong Butte resident and ardent conservationist, was the undesignated leader of this contingent. He fished the river from the 1920s until his one-hundredth birthday in 2006. A dedicated river rat, Grant allegedly spent more time on the Big Hole than any other person. Grant once wrote, "In the nine great trout states of the western United States, it would be difficult to find a single stream that exceeds the overall quality of the Big Hole River. It must be classified as a big river, but it is certainly not as large or impersonal as the Yellowstone or Missouri, nor as barren-banked and monotonous as the famous Madison. The Big Hole rises at high altitude and flows clear and cold through wide valleys and narrow canyons, seldom presenting similar water or scenery throughout its entire 150 fascinating miles."

Adventuresome floaters can start as high in the Big Hole drainage as Jackson, where the river is small and sinuous with many channels and obstacles. Barbed-wire fences are common, and sharp bends into overhanging branches are the rule. At high water it's a challenge to stay out of the bushes; at low water it's a challenge to stay off the bottom. Nevertheless, the section from Jackson to Wisdom is isolated, interesting, and navigable by intermediates in canoes or kayaks. It's mighty small for a raft.

A Big Hole tributary that merits exploration (for those who don't mind carrying their boats occasionally) is the North Fork of the Big Hole in the vicinity of the Big Hole Battlefield. The river snakes through a maze of willow thickets and beaver ponds. It's not hazardous except during peak flows. At normal flows, there are no rapids, just an unrelenting current that always cuts into the bank and under the bushes. From year to year, there may be beaver dams to ford. During spring and fall migration periods, ducks, geese, sandhill cranes, and all kinds of interesting songbirds use this rich habitat. It's also a great place to see moose.

Floating the Big Hole in autumn can be a way to avoid the crowds. PHOTO BY HUGH ZACKHEIM

About 10 miles north of Wisdom, the main stem river changes from a braided, winding stream to a broad, flat river. From here to the town of Wise River, the Big Hole flows peaceably and presents few obstacles. This scenic section flows through high-altitude meadows where colorful wildflowers dot the landscape. The sky-scraping peaks of the Anaconda-Pintler Wilderness complete the scene. This is a good section for beginners in canoes or rafts, as it has easy access and few hazards. The upper river has some good fishing and rarely gets discolored, even during runoff.

This section of the river supports not only brook and rainbow trout but also the occasional grayling. The upper Big Hole is virtually the only large river in the lower forty-eight where grayling can still be caught with regularity. The native stream-dwelling grayling has been petitioned for listing as an endangered species and must be released if caught. Handle them quickly and carefully to ensure a successful release. These beautiful fish, with their large dorsal fin and delicate black spots, are truly spectacular.

Because the river between Wisdom and Wise River is wide and shallow, it can experience high water temperatures in summer. While fishing may tail off, rafting and swimming come into their own, making this an ideal spot for a family float.

Below Wise River, the Big Hole increases in velocity and gets narrower as it approaches Divide. In the canyon between Wise River and Divide, there are some large waves and moderate rapids. Intermediates can handle this section, although open canoes may get swamped by high waves at peak flows. The most difficult water can be scouted from the highway. Watch carefully for the diversion dam at the Big Hole Pumping Station about 0.5 mile above the highway bridge before Divide. It's a mandatory portage over concrete slabs on the left side and very dangerous—people have drowned here. As water levels drop during the summer, the upright concrete slabs rise higher out of the water, making the portage over them nearly impossible. Check with local fly shops before floating this dangerous section.

The most heavily floated section of the Big Hole lies between Divide and Glen. It's a beautiful, isolated canyon where bighorn sheep graze along rocky outcroppings and golden eagles soar on the thermals. Unofficial estimates run as high as 150 floaters per day during peak periods. Unquestionably, the peak of the high-use period occurs when the salmon fly hatch starts in mid-June. When these large insects hatch, big trout become less wary and can be taken more readily on dry flies. This hatch is one of the state's most poorly kept secrets, however, and outfitters from all over haul their dudes in to get a piece of the action.

Because of the intensive fishing pressure, Montana Fish, Wildlife and Parks has designed special fishing regulations geared toward protecting trophy trout. Although Montana Fish, Wildlife and Parks has designated specific days for residents, nonresidents, and outfitters to float and fish , the problem is somewhat self-regulating: When the crowds get too thick, those who want solitude go elsewhere, knowing that in a few weeks fishing pressure will slacken.

Because many Big Hole anglers fish on foot, floaters need to be courteous and considerate. Keep as far away from anglers as possible, and go behind them when it's convenient.

The canyon section between Divide and Melrose can be too rough for even intermediate canoeists at high flows. Intermediates in rafts and riverboats do fine, despite occasional downed trees and logjams. Melrose to Glen is easier, although it still has plenty of snags. Beginners in rafts or canoes can handle Melrose to Glen at low flows, but watch out for those logjams!

From Glen to the Big Hole's confluence with the Beaverhead, floating pressure is lighter and access is more difficult. The river meanders through thick cottonwood bottoms, changing its course from year to year. While it doesn't have many rapids, the river braids and winds and has some troublesome logjams and fallen trees. It's a little too much for beginner canoeists or rafters. Fishing remains good, particularly for brown trout. The lower part of the river is an excellent spot to see mink and river otters.

Biologists estimate that below Glen the river hosts a wild brown trout population maximum of about 2,000 fish per mile. As you move upriver, brown trout populations decrease but size increases. It's just the opposite for rainbows. In the lower reaches they're scarce, but they increase to a maximum of 2,000 per mile as you move upriver. While the trout may not always bite, the Big Hole mosquitoes are pretty dependable,

Big Hole equals big fish.

especially in June and July. Take some repellent and wear long sleeves.

As popular and delightful as the Big Hole may be, it has problems. Dewatering of the river is the Big Hole's most serious issue, as farmers and ranchers compete with fish and wildlife for water. In recent years Montana Fish, Wildlife and Parks has closed the river to fishing during a portion of the summer because of severe drought conditions, and might do so in the future under similar conditions. Floaters and anglers should voluntarily limit use during these times of drought.

Montana has no state law that guarantees minimum stream flows, and the Big Hole gets seriously dewatered in dry years. Depleted river flows not only have the obvious impact of less water in the river, they also cause higher water temperatures and less dissolved oxygen in the stream. Montana sorely needs adequate in-stream water reservations to protect its rivers. The Big Hole River Foundation is a watchdog group looking out for the river. If you want to help, the foundation's address is in appendix B.

3 Bighorn River

A ribbon of green slicing through parched land, the Bighorn rushes past scenic bluffs and thick cottonwood bottoms, providing anglers some of Montana's best trout fishing.

Vital statistics: 84 miles long from Yellowtail Dam to its juncture with the Yellowstone River near Custer.

Level of difficulty: A Class I river, suitable for practiced beginners.

Flow: Annual mean flow: 3,482 cfs near St. Xavier. Dam-controlled; floatable all year. Can have excellent conditions in May and June when other rivers are high with runoff. Optimal flows for fishing are 3,500 to 4,000 cfs.

Hazards: Snags and occasional logjams, swift flows in the upper section. Sudden high winds associated with storms. Three diversion dams (portage necessary).

Where the crowd goes: Afterbay to Bighorn.

Avoiding the scene: Downstream from Hardin.

Inside tip: Good fishing on warm winter days and in early spring. One of Montana's warmest areas.

Maps: BLM: #79 (Hysham), #80 (Hardin), #81 (Lodge Grass)

USGS: Billings, MT; Hardin, MT; Forsyth, MT

Montana Afloat: #14, The Bighorn River

River rules: No motorboats from Afterbay to Bighorn. A National Park Service $5-per-vehicle user fee or $30 annual fee is required for floating between Afterbay and Bighorn. Permits can be purchased at Quill Gordon Fly Fishers and near the NPS Afterbay access.

For more information: Bighorn Trout Shop, Fort Smith; Bighorn Angler, Fort Smith; Quill Gordon Fly Fishers, Fort Smith; Montana Fish, Wildlife and Parks, Billings; National Park Service, Fort Smith.

The Paddling

Steeped in history and shrouded in controversy, the magnificent Bighorn River springs from the glaciers of the Wind River Range in western Wyoming. It may be the very best river in the United States for trout fishing. With tributaries including the Wind, Shoshone, and Little Bighorn Rivers, this is a big river, nearly as large as the Yellowstone when the two merge near Custer.

As the Bighorn flows from Wyoming into Montana, it carves a rugged and scenic canyon that extends for nearly 50 miles. This great chasm winds and twists through the mountains in a tortuous course, its limestone and sandstone cliffs exuding the same brilliant colors and hues as the Grand Canyon of the Yellowstone in Yellowstone Park.

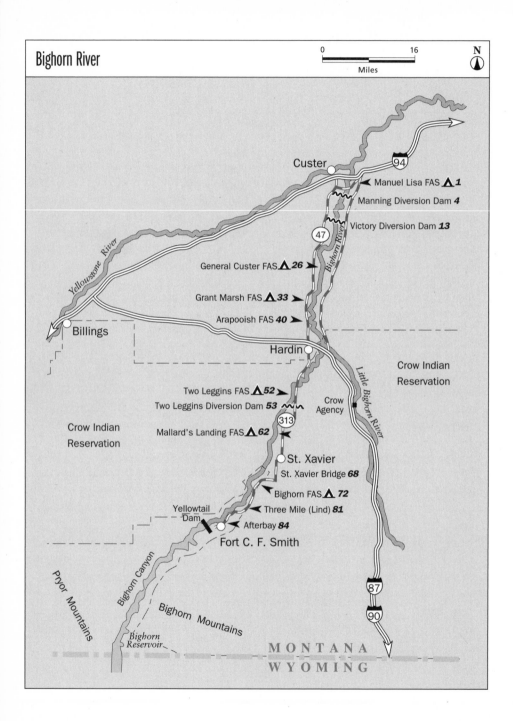

Bighorn River

0   16
Miles

N

Custer

Manuel Lisa FAS ▲ **1**

Manning Diversion Dam **4**

Victory Diversion Dam **13**

47

Bighorn River

Yellowstone River

General Custer FAS ▲ **26**

Grant Marsh FAS ▲ **33**

Arapooish FAS **40**

Billings

Hardin

Crow Indian
Reservation

Two Leggins FAS ▲ **52**

Two Leggins Diversion Dam **53**

Crow
Agency

313

Little Bighorn River

Crow Indian
Reservation

Mallard's Landing FAS ▲ **62**

St. Xavier

St. Xavier Bridge **68**

Bighorn FAS ▲ **72**

Three Mile (Lind) **81**

Yellowtail
Dam

Afterbay **84**

Fort C. F. Smith

Pryor Mountains

Bighorn Canyon

Bighorn Mountains

87

90

*Bighorn
Reservoir*

M O N T A N A

W Y O M I N G

Key Access Points along the Bighorn River

Access Point (River Mile)	Next Access Point	Access Point (River Mile)	Next Access Point
Afterbay (84)	3 Miles	Arapooish FAS (40)	7 miles
Three Mile (81)	9 miles	Grant Marsh FAS (33)	7 miles
Bighorn FAS (72)	10 miles	General Custer FAS (26)	25 miles
Mallard's Landing FAS (62)	10 miles	Manuel Lisa FAS (1)	none
Two Leggins FAS (52)	12 miles		

According to a 1932 newspaper account, the Bighorn Canyon once contained formidable rapids: "This river is one of the most dangerous in America to traverse. Many have lost their lives in attempts to go down the rapids, while a few others succeeded in accomplishing the feat." Famous mountain man Jim Bridger claimed he shot the Bighorn Canyon on a raft made of driftwood logs. Bridger, however, was known to stretch the truth. He also said the rivers in Yellowstone Park steamed because they flowed so fast they got the river bottom hot.

Yellowtail Dam transformed the treacherous Bighorn Canyon into a flatwater paddle. The 525-foot-high dam, completed in 1967, backs up 71 miles of river. While a canoe paddle through the canyon remains extremely scenic, the area is used primarily by powerboaters and water-skiers.

Jim Bridger was only one of the dozens of mountain men who trudged up the Bighorn on their way to outstanding fur-producing areas along the Wind and Green Rivers. This river valley is alive with Montana history. While Lewis and Clark did not explore the Bighorn, it's obvious from Captain Clark's journals that the Corps of Discovery knew the approximate length of the Bighorn and some of its tributaries. The river was named for its healthy population of bighorn sheep in the canyon area.

In 1807 an enterprising Spaniard named Manuel Lisa constructed Montana's first trading post at a point near where the Bighorn and Yellowstone Rivers join. In future years this spot became the site of several other forts, a projected city, and an army headquarters. All are gone today. Near Yellowtail Dam, the remains of Fort C. F. Smith can still be viewed. The fort was built in 1866 to protect travelers using the Bozeman Trail, which crossed the river about 3 miles below the present site of Yellowtail Dam.

Construction of Yellowtail Dam changed the entire character of the Bighorn River in Montana. The river once carried a heavy silt load to the Yellowstone. Now the dam traps the dirt. Below the dam, the Bighorn winds through arid benchlands and thick cottonwood groves. The river is an oasis in the middle of a parched land, a belt of green that attracts many species of wildlife, including deer, beaver, and songbirds. Migrating waterfowl flock to the Bighorn.

The combination of less sediment and regular flows means the river no longer braids or creates islands. In fact, about 1,500 acres of islands have disappeared since 1967, a 50 percent decrease. While this habitat loss is especially significant to beavers, muskrats, and geese, other native wildlife associated with the river have also suffered.

On the other hand, the combination of less sediment and cold flows from the reservoir has created an outstanding trout fishery. The river is not only rich in vegetation, but it squirms with aquatic life, including freshwater shrimp and caddis fly larvae. The river flows through limestone country, and the water is quite mineralized and rich in nutrients, which makes for excellent insect life. Such a favorable climate creates extraordinary

Bald eagles also like the fishing on the Bighorn.

growing conditions for trout. For instance, a 7-inch Bighorn River rainbow trout can grow to 14 inches in a year, about three times the normal growth rate. A fingerling brown trout can grow to 16 inches in three years. Only the Beaverhead can match the Bighorn for productivity.

The Bighorn's reputation rests on its abundance of trout and their exceptional size. The record Bighorn trout is a 29-inch, sixteen-pound rainbow. Although few trout exceed 21 inches, the average trout is slightly more than 14 inches. The Bighorn has almost 6,000 fish per mile, and over half of these are 13 inches or more, almost twice as many as the Madison and nearly three times as many as the Beaverhead.

These Bighorn fish facts are well known to trout fishing's cognoscenti, and this river's popularity has zoomed during the last two decades. During the peak periods of July, August, and September, the popular sections of the river may see well over one hundred boats a day. Fortunately, this river has good fishing almost all year, so it is possible to avoid the crowds if you are willing to brave inclement weather. A National Park Service $5-per-vehicle user fee is required for floaters between Afterbay and Bighorn. Purchase permits at Quill Gordon Fly Fishers in Fort Smith or at the National Park Service Afterbay access. No permits are required for those boating downstream from Bighorn.

Summertime moss and algae buildups can frustrate anglers—especially those with spinning gear. But the copious amounts of river vegetation attract wildlife, and the birdlife along the Bighorn can be spectacular. Shorebirds pass through this drainage in large numbers, and the river sees heavy waterfowl use during migration. Up to 20,000 mallards winter on the river, and these ducks attract raptors like bald eagles and, occasionally, peregrine falcons. Afterbay is a favorite winter and spring spot for serious bird-watchers.

The upper 44 miles of the river in Montana flow through the Crow Indian Reservation. Recreational use of this portion of the Bighorn, particularly for fishing and hunting, has been a controversial topic for several decades. In 1976 the Crow Tribe declared the river off-limits to non–tribal members. This initiated a legal debate that was resolved by a 1978 Supreme Court decision that ruled the riverbed belongs to the State of Montana, not the Crow Tribe.

The state reopened the section of the Bighorn that flows through the reservation to public fishing in 1981. Be aware that on the reservation, recreational use is only permissible below the high-water mark. Hunting big game is not allowed, and upland bird hunting is only allowed on deeded land. Waterfowl hunting is only permitted within the high-water mark.

Access to the Bighorn is limited but adequate. Most floating occurs immediately below the dam in the 12-mile section between Afterbay and the Bighorn access. While the trout habitat between Bighorn and Mallard's Landing isn't as good, the fishing pressure is considerably lower and the fishing still excellent.

Below Hardin, it is a warmwater fishery with limited populations of sauger, channel catfish, burbot, and smallmouth bass. This section also has good waterfowl concentrations and receives some hunting pressure. The Crow Reservation stops at Hardin. Floating pressure below Hardin is light. Access can be difficult, however, as the river flows mostly through private land.

Floaters use all kinds of crafts on the Bighorn, including motorboats and jet boats (no motors allowed above Bighorn access). Practiced beginners can handle the Bighorn. The main channel splits occasionally, and snags in the river can cause problems for the unwary. High winds can be a problem, too. Watch for the low diversion dam on the downstream side of the old Two Leggins Bridge. Below Hardin, watch for the Victory and Manning diversion dams.

4 Bitterroot River

A notably clear stream that flows over graveled bottoms and through cottonwood bottoms in a very picturesque valley.

Vital statistics: 80 miles long from Conner to its confluence with the Clark Fork River near Missoula.

Level of difficulty: All Class I, but swift water, frequent logjams, and occasional snags above Stevensville require intermediate skills. Beginners can try below Stevensville, but avoid high flows.

Flow: Annual mean flow: 876 cfs near Darby. May get too low in exceptionally dry years, especially between Corvallis and Stevensville. Minimum flow is 175 cfs (Darby gauge). Stay home when the river is above 2,200 cfs at Darby.

Hazards: Logjams and snags, narrow channels and sharp bends. Five diversion dams (Miles 65, 60, 54, 45, 44).

Where the crowd goes: Use is well dispersed, but Stevensville to Florence and Darby to Wally Crawford see the most traffic.

Avoiding the scene: Difficult in summer.

Florence to Lolo has slightly less pressure because you have to carry your boat a substantial distance at the takeout.

Inside tip: Nothing is more spectacular than a Bitterroot float trip with the leaves in full color—usually the first week of October.

Maps: BLM: #13 (Missoula West), #14 (Hamilton), #15 (Nez Perce)

USFS: Bitterroot

USGS: Hamilton, MT; Elk City, MT

Montana Afloat: #1 (The Bitterroot River)

River rules: Motors allowed only from May 1 to June 30 between Florence Bridge and the confluence with the Clark Fork at Kelly Island and from October 1 to January 31 (15 horsepower or less) on the entire river. Complex fishing regulations—check with Montana Fish, Wildlife and Parks.

For more information: Grizzly Hackle, Missoula; Missoulian Angler; Montana Fish, Wildlife and Parks, Missoula.

The Paddling

When famous mountain man Old Bill Williams found a river that pleased him, he would exclaim, "Thar my stick floats!" For many denizens of Missoula and Hamilton,

Key Access Points along the Bitterroot River

Access Point (River Mile)	Next Access Point	Access Point (River Mile)	Next Access Point
Hannon Memorial FAS (77)	11 miles	Bell Crossing FAS (38)	6 miles
Darby Bridge FAS (74)	3 miles	Stevensville Bridge (32)	5 miles
Wally Crawford FAS (68)	10 miles	Poker Joe FAS (27) (walk-in)	4 miles
Angler's Roost (58)	4 miles	Florence Bridge FAS (23)	3 miles
Silver Bridge (52)	3 miles	Chief Looking Glass FAS (20)	10 miles
Woodside Bridge FAS (49)	5 miles	Riverside Park (10) (walk-in)	5 miles
Tucker Crossing West FAS (44)	3 miles	Buckhouse Bridge (5)	3 miles
Victor Crossing (41)	3 miles	Maclay Flat (2)	none

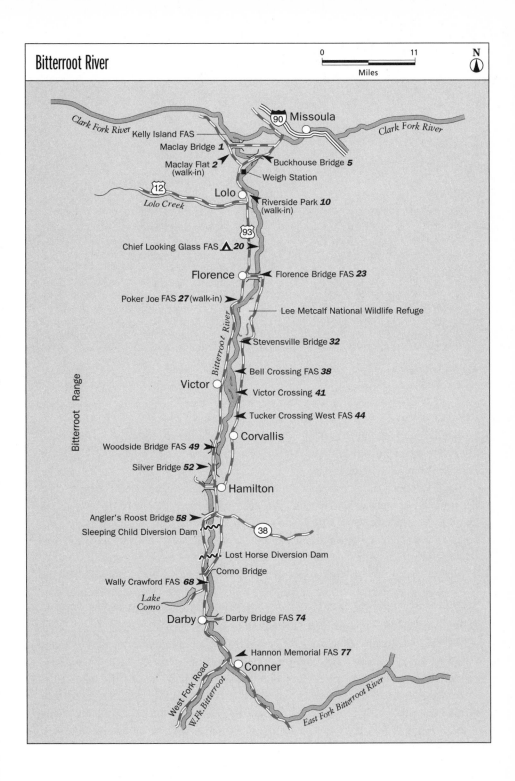

Bitterroot River

0   11
Miles

N

Clark Fork River

Clark Fork River

90 Missoula

Kelly Island FAS
Maclay Bridge **1**
Maclay Flat **2**
(walk-in)

Buckhouse Bridge **5**
Weigh Station

12

Lolo

Lolo Creek

Riverside Park **10**
(walk-in)

93

Chief Looking Glass FAS ▲ **20**

Florence

Florence Bridge FAS **23**

Poker Joe FAS **27** (walk-in)

Bitterroot River

Lee Metcalf National Wildlife Refuge

Stevensville Bridge **32**

Bell Crossing FAS **38**

Victor

Victor Crossing **41**

Tucker Crossing West FAS **44**

Bitterroot Range

Corvallis

Woodside Bridge FAS **49**

Silver Bridge **52**

Hamilton

Angler's Roost Bridge **58**
Sleeping Child Diversion Dam

38

Lost Horse Diversion Dam

Como Bridge

Wally Crawford FAS **68**

Lake
Como

Darby

Darby Bridge FAS **74**

Hannon Memorial FAS **77**

Conner

West Fork Road

W.Fk.Bitterroot

East Fork Bitterroot River

The upper Bitterroot maintains cool flows even in the heat of summer.

their stick floats in the Bitterroot, an occasionally battered but still beautiful river. Even though this stream sometimes flows near civilization, it is an excellent spot for a daylong or weeklong float trip.

Early trappers and explorers frequently spoke of the Bitterroot's beauty. The description Captain Lewis wrote in 1805 still works well: "It is a handsome stream about 100 yards wide and affords a considerable quantity of very clear water, the banks are low, and it's bed entirely gravel." Lewis originally dubbed the Bitterroot "Clark's River" to honor his esteemed co-leader.

The proximity of the mountains makes Bitterroot River trips especially scenic. The saw-toothed Bitterroots flank the river on the west, while the more rolling and open Sapphires dominate the eastern horizon. The grass-covered Sapphires frequently glow spectacularly as the sun slides below the peaks of the Bitterroots.

Fall may be the best time for a Bitterroot float. The streamside vegetation comes alive with color, and fish are feeding in preparation for winter. Since most ranchers stop irrigating about this time, water conditions are usually excellent. Those seeking an extended trip might want to take five or six days and float the river's entire 80-mile length. Dry-fly fishing seems to reach its peak about the same time the colors of the leaves achieve their most brilliant (usually the first week or two in October). It's possible to find public land for camping along most of the river, but check maps to avoid private land. If camping within the river's high-water mark, do not camp within sight of occupied residences.

Although the Bitterroot retains its clear and impressive vistas, civilization's heavy hand is sometimes evident. Extensive riprapping done by the Northern Pacific Railway in the 1960s, using both crushed rock and car bodies, created eyesores. Between Stevensville and Florence there used to be over 2,000 rusting car bodies. Thanks largely to local volunteers, most of these rusting hulks have been removed.

Irrigation places heavy demands on the Bitterroot's finite water supply. In dry years fish and wildlife suffer, and floating may not be possible. The problem is most acute near Victor, where the river branches into several small channels. State purchase of water from Painted Rocks Reservoir has helped alleviate this issue.

Despite its problems, the Bitterroot retains good wildlife populations. Deer, mink, and muskrat are common, as are dippers and spotted sandpipers, which scurry along the shores. Canada geese nest in secluded areas and on islands, and beavers can be observed along most of the river. Great blue heron rookeries occur in several areas where the river winds away from civilization. Near Stevensville, the river skirts the Lee Metcalf National Wildlife Refuge for several miles.

The Bitterroot is a great place for the unusual. Once we spotted a yellow-bellied marmot sunning itself in a tree. Another time, a young bull moose waded across the river in front of our canoe. Elk sometimes sneak down to the river bottom as well.

The Bitterroot can be floated for its entire distance, and intermediates can navigate its two forks if they can avoid logjams and maneuver through fast water. While access is adequate, it is limited enough so that the river doesn't get overrun the way the Blackfoot sometimes can. Most floaters start below the U.S. Highway 93 bridge between Conner and Darby. This upper section of the river generally has less development than below Hamilton. A catch-and-release fishing section between Darby and Como Bridge and Tucker Crossing to Florence Bridge receive heavy summertime float-fishing pressure from outfitters.

The Bitterroot upstream from Hamilton has more sharp bends, logjams, and fast water than the water downstream. It's all Class I water, but it's not the place for a maiden voyage. Logjams can be lethal, especially at high flows. Watch carefully for diversion dams between Darby and Hamilton. The Sleeping Child Diversion (about 5 miles south of Hamilton) drops several feet and must be portaged.

Downstream from Hamilton, the river gets progressively easier. River channels change remarkably from year to year, however, and new, dangerous logjams create hazards. Below Stevensville beginners can handle the Bitterroot if they watch out for snags and sharp turns. Many canoeists and rafters have a bad habit of underrating the Bitterroot, particularly during high water.

While it's too late to preserve all the Bitterroot's natural attributes, some areas remain secluded and lightly developed. Large agricultural landowners who have refused to subdivide their land deserve the credit. It is remarkable and commendable that a large segment of the river close to Missoula—the stretch between Florence and

Lolo—remains much as Lewis and Clark saw it. The explorers camped twice at a spot near where Lolo Creek meets the Bitterroot. In their journals they called it "Traveler's Rest." When traveling west to the Pacific, the Corps of Discovery used this campsite to make preparations for crossing the mountains. When returning east, Lewis and Clark camped here in preparation for splitting up and taking separate routes across Montana before meeting up at the juncture of the Yellowstone and Missouri Rivers.

The Bitterroot's proximity to Missoula and Hamilton makes it an extraordinary recreational and aesthetic resource. Private landowners need better incentives—conservation easements or perhaps even tax credits—for refraining from subdividing land with high public values. Significant parts of the Bitterroot River corridor deserve protection.

5 Blackfoot River

The Blackfoot is a glacial stream, lined with large rocks, that occasionally gets squeezed into short canyons. The result is a dashingly beautiful stream that provides outstanding whitewater excitement, incredible scenery, and dependable fishing. It's Missoula's favorite recreational river, and there's no better place on a hot summer day.

Vital statistics: 132 miles long from Anaconda Creek near Rogers Pass to its junction with the Clark Fork near Milltown.

Level of difficulty: Class I and II except at peak flows, when it's Class III+. The best whitewater lies between Russell Gates and Johnsrud Park.

Flow: Annual mean flow: 1,573 cfs near Bonner. Floatable all year below the North Fork of the Blackfoot. Flows above 1,000 cfs are optimum; 10,000 cfs is a maximum.

Hazards: Numerous logjams, sharp turns, and narrow channels in the upper river. Rapids in the middle section. The diversion dam at Bonner has been removed, and the Milltown dam, which lies at the confluence of the Blackfoot and Clark Fork Rivers, was removed in 2007.

Where the crowd goes: From Roundup to the weigh station. The closer to Missoula, the higher the number of people.

Avoiding the scene: Few float between Lincoln and River Junction. In summer, go early in the morning before the river warms enough to attract inner-tubers and swimmers.

Inside tip: Great diving rock and swimming hole at Rainbow Bend Road.

Maps: BLM: #20 (Seeley Lake), #21 (Missoula East), #31 (Elliston), Garnet Travel Plan Map
USFS: Lolo, Flathead
USGS: Butte, MT; Choteau, MT
Montana Afloat: #2 (The Blackfoot River)

River rules: Special rules for river access, camping, and day-use along the mostly private 26-mile stretch of river from Russell Gates to Johnsrud Park. Generous property owners have made their property available for recreational use, so please respect these rules. Maps and river regulations can be found at most access points and at Montana Fish, Wildlife and Parks in Missoula.

For more information: Grizzly Hackle, Missoula; Missoulian Angler, Missoula; Montana Fish, Wildlife and Parks, Missoula.

Johnsrud Park is the epicenter of Blackfoot floats.

The Paddling

The Blackfoot has earned a reputation as one of Montana's top whitewater canoe and kayaking streams, particularly in May and June during high water.

While most streams run swiftly in their upper reaches and then slow down in the lower parts, the Blackfoot River does just the opposite. A brushy meadow stream where it originates near Lincoln, the Blackfoot picks up steam and offers some challenging whitewater before its juncture with the Clark Fork River near Bonner, just a few miles east of Missoula. During the heat of summer, it is one of the most heavily used rivers in the state.

The Indians knew the Blackfoot as Cokalihishkit, meaning "river of the road to the buffalo." Tribes followed the river for its entire length, crossed the Continental Divide near the place we now call Rogers Pass, and then traveled to the plains surrounding present-day Great Falls in search of bison. Fur trappers willing to risk encounters with Blackfeet Indians also worked the river in the early days, and later on timber companies floated logs down the river to a mill at Bonner.

Many Montanans call this stream the "Big" Blackfoot River to avoid confusion

Blackfoot River

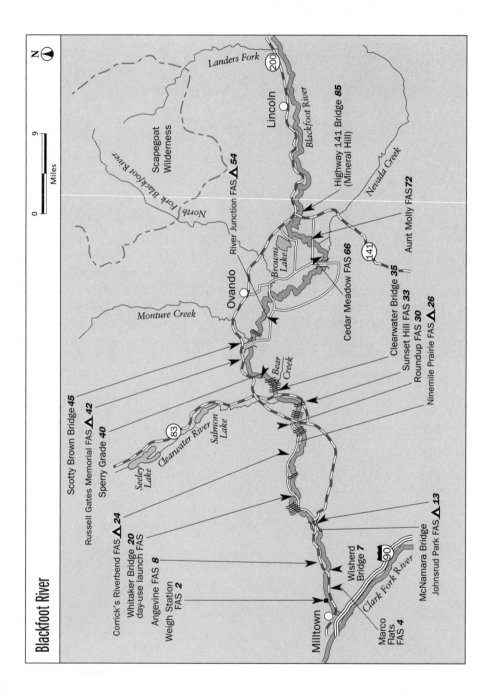

Key Access Points along the Blackfoot River

Access Point (River Mile)	Next Access Point	Access Point (River Mile)	Next Access Point
Mineral Hill (85)	13 miles	Roundup FAS (30)	6 miles
Aunt Molly FAS (72)	6 miles	Corrick's Riverbend FAS (24)	4 miles
Cedar Meadow FAS (66)	12 miles	Whitaker Bridge day-use launch (20)	7 miles
River Junction FAS (54)	9 miles	Johnsrud Park FAS (13)	5 miles
Scotty Brown Bridge (45)	3 miles	Angevine FAS (8)	1 mile
Russell Gates Memorial FAS (42)	2 miles	Wisherd Bridge (7)	3 miles
Sperry Grade (40)	5 miles	Marco Flats FAS (4)	2 miles
Clearwater Bridge (35)	2 miles	Weigh Station FAS (2)	none
Sunset Hill FAS (33)	3 miles		

with the Little Blackfoot River, which runs into the upper Clark Fork near Garrison Junction.

Although the Blackfoot doesn't have the huge whitewater of an Alberton Gorge or a Bear Trap Canyon, it can be quite challenging and very dangerous when flows are high and the water is cold. Because of possible hypothermic conditions in spring, only strong intermediates or better should try the river at this time. Wetsuits, ropes, a throw bag, and a dry bag with matches and warm clothes are standard gear. Keep in mind the 100-degree rule: If the air temperature and water temperature combined do not exceed 100 degrees, there's a real danger of hypothermia. It's a smart policy to go with several boats to a party. Each boat should have experienced people who know the river.

During high water the Blackfoot offers a first class wave for kayak and canoe "park-and-play" boaters. Known by locals as "The Ledge," this rock shelf extends halfway across the river and provides playboaters with a pour-over hole and a large green wave. It's located 0.5 mile upstream from Johnsrud Park FAS, and there's a clearly marked parking area on the right side of the road. This play spot has great eddy access and is an excellent spot for intermediates to hone their surfing skills. Optimum flows for The Ledge are above 3,000 cfs; the best is usually around 5,000 cfs.

Once the water drops (usually by mid-July), less-experienced rafters and canoeists can try their luck. While parts of the Blackfoot can be floated by beginning rafters, beginning canoeists should first practice on easier rivers like the lower Bitterroot and lower Clark Fork. Get some experience before challenging yourself too much.

Blackfoot floats can start as high in the drainage as a few miles east of Lincoln, where the Landers Fork meets the main river. Although some of the upper river is slow and flat, the numerous logjams, occasional sharp turns, and narrow channels create too many hazards for beginners. Because canoes are the easiest craft to portage over logjams, they're the boat of choice for the upper river, although a small, light raft is a possibility. Beginners can handle this section at low flows only. Be prepared to portage your boat repeatedly.

Above its confluence with the North Fork of the Blackfoot (about 25 miles west of Lincoln), the Blackfoot braids frequently and floating may be impossible in dry years. Below the North Fork, floating is almost always possible.

The North Fork of the Blackfoot has floating potential for those willing to drag across logjams and occasional blocked channels. It frequently gets too low to float by late summer. When the water is high, the section above the Highway 200 bridge can be challenging even for intermediate rafters and canoeists.

Between Lincoln and Russell Gates FAS, the main Blackfoot offers outstanding scenery as it meanders through undeveloped river bottoms, occasional farmland, and secluded canyons. It's an excellent area to see bald eagles and owls, as both like the river-bottom habitat. Look for white-tailed deer, elk, sandhill cranes, and waterfowl as well, and be advised that grizzly bears have started to recolonize this part of the upper Blackfoot Valley. Please be considerate of private landowners by staying within the river's high-water mark.

Between River Junction and Russell Gates lies a 5-mile section of river known as Box Canyon. One of the most memorable scenes in Norman Maclean's excellent book *A River Runs Through It* takes place here (the movie was filmed on the Gallatin River). Steep cliffs rise from both sides of the river, and thick timber blankets surrounding hillsides. Cliff swallows construct mud nests on the cliff walls, and hawks and eagles often soar overhead. While the river has several rocky ledges and drop-downs, the canyon has only one moderately difficult rapid. It's at the lower end of the canyon, about a 0.5 mile above Scotty Brown Bridge, and it will swamp the inexperienced or the unprepared. We once saw a canoe wrapped around the biggest rock in the rapid. Those not interested in earning whitewater merit badges can easily walk around it.

Some of the river's toughest rapids lie 3 miles downstream from Russell Gates FAS near the Bear Creek Bridge pilings. Between here and the Clearwater Bridge, watch for a couple of drops with big rocks and high waves. Most drops are followed by big pools, allowing time for recovery if problems occur. In high water, only strong intermediate canoeists or better should try this section. Spray skirts or float bags may be necessary to avoid getting swamped by big waves.

Between Russell Gates and Roundup, it's all Class I and Class II water at normal flows, but the drops bump up to Class III during runoff. Immediately upstream from the Highway 200 bridge at Roundup lies a big rock garden that lasts for several hundred yards.

Whitewater continues for several miles below Roundup, with plenty of big rocks. At high flows the rapids can be fairly continuous, allowing little time for recovery if there's an upset. But you can catch your breath in the 6-mile stretch of quiet water between Ninemile Prairie and Whitaker Bridge. Right after Whitaker, look for the Blackfoot's best-known piece of whitewater—Thibodeau Rapids. Look for big rocks and a drop; the safest route is on the left. Watch for several other frisky rapids in the next few miles below Whitaker and Johnsrud Park. Most of the river between

The Blackfoot offers exceptional intermediate water for canoeists, rafters, and kayakers.

Roundup and Johnsrud is Class I or II except during high water, when the larger drops become Class III. By midsummer, however, experienced inner-tubers can tackle the entire river, as long as they don't mind a pinball-style ride through the rock gardens.

At high flows, even the 10-mile section between Johnsrud Park and the weigh station at Bonner can be exciting. It's mostly Class II or less, but high waves can develop, and the current is very fast.

Fishing is good on the Blackfoot. Insect carapaces on the cliff walls tell the story of a significant salmon-fly hatch. Salmon flies are a species of giant stonefly that generally hatch in mid-June. In most years this hatch coincides with high water, making fishing difficult. The upper Blackfoot contains mostly brown trout, with some rainbows and an occasional cutthroat and bull trout (which must be released). The lower river is predominately a rainbow trout fishery.

Access to the lower Blackfoot (below Russell Gates) is quite good, thanks mainly to private landowners—along with federal, state, and local agencies, they have formed a cooperative river management zone that protects the river and makes it accessible to the public. Along this 26-mile corridor (from Russell Gates to Johnsrud Park), various sites have been designated for boat launching, day use, overnight camping, and other uses. A pamphlet that details regulations and provides a floating map is available from the Montana Fish, Wildlife and Parks Missoula office. Be sure to follow regulations—it's only through the goodwill of the various landowners and corporations that this outstanding section of the river has been protected and made available to floaters. Many experts point to the Blackfoot's innovative management as a national example of how cooperation can protect a river.

The Blackfoot between Roundup and the Bonner weigh station receives more use than any other portion of the river. From Ninemile Prairie to Whitaker Bridge, floating is easy, suitable for beginners. This stretch's real claim to fame, however, is Montana's only nude beach.

Beginners should pull out at a day-use launch just below Whitaker Bridge, as Thibodeau Rapids lie less than a mile below. Watch out for the big rock on the right side of the river.

Next comes Johnsrud Park, the most common starting point for a Blackfoot float. The standard trip starts here and ends 10 miles downstream at Bonner. At normal flows it takes around five hours. At low flows this section is suitable for beginning rafters and canoeists, but watch carefully for rocks and snags. Many people use inner tubes during the heat of summer. Be prepared for heavy use, and take along a bag to pick up trash left by our unthinking beer-drinking brethren.

Since the 2005 removal of a run-of-the-mill dam behind Stimson Lumber Company, the Blackfoot flows freely into the Clark Fork River at Bonner. You'll be able to continue down the Blackfoot River once the Milltown Dam is removed and restoration is complete. (Estimated date for river recreation through the Milltown Dam site is 2010.) Until the dam is removed, take out at the FWP weigh station at Mile 2.

Despite the cooperative management plan, the Blackfoot has problems. Private housing development and subdivision are the biggest threat. But worse, large mining companies have proposed a mammoth open-pit gold mine on the headwaters of the river near Lincoln. The leach pits from the mine would be a quarter mile from the river, and the river itself would be used to dilute mine wastes. Fortunately, recent initiatives have blocked mining on the upper Blackfoot, but it is unknown how long this beautiful river will remain undisturbed. While a mine on the Blackfoot seems unthinkable, it could happen if river lovers fail to remind decision makers that this river is far more precious than gold.

6 Clark Fork River

The Clark Fork starts out small, but exits the state as Montana's largest river. It meanders through pastures and woodlands with Interstate 90 paralleling much of its route.

Vital statistics: 333 miles from Warm Springs Creek to the Montana-Idaho border.

Level of difficulty: Mostly Class I water except for a difficult whitewater section through the Alberton Gorge that has Class III and IV rapids. Other than the gorge, practiced beginners can handle much of the Clark Fork.

Flow: Annual mean flow: 7,128 cfs at St. Regis. Floatable all year long below Rock Creek. May get too low above Rock Creek in dry years by late summer (1,200 cfs min). Maximum flow for floating Alberton Gorge in less than 16-foot rafts is 18,000 cfs (St. Regis gauge).

Hazards: Continuous meanders, swift current, logjams, and snags above Milltown. Numerous dams and diversions below Milltown. Large standing waves in the lower river.

Where the crowd goes: Rock Creek to Turah and Spurgin Road to Huson. Alberton Gorge in summer.

Avoiding the scene: Get outside the Missoula zone of influence; upstream from Rock Creek and downstream from Forest Grove access.

Inside tip: Excellent waterfowl hunting between old Harper Bridge and Huson. Good fall fishing below Forest Grove.

Maps: BLM: Lower Clark Fork—#5 (Libby), #6 (Thompson Falls), # 11 (Polson), #12 (Plains), #13 (Missoula West); Upper Clark Fork—#21 (Missoula East), #31 (Elliston), #32 (Butte North)

USFS: Deerlodge, Lolo, Kootenai

USGS: Butte, MT; Hamilton, MT; Wallace, ID; Kalispell, MT

Montana Afloat: #4 (The Clark Fork River)

River rules: No motors between St. John's Fishing Access Site and the mouth of Fish Creek (Alberton Gorge).

For more information: Montana Fish, Wildlife and Parks, Missoula; Grizzly Hackle, Missoula; Missoulian Angler, Missoula; Lewis & Clark Trail Adventures, Missoula; 10,000 Waves-Raft & Kayak Adventures, Missoula; Montana River Guides, Missoula; Western Waters, Missoula.

The Paddling

As recently as 1972, the Clark Fork River ran red with pollution, and even the most daring river runners didn't risk their necks on the placid-but-acid upper river. Thanks to the Anaconda Company, all forms of aquatic life were wiped out in parts of the upper river; nearly 100 miles of stream were affected. The Environmental Protection Agency eventually designated the entire upper Clark Fork drainage as a Superfund site. Stretching from Butte all the way to Milltown Dam, it's the nation's largest toxic waste problem area.

But this unfortunate situation has improved. Responding to public pressure, the Anaconda Company began to clean up its act. Initial results were encouraging. A section of river below Warm Springs Ponds that had an average of four trout per mile in 1972 had increased to an average of 984 catchable (over 6 inches) trout per mile by 1978. Aquatic insects returned in some areas, as did beaver and waterfowl.

Clark Fork River (Upper)

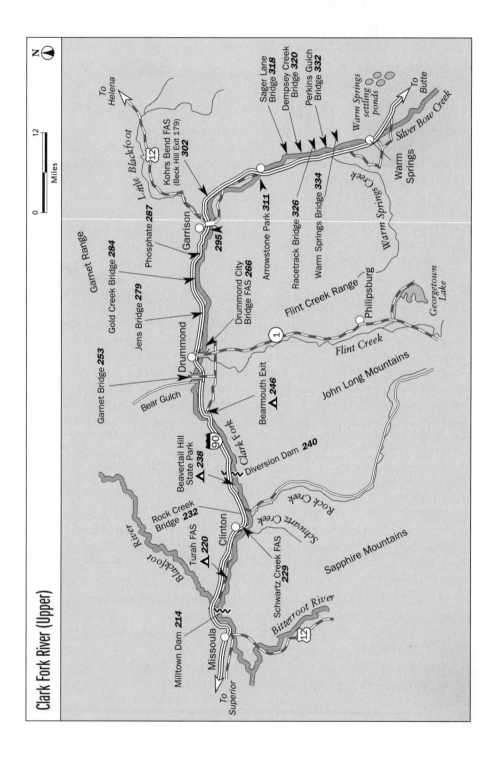

N

0 12
Miles

To Helena

Little Blackfoot

Garnet Range

Kohrs Bend FAS
(Beck Hill Exit 179)
302

Phosphate **287**

Gold Creek Bridge **284**

Jens Bridge **279**

Garrison

295

Drummond City Bridge FAS **266**

Arrowstone Park **311**

Sager Lane Bridge **318**

Dempsey Creek Bridge **320**

Perkins Gulch Bridge **332**

Warm Springs settling ponds

To Butte

Silver Bow Creek

Warm Springs

Warm Springs Creek

Racetrack Bridge **326**

Warm Springs Bridge **334**

Flint Creek Range

Philipsburg

Georgetown Lake

Flint Creek

John Long Mountains

Garnet Bridge **253**

Bear Gulch

Drummond

Bearmouth Exit ▲ **246**

1

Beavertail Hill State Park ▲ **238**

Diversion Dam **240**

Clark Fork

90

Rock Creek Bridge **232**

Rock Creek

Schwartz Creek

Turah FAS ▲ **220**

Clinton

Schwartz Creek FAS **229**

Sapphire Mountains

Blackfoot River

Milltown Dam **214**

Missoula

To Superior

Bitterroot River

12

The upper Clark Fork near Drummond receives little floating pressure.

The bad news is that trout populations remain low between Garrison and Rock Creek, and fish kills occurred with some regularity during the 1990s. Biologists believe that high-water episodes associated with spring runoff or heavy storms wash toxic materials that have accumulated along stream banks into the river. Meanwhile, the Atlantic Richfield Company (ARCO) has merged with Anaconda, and there's a heated debate over how much responsibility ARCO bears for cleaning up existing pollution.

Key Access Points along the Clark Fork River (Upper)

Access Point (River Mile)	Next Access Point	Access Point (River Mile)	Next Access Point
Warm Springs Bridge (334)	2 miles	Jens Bridge (279)	13 miles
Perkins Gulch Bridge (332)	6 miles	Drummond City Bridge FAS (266)	13 miles
Racetrack Bridge (326)	6 miles	Garnet Bridge (253)	7 miles
Dempsey Creek Bridge (320)	2 miles	Bearmouth Exit (246)	8 miles
Sager Lane Bridge (318)	7 miles	Beavertail Hill State Park (238)	6 miles
Arrowstone Park (311)	9 miles	Rock Creek Bridge (232)	3 miles
Kohrs Bend FAS (302)	7 miles	Schwartz Creek FAS (229)	9 miles
Garrison (295)	8 miles	Turah FAS (220)	6 miles
Phosphate (287)	3 miles	Milltown (214)	none (after 2009)
Gold Creek Bridge (284)	5 miles		

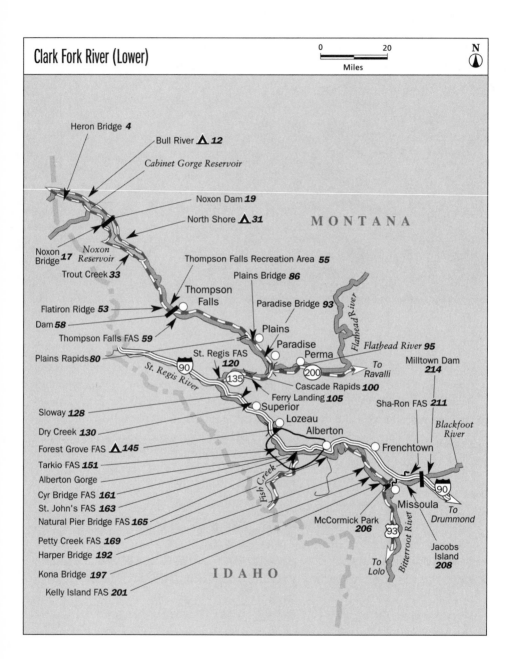

Clark Fork River (Lower)

0   20
Miles

N

Heron Bridge *4*

Bull River △ *12*

Cabinet Gorge Reservoir

Noxon Dam *19*

North Shore △ *31*

MONTANA

Noxon Bridge *17*   *Noxon Reservoir*

Trout Creek *33*

Thompson Falls Recreation Area *55*

Plains Bridge *86*

Flatiron Ridge *53*

Thompson Falls

Paradise Bridge *93*

Dam *58*

Plains

Thompson Falls FAS *59*

Paradise

Flathead River

Plains Rapids *80*

St. Regis River

St. Regis FAS *120*

Perma

Flathead River 95

Milltown Dam *214*

90

135

200

To Ravalli

Cascade Rapids *100*

Sha-Ron FAS *211*

Ferry Landing *105*

Sloway *128*

Superior

Lozeau

Blackfoot River

Dry Creek *130*

Alberton

Forest Grove FAS △ *145*

Frenchtown

Tarkio FAS *151*

Alberton Gorge

Fish Creek

Cyr Bridge FAS *161*

St. John's FAS *163*

Natural Pier Bridge FAS *165*

90

McCormick Park *206*

Missoula

To Drummond

Petty Creek FAS *169*

Harper Bridge *192*

93

Bitterroot River

Jacobs Island *208*

Kona Bridge *197*

IDAHO

To Lolo

Kelly Island FAS *201*

Key Access Points along the Clark Fork River (Lower)

Access Point (River Mile)	Next Access Point	Access Point (River Mile)	Next Access Point
Milltown (214)	3 miles	Dry Creek (130)	2 miles
Sha-Ron FAS (211)	3 miles	Sloway (128)	8 miles
Jacobs Island (208)	2 miles	St. Regis FAS (120)	15 miles
McCormick Park (206)	5 miles	Ferry Landing (105)	12 miles
Kelly Island FAS (201)	4 miles	Paradise Bridge (93)	7 miles
Kona Bridge (197)	5 miles	Plains Bridge (86)	27 miles
Harper Bridge (192)	10 miles	Thompson Falls FAS (59)	4 miles
Petty Creek FAS (169)	4 miles	Thompson Falls Recreation Area (55)	2 miles
Natural Pier Bridge FAS (165)	2 miles	Flatiron Ridge FAS (53)	20 miles
St. John's FAS (163)	2 miles	Trout Creek (33)	2 miles
Cyr Bridge FAS (161)	4 miles	North Shore (31)	14 miles
Triple Bridges (157) (walk-in)	4 miles	Noxon Bridge (19)	5 miles
Ralph's Takeout (153)	2 miles	Bull River (12)	8 miles
Tarkio FAS (151)	6 miles	Heron Bridge (4)	none
Forest Grove FAS (145)	15 miles		

While the upper Clark Fork's water quality problems can be deadly for fish, they don't impede floating. This river remains one of western Montana's popular float streams. The Clark Fork (this is the Clark Fork of the Columbia, not to be confused with the Clarks Fork of the Yellowstone) begins its 333-mile trek across the state near Warm Springs and can be floated its entire distance in Montana. The upper sections are brushy and winding, the lower sections broad and deep.

The Clark Fork grows from a medium-size river (about 3,000 cfs) to a large river (about 10,000 cfs) just above its confluence with the Flathead River, bolstered by the influx of both the Bitterroot and Blackfoot Rivers. By the time it departs Montana on its way to meet the Columbia River, the Clark Fork carries more water than any other river in Montana, with a flow nearly equal to the Missouri and Yellowstone Rivers combined.

Milltown Dam, a small, obsolete power project about 5 miles east of Missoula, creates the artificial distinction between the upper and lower river. Soon this distinction will become even more artificial with the removal of the dam. According to the Clark Fork Coalition, projected completion of the EPA Superfund site is 2009. It will require the removal of 150,000 truckloads of arsenic-contaminated soil above the dam and redevelopment of the Blackfoot and Clark Fork Rivers around the Milltown/Bonner community.

The dam lies at the head of Hellgate Canyon, an area named by French trappers. In early times the canyon was an ideal spot for ambushes and horse stealing. Since enemies didn't worry too much about funeral arrangements, the place became so cluttered with bones and skulls that the Frenchmen named it "the Gates of Hell." If the origin of this name depresses you, keep in mind that Paradise—a small town near where the Clark Fork joins the Flathead—is a mere 121 miles downstream.

Interstate 90 parallels the Clark Fork for most of its distance in Montana. Fortunately it's usually far enough from the river that one has a sense of solitude. Surprisingly, even with an interstate nearby, access isn't always easy. County road bridges, along with a few Department of Fish, Wildlife and Parks sites, provide most of the access.

On the upper river, floating can start right below the settling ponds at Warm Springs. The river is very small and windy for its first 15 miles between Warm Springs and Deer Lodge. In dry years count on scraping and carrying your craft across riffles. Canoes are best at negotiating the sharp turns and avoiding the overhanging brush in this section. It's a great section for solo boating with a small craft.

The scenery of the upper river is exceptional as the river wanders by the Flint Range, and sunsets can be spectacular. Beginners can handle this section when the weather is favorable and the water is low. From Deer Lodge to Garrison, the river broadens and gets shallower, and it may get too low to float in dry years. There's little floating pressure anywhere in the upper river. The Native Americans of the area knew the upper Clark Fork as the Arrowstone River because of a semitransparent stone found near the river they used to make arrowheads.

At Garrison the Little Blackfoot River flows into the Clark Fork, improving both water quality and quantity from Garrison to Drummond. The river gradually winds away from civilization as it flows through thick cottonwood bottoms alive with white-tailed deer and beaver. An elk herd uses this river bottom as well. This section has a fair brown trout fishery, and anglers occasionally reel in cutthroat trout. In fall and winter, waterfowl use the river heavily. Between Drummond and Rock Creek, the river flows closer to I-90, fish populations are low, and few people float it.

The repeated bends, occasional diversion dams, and possible barbed-wire fences make the Garrison-to-Drummond stretch a little too difficult for beginners except when the water is low. Much of this section flows through private land where landowners are very sensitive about trespassing, so stay within the high-water mark.

The Clark Fork from Rock Creek to Milltown Dam is by far the most heavily used portion of the upper river. Rock Creek provides a slug of high-quality water, and the fishing improves. Numerous downed trees, logjams, and tricky channels make the Rock Creek-to-Milltown run challenging, especially when the river is high. Beginners should avoid this section.

The Clark Fork changes complexion and becomes a large, broad river after being joined by the Blackfoot and Bitterroot Rivers near Missoula. The lower river flows mainly through cottonwood bottoms, although in some areas steep, pine-covered hillsides come down to the river's edge.

Although access to the lower Clark Fork is generally good, floating pressure is much heavier near Missoula. The section between Milltown Dam and Missoula is quite popular, particularly in the heat of summer. The lower Clark Fork probably offers the easiest floating close to Missoula, but beginners should stay away until after spring runoff. Man-made hazards such as diversions dams and weirs pose the biggest threat.

Those floating through Missoula should watch for a diversion just upstream from the Eastgate Shopping Center. Then, as you leave town, take the left channel that goes by the Spurgin Road access. The right channel has a diversion dam just above the confluence of the Bitterroot and Clark Fork Rivers that must be portaged.

Another popular, close-to-town float starts on the Bitterroot River at Buckhouse Bridge (Highway 93 bridge near Missoula) and ends 9 miles downstream at Kona Bridge on the Clark Fork. It's suitable for beginners and has decent fishing. Experienced floaters may want to try it in winter, when the goldeneyes, mergansers, Canada geese, and bald eagles concentrate along the river. It's possible to see a half dozen or more mature baldies along this stretch on a bright winter day.

Below Harpers Bridge (which largely burned down in the 1990s), the Clark Fork winds past the odiferous Frenchtown pulp mill and flows placidly until it reaches Alberton. Although the paper plant's stench may discourage you, the river here is quite isolated and fishing can be good. The pulp mill's desire to dump more wastewater from the mill into the river has caused a continuing controversy.

Not far below Alberton the river enters the Alberton Gorge, also known as Cyr Canyon. Experts with large rafts or kayaks will have a ball, but inexperienced floaters with canoes or small rafts don't have a chance. Several commercial outfitters take groups or individuals through the gorge. (Paddling details are provided in a separate section below.)

Safe floating starts again near Tarkio and continues to Thompson Falls with only minor rapids. Beginners should portage Cascade Rapids, 200 yards of difficult water between St. Regis and Paradise. The other tough spot occurs about 5 river miles after the Plains Bridge access. Beginners may want to use the shoreline and portage river left. Floating ends near Thompson Falls, where dams form continuous reservoirs to the Idaho border.

Much of the lower Clark Fork still has undisturbed shoreline, with mountains rising up from both sides of the river. The river has excellent rainbow trout populations. In fall, copious mayfly hatches bring the trout to the surface, where they feed with abandon. The cold nights and warm afternoons create some of the most consistently good fishing conditions of the year.

Motorboats and jetboats threaten to become a nuisance on the Clark Fork and should be regulated before their use becomes established. The only section of the Clark Fork where no motors are allowed is the Alberton Gorge area from St. Johns access to Fish Creek.

In 1984 a citizens' group called the Clark Fork Coalition formed to protect the Clark Fork River watershed. They do a commendable job. To join, write to the coalition at the address in appendix B.

ALBERTON GORGE

When anyone talks about whitewater on the Clark Fork, you can be sure they're talking about Alberton Gorge, sometimes known as Cyr Canyon or the Fish Creek Gorge. This 20-mile whitewater section, which begins just west of Alberton, has some outstanding rapids in a very beautiful, isolated setting. Although I-90 parallels the river, it's only noticeable in a few places where bridges span the river. For the most part, the gorge provides a primitive experience, with little development or other signs of human use.

Access to the gorge is limited. The standard Alberton Gorge trip starts at Cyr and ends at Tarkio (although those who want a longer float often go to Forest Grove). Most of the heavy whitewater action comes in the first part of the trip. After Fish Creek the rapids aren't nearly as difficult.

Those starting at Cyr will miss the Rest Stop Rapids (creatively named for an adjacent I-90 pullout). At high flows it's a Class IV (for experts only) with big waves and a huge hole. To hit the Rest Stop Rapids, put in at the St. Johns Fishing Access Site. The rapids lie immediately below the put-in, however, leaving little time to get acclimated to the river before the action starts. An alternative would be to put in at Petty Creek. At normal flows, Rest Stop is a routine Class II.

For the first couple miles below Cyr expect only minor Class II rapids. Steep cliffs and a dull roar will let you know you are approaching the Ledge Rapids. Expect big waves and some jagged sleeper rocks that create a narrow passage in a rock shelf that extends across the entire river. The rocks that form this solid Class III run have shredded the rafts of unwary rafters at low flows. After the Ledge, look for Cliffside 1 and Cliffside 2, two Class III rapids that get bigger and steeper with lower flows.

The most difficult rapids in the gorge come right after the triple bridges. The canyon narrows significantly, and at high flows the rapids are continuous and the current extremely swift. The gorge's toughest rapid, Tumbleweed, lies in this 2-mile section. It's easy to spot because the river gets very narrow and there's a huge rock on the right (submerged at high water). Scout Tumbleweed by pulling out on the left. At low flows it's a Class III, but at high flows it's a very difficult Class IV. A flip at high water can mean a long and dangerous swim. It's best to stay left; watch out for a big hole behind the rock.

Not far downstream from Tumbleweed come three more of the gorge's toughest rapids: Boat Flipper, Boateater, and Fang. At high flows they have tremendously big waves that can flip even large boats. Exciting but not technically difficult, they are strong Class III rapids at high flows; at low water Boat Flipper doesn't exist. After Fang it's only a short run to where Fish Creek enters the river; from Fish Creek on, it's Class I and II water.

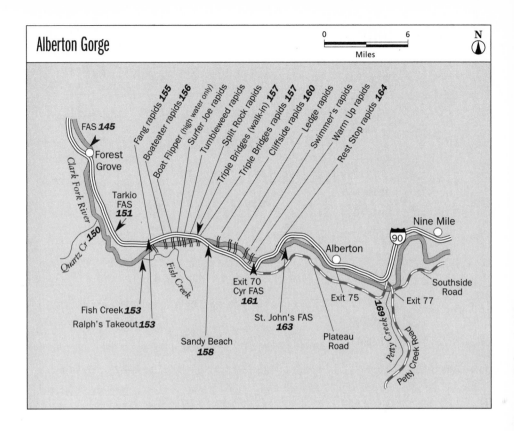

Again, the two standard take-out points for gorge trips are Tarkio and Forest Grove. The 4 miles in between have outstanding scenery and good fishing. While not recommended as a normal access point, in case of emergencies there's a steep narrow trail where Fish Creek enters the river. The mouth of Fish Creek is a popular stopping point that's showing signs of overuse. Consider stopping elsewhere.

Alberton Gorge changes dramatically based on the water flows. Places like Rest Stop Rapids and Boat Flipper become formidable in high water, while other rapids, like Cliffside, may wash out. Conversely, some rapids become more technical at low flows.

Average whitewater conditions can be found at flows between 2,000 and 10,000 cfs. These flows are measured at a gauge station at St. Regis. Between 10,000 and 20,000 cfs, the river gets much more difficult and dangerous. The normal peak flow generally is between 18,000 and 22,000 cfs. Above 20,000 cfs, the current and high waves make the river extremely treacherous. At maximum flows, which may approach 40,000 cfs, the flows are so fast and the water so turbulent that a long swim is likely if your boat flips. Given the cold water temperatures and the likelihood of debris in the river, this creates a very dangerous situation.

At higher flows the gorge is for advanced intermediates and experts. Be sure to have more than one raft in your party in case of trouble, and be sure to have a high-quality life jacket. Big self-bailing rafts with rowing frames (16-foot and up with 20-inch tubes) are the standard equipment for runs from mid-May through June.

Less adventuresome people should try the gorge when the water drops and the temperatures rise. In a normal year, paddle rafts are a possibility after early July; smaller boats get to be more fun as the water drops more. At very low flows you may even see thrill-seekers in canoes testing their abilities. This is for experts who don't mind getting wet. Do not mix alcohol with an Alberton Gorge trip; the rapids are difficult, and people get thrown out of boats.

Kayaking the Gorge

The gorge offers exceptional kayaking year-round and is highly esteemed in the kayak community as a playboater-friendly river. Most kayakers put in just above the place where three bridges cross the Clark Fork (take the Fish Creek exit off I-90) and carry their boats a short distance down to the river. The first rapid is located hundreds of feet beneath the interstate bridges and is aptly named "Triple Bridges." At most water levels the wave train is eddy accessible, and several features come and go during the season. The first wave is the most desirable and becomes a green wave with a small pile at 3,000 cfs. A larger hole is often present at high water, located upstream on river right, but should only be attempted by experts.

Less than a 0.5 mile below Triple Bridges, Split Rock Rapid provides playboaters with a small, eddy-access hole on river right, best suited for smaller boats. The hole isn't very big, but at the right level (4,000 cfs) can be very retentive. Right-handed cartwheels are the move of choice.

The next 1.5 miles of the river have great whitewater, but no easily accessed play spots. Surfer Joe is great for beginners, and often Boat Eater has a surging hole toward the bottom of the run that can be accessed via an eddy on river left.

The last and arguably most exciting rapid is Fang—an experienced playboater's paradise. The upper section of the rapid has several large play holes, and the first wave on the lower wave train is a surging monster above 4,000 cfs. The wave is eddy accessible (if you call a surging whirlpool an eddy!), and nearly any move can be done at the right level. The rapid seems to change year to year as the streambed is slowly transformed, but there is always at least one feature that will leave you gasping for air.

Most kayakers (and some beefy rafters) pull off the river at Ralph's Takeout, about 1 mile below Fang on river right. The takeout isn't marked, so look for a wooden staircase leading up the side of a steep embankment just after a small set of rapids. The parking area is about 200 yards up the trail. To drive to Ralph's, exit I-90 at Fish Creek, head toward the river, turn left at the stop sign, and head west down the frontage road crossing the gorge. The road soon turns to dirt; keep driving (about 3 miles) until there is an obvious left turn. The road deteriorates quickly for one more mile (four-wheel drive is recommended) as it leads closer to the river.

Alberton Gorge is for seasoned boaters. If you don't have friends with experience, there are at least two alternatives. A number of outfitters take people down the gorge. Another choice is the University of Montana's Campus Recreation Outdoor Program. See appendix A for phone numbers and addresses.

7 Clarks Fork of the Yellowstone

East of Yellowstone National Park in the shadow of the Beartooth Mountains, the Clarks Fork meanders through isolated cottonwood groves and beautiful prairie country.

Vital statistics: 73 miles long from Montana border near Belfry to its junction with the Yellowstone near Laurel.
Level of difficulty: Class I for its entire length in Montana (the whitewater is in Wyoming). Suitable for practiced beginners at normal flows.
Flow: Annual mean flow: 929 cfs near Belfry. Can be too low for floating in September between Bridger and Fromberg. Minimum flow for floating is 100 cfs; maximum is 4,000 cfs.
Hazards: Eleven diversion dams. Lind (Golden) diversion just north of Belfry and Orchard diversion south of Bridger are portages.

Where the crowd goes: Nowhere.
Avoiding the scene: Just show up.
Inside tip: This is the perfect trip for those seeking solitude and good wildlife viewing. What most Montana rivers were like thirty years ago.
Maps: BLM: #63 (Red Lodge), #72 (Bridger), #71 (Billings), RAG-36
USFS: Custer (Beartooth)
USGS: Billings, MT
River rules: Mostly private land. Stay within the high-water mark.
For more information: Montana Fish, Wildlife and Parks, Billings.

The Paddling

When Captain Clark floated down the Yellowstone on his 1806 return trip across Montana (he met Captain Lewis at the juncture of the Yellowstone and the Missouri), he mistook the Clarks Fork for the Bighorn River. He realized his mistake when he hit the actual Bighorn a few days downstream and compensated for his error by naming this mistaken river for himself. The captain describes the Clarks Fork in his journal as "a bold river, 150 yards wide at the entrance, but a short distance above is contracted to 100 yards. The water is of a light muddy color and much colder than that of the Yellowstone; its general course is south and east of the Rocky mountains."

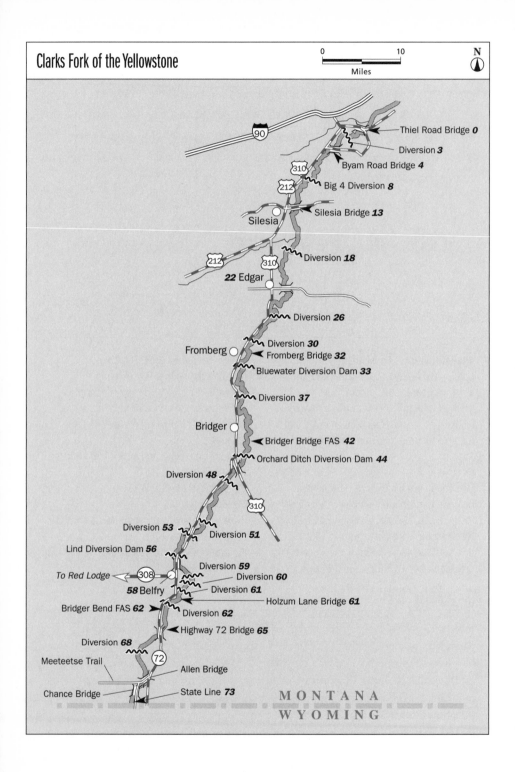

Clarks Fork of the Yellowstone

0   10
Miles

N

Thiel Road Bridge **0**
Diversion **3**
Byam Road Bridge **4**
Big 4 Diversion **8**
Silesia Bridge **13**
Silesia
Diversion **18**
22 Edgar
Diversion **26**
Diversion **30**
Fromberg
Fromberg Bridge **32**
Bluewater Diversion Dam **33**
Diversion **37**
Bridger
Bridger Bridge FAS **42**
Orchard Ditch Diversion Dam **44**
Diversion **48**
Diversion **53**
Diversion **51**
Lind Diversion Dam **56**
Diversion **59**
To Red Lodge
Diversion **60**
58 Belfry
Diversion **61**
Holzum Lane Bridge **61**
Bridger Bend FAS **62**
Diversion **62**
Highway 72 Bridge **65**
Diversion **68**
Meeteetse Trail
Allen Bridge
Chance Bridge
State Line **73**
MONTANA
WYOMING

Key Access Points along the Clarks Fork of the Yellowstone River

Access Point (River Mile)	Next Access Point	Access Point (River Mile)	Next Access Point
State Line (73)	8 miles	Fromberg Bridge (32)	19 miles
Highway 72 bridge (65)	3 miles	Silesia Bridge (13)	9 miles
Bridger Bend FAS (62)	1 mile	Byam Road Bridge (4)	4 miles
Holzum Lane (61)	19 miles	Thiel Road Bridge (0)	none
Bridger Bridge FAS (42)	10 miles		

The Clarks Fork remains the same color at its mouth that Clark observed: light coffee to medium chocolate. What the captain didn't know is that the Clarks Fork starts clear and pure as a mountain stream. It originates 3 miles east of Cooke City, enters Wyoming, and then reenters Montana 67 miles later as a prairie stream with little sign of its mountainous origin.

The best-known sections of the Clarks Fork are in Wyoming and possess challenging whitewater. In Montana floating can start right at the state line. The 31 miles of river between the border and Bridger contain the best water quality and easiest access. County roads and highway bridges provide nearly all the access. Upstream from Bridger, access points are well defined. Below Bridger, most accesses lack automobile pullouts, and routes to the river may be blocked by barbed wire. Fromberg and Silesia Bridges both provide access to the lower river.

Most fishing takes place upstream from Bridger, where the river is clearer. Although the trout populations aren't outstanding, persistent anglers catch rainbows, browns, cutthroat, and whitefish up to 15 inches or more. The Clarks Fork in Montana isn't on anyone's list of famous trout rivers, so you'll probably have the river to yourself if float-fishing.

Diversion dams and irrigation jetties provide the greatest obstacles to a pleasant float. This river may have more diversions per mile than any river in Montana. Some require portaging (Lind and Orchard), and some you can scrape over, based on flows. Abundant diversion dams are a sure sign of a river with high irrigation demands. Serious dewatering, especially between Bridger and Fromberg, often occurs on the Clarks Fork, so expect a scratchy float in late summer, except in wet years.

Below Bridger the river gets murkier and loses more water to irrigation. From Edgar to the Yellowstone River, the river is more isolated, rarely coming near the highway. Rock Creek flows in above Silesia and provides a blast of cold, clear water.

Practiced beginners can handle the entire Clarks Fork in Montana. Watch for downed cottonwoods, diversions, and almost-invisible sandbars. The river's milky color makes it difficult to read the water. It's easy to miss the shallow spots and get hung up.

Even though the Clarks Fork isn't far from Billings, it receives light use. While not a great fishing stream, it offers beautiful scenery, wildlife, and isolation. For those who seek rivers far from the madding crowd, this may be a spot for you.

8 Clearwater River

This aptly named river flows through pine forests and mountain meadows with the famous Bob Marshall Wilderness to the east and the towering Mission Mountains to the west.

Vital statistics: 42 miles long from Clearwater Lake to its juncture with the Blackfoot River.

Level of difficulty: Mostly Class I water suitable for practiced beginners. A 2-mile section of Class II and III whitewater starts in a canyon just after Salmon Lake.

Flow: Annual mean flow: 287 cfs near Clearwater. Adequate all year except in the driest years.

Hazards: Logjams and beaver dams. The short whitewater stretch. Three diversion dams.

Where the crowd goes: The Clearwater Canoe Trail (3 miles north of Seeley Lake).

Avoiding the scene: Between Seeley and Salmon Lakes.

Inside tip: Watch migrating songbirds along the Clearwater Canoe Trail in spring.

Maps: BLM: #20 (Seeley Lake)
USFS: Flathead
USGS: Choteau, MT; Butte, MT

River rules: No wake on the Clearwater Canoe Trail.

For more information: Lolo National Forest, Seeley Lake; Montana Fish, Wildlife and Parks, Missoula.

The Paddling

To any person driving around western Montana in May and June, the Clearwater seems appropriately named. While other rivers gush brown with runoff, the Clearwater runs strikingly clear. The reason? It flows through a heavily forested landscape and gets filtered through a chain of lakes that include Rainy, Alva, Inez, Seeley, and Salmon Lakes.

Key Access Points along the Clearwater River

Access Point (River Mile)	Next Access Point	Access Point (River Mile)	Next Access Point
East Fork Bridge (42)	2 miles	Bridge (20)	4 miles
Rainy Lake (40)	2 miles	Placid Lake Road Bridge (16)	5 miles
Lake Alva Campground (38)	1 mile	Salmon Lake Campground (11)	1 mile
West Fork Bridge (37)	2 miles	Salmon Lake Outlet (10)	3 miles
Lake Inez Campground (35)	2 miles	Elbow Lake Access (7)	2 miles
Beargrass Lane (33)	4 miles	Harper's Lake Campground FAS (5)	1 mile
Canoe Trail Put-in (29)	3 miles	Clearwater Crossing FAS (4)	4 miles
Canoe Trail Take-out (26) ranger station	2 miles	Clearwater Bridge (0)	none
Camp Paxson Bridge (24)	4 miles		

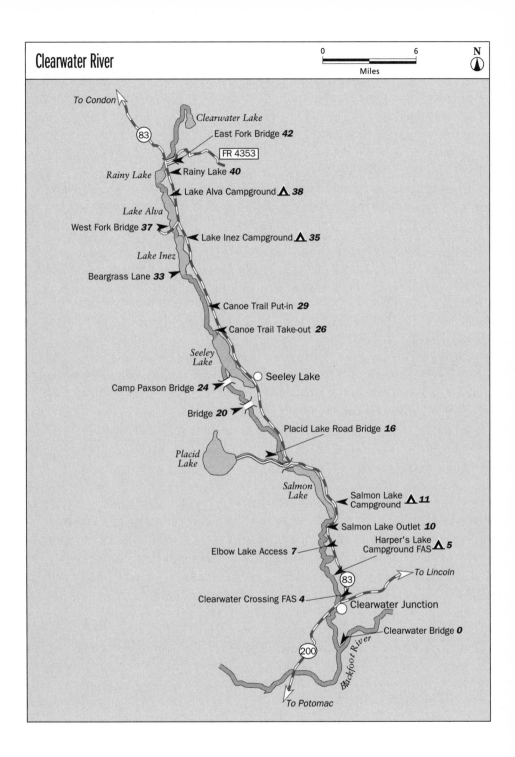

Clearwater River

0   6
Miles

N

To Condon

Clearwater Lake

East Fork Bridge *42*

83

FR 4353

Rainy Lake ◄ Rainy Lake *40*

Lake Alva Campground ▲ *38*

Lake Alva

West Fork Bridge *37* ➤

◄ Lake Inez Campground ▲ *35*

Lake Inez

Beargrass Lane *33* ➤

◄ Canoe Trail Put-in *29*

◄ Canoe Trail Take-out *26*

Seeley
Lake

○ Seeley Lake

Camp Paxson Bridge *24* ➤

Bridge *20* ➤

Placid Lake Road Bridge *16*

Placid
Lake

Salmon
Lake

◄ Salmon Lake
Campground ▲ *11*

◄ Salmon Lake Outlet *10*

Harper's Lake
Campground FAS ▲ *5*

Elbow Lake Access *7*

To Lincoln

83

Clearwater Crossing FAS *4*

○ Clearwater Junction

Clearwater Bridge *0*

200

Blackfoot River

To Potomac

Although the source of the 46-mile-long Clearwater River is Clearwater Lake (upstream from Rainy Lake), there isn't any decent floating until below Lake Inez. Don't miss the Clearwater Canoe Trail, a truly exceptional canoe trip with an ingenious design. First you float about 4 miles down the river (about one to two hours), and then you walk about 1.5 miles back on a groomed trail to get your car (about thirty minutes). Both the water and the walk lead through a dense willow marsh on an isolated portion of the Clearwater. It's a great opportunity to see warblers, loons, bitterns, catbirds, snipe, kingfishers, and wood ducks. You'll likely see turtles, fish, and muskrats as well.

This is a great trip for beginners. Even kids can handle the placid flows here. The last part of the trip crosses the top of Seeley Lake, so skirt the shore if the wind is strong.

There's also good floating and easy access between Seeley and Salmon Lakes. Fishing can be good in this section. Below Salmon Lake lies a difficult 2-mile-long whitewater canyon that's only for highly experienced boaters. The whitewater ends at Elbow Lake, and a small dam creates a large marsh that's an excellent place for bird-watchers to paddle their canoes. In fact, some people pull off the picnic area right at Highway 200 and paddle upstream in the lazy current. It's an excellent spot for beginners.

The last 3.5 miles of the Clearwater below the Highway 200 bridge aren't difficult, but be aware that the Blackfoot contains several difficult rapids in the section immediately below where the Clearwater enters. Beginners should get out at the access point where the Blackfoot meets the Clearwater.

9 Dearborn River

Crystal-clear waters rush through narrow canyons with sheer walls and spectacular rock formations on this highly scenic small stream.

Vital statistics: 67 miles long from Scapegoat Mountain north of Lincoln to its juncture with the Missouri.

Level of difficulty: Class I and II water, with rock gardens, rapids and sharp drops. Not for beginners.

Flow: Annual mean flow: 220 cfs near Craig. Typically too low to float by late July. Minimum flow is 250 cfs. Ideal flows are around 400 cfs. Flows over 1,000 cfs should be avoided by those in canoes.

Hazards: A small waterfall at Mile 34, 10 miles downstream from the Dearborn Canyon Road put-in. Fences, rock gardens, rapids, and shallow waters.

Where the crowd goes: U.S. Highway 287 bridge to the Missouri River.

Avoiding the scene: Dearborn Canyon Road Bridge to US 287 bridge.

Inside tip: Extend your Dearborn trip and continue down the Missouri. Excellent fishing and scenery.

Maps: BLM: #30 (Dearborn River), #40 (Great Falls South)
USFS: Lewis and Clark (Rocky Mountain Division)
USGS: Great Falls, MT; Choteau, MT

River rules: Be sure to stay within the high-water mark, as almost all of the land along the Dearborn is privately owned.

For more information: Montana Fly Goods, Helena; Montana Fish, Wildlife and Parks, Great Falls.

The Paddling

Anyone who floats the Dearborn River at low flows can't help but be mesmerized by the extreme clarity of this small stream. Even in the deep pools, it's almost always possible to see the brightly colored rocks that dot the streambed.

The Dearborn's clarity impressed Meriwether Lewis, and he made this observation after a brief exploratory trip on July 18, 1805:

> "At the distance to 2.5 miles we passed the entrance of a considerable river on the Stard. side; about 80 yds. wide being nearly as wide as the Missouri at that place. it's current is rapid and water extreamly transparent; the bed is formed of small smooth stones of flat rounded or other figures. it's bottoms are narrow but possess as much timber as the Missouri. the country is mountainous and broken through which it passes. it appears as if it might be navigated but to what extent must be conjectural. this handsome bold and clear stream we named in honor of the Secretary of war calling it Dearborn's river."

The highly picturesque Dearborn gets its start high on Scapegoat Mountain near the Bob Marshall Wilderness, and it carves a deep and beautiful path as it winds its

Dearborn River

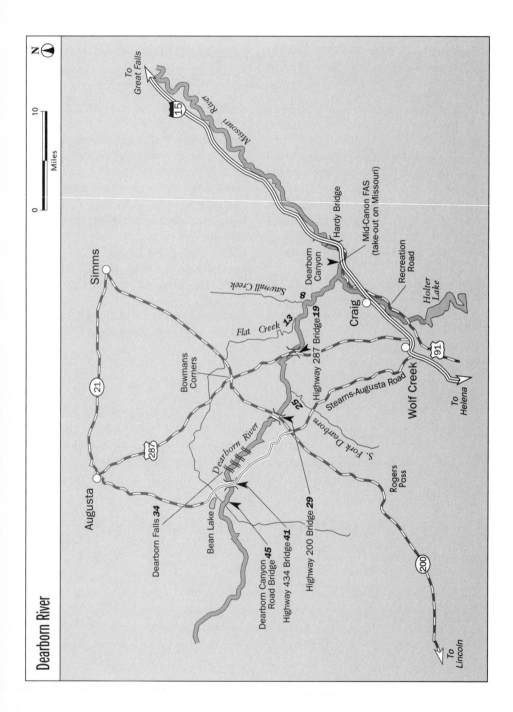

way out of the mountains and onto the open country that once was the buffalo hunting grounds of the Blackfeet Indians. Although the Dearborn is rather small, it's a high-quality stream with a floatable distance of 45 miles.

The Dearborn can be logically divided into three sections, each floatable in a day during the peak of summer when days are long. The uppermost section begins at the Dearborn Canyon Road bridge (also known as Clemons Creek Bridge) and flows for about 16 river miles to the Highway 200 bridge. The Highway 434 bridge, about 4 miles downstream from the Dearborn Canyon Road bridge, offers another potential access point, but the banks are rather steep, making access more difficult.

The river in this section is quite small and shallow, so it's primarily an early-season trip. It's a popular run for good intermediate canoeists. The river passes through a narrow canyon with many rocks and sharp turns. Watch out for fences, and beware of a waterfall about 10 miles downstream from the Dearborn Canyon Road put-in. It's a mandatory portage. The shortest portage is on river right over bedrock, but if the river is up, you may have to use the trail on river left.

The middle section, from the Highway 200 bridge (another steep put-in spot) to the US 287 bridge, flows for about 10 miles. It's another popular canoe stretch, though not as difficult as upstream. The only real hazard other than fences, fallen trees, and swift water is a 3-foot drop about 3 miles below the Highway 200 bridge. The river generally runs through open country with occasional bluffs. This section is still too tough for beginners except at low flows.

The most popular and scenic Dearborn float is the 19-mile section that runs from the US 287 bridge to the Missouri River. Although the distance is less than 12 miles as the crow flies, the river twists and turns through a narrow canyon.

The river cuts through a highly scenic gorge, replete with sheer walls that rise hundreds of feet with unusual rock formations. Most people either take out right where the Dearborn meets the Missouri (a difficult takeout on the southeast shore) or float a few miles down the river to Mid-Canon Access and take in the good fishing and scenery there.

This lower section of the Dearborn is suitable for small rafts or canoes. Several tricky rock gardens and a few rapids occur below where Flat Creek enters the Dearborn, about 6 miles downstream from the US 287 bridge. These rapids pose a serious hazard to beginning canoeists and an exciting challenge to intermediates. They aren't so hard in a raft. The rock gardens require quick boat handling and become more challenging as the water level drops below 400 cfs.

Key Access Points along the Dearborn River

Access Point (River Mile)	Next Access Point	Access Point (River Mile)	Next Access Point
Dearborn Canyon Road Bridge (45)	4	Highway 287 bridge (19)	21
Highway 434 bridge (41)	12	Mid-Canon FAS	
Highway 200 bridge (29)	10	(takeout on Missouri River)	none

The Dearborn's whitewater offers a good challenge to intermediate paddlers.

While many people do this lower section in one day, if you take much time for photography, fishing, or swimming, you won't make it. The Dearborn canyon is so spectacular that you will want to take your time, but public land camping opportunities are extremely limited and make it difficult to stay overnight on the river. Montana law does allow camping within the high-water mark of the river (defined as the place where the presence of water upon the land changes its characteristics below the line), as long as the camping is not within sight, or within 500 yards, of an occupied dwelling. Islands and gravel bars are the best bets. Respect private property and do not trespass. This river has some VERY sensitive landowners.

Beaver, deer, and raptors abound along the Dearborn, and you may spot one of Montana's less common streamside denizens, the river otter. Unfortunately, trapping of these fascinating creatures is still permitted, even though they are extinct in most states and rare in almost all the rest. This is a predator that everyone can like: They don't eat sheep, grass, or people. Although Lewis and Clark regularly encountered river otters in Montana, count yourself fortunate to see one today.

The typical Dearborn River float season is quite short. The water is often high and dirty into early June, and it often gets too low to float by mid-July. The river offers excellent fly fishing for small rainbows and some cutthroats. A few large brown trout reside in the deep pools. Occasionally a really large fish will grab onto a smaller fish as you reel it in.

For most of its floatable distance, the Dearborn offers a semiwilderness float. Much of the canyon is relatively pristine and very scenic. Along parts of the lower river, however, subdivision and other signs of human activities scar the river. Management of the river corridor is sorely needed if this spectacular river is going to keep its outstanding natural attributes. A cooperative management effort, like that on the Blackfoot River, would be a big step forward.

10 Flathead River, Main Stem

This wide river with aquamarine waters flows tranquilly past the spectacular Mission Mountains.

Vital statistics: 158 miles long from the confluence of the Middle and North Forks to its juncture with the Clark Fork near Paradise.
Level of difficulty: Almost all Class I water except for a whitewater section (Buffalo Rapids) with Class III and IV rapids immediately below where the river exits Flathead Lake.
Flow: Annual mean flow: 11,070 cfs at Perma. Plenty of water all year. Optimum flows for Buffalo Rapids: 10,000 to 13,000 cfs. Maximum flows for floating are 30,000 cfs.
Hazards: Fluctuating water levels caused by dam releases. Occasional big standing waves.
Where the crowd goes: Upper river: Pressentine to Old Steel Bridge. Lower river: Buffalo Rapids
Avoiding the scene: Upper river: Old Steel Bridge to Sportsmans Bridge. Lower river: Dixon to Paradise.
Inside tip: Buffalo Bridge to Sloan Bridge is an excellent overnight trip.

Maps: BLM: #10 (Kalispell), #11 (Polson), #12 (Plains)
USFS: Flathead, Lolo
USGS: Kalispell, MT; Wallace, ID
River rules: Most of the river flows through the Flathead Indian Reservation; floaters age 12 and older need a tribal recreational use permit on the section of the river within the reservation. No motors on the reservation (Kerr Dam to 7 miles downstream from Perma Bridge) March 15 to June 30. Motors over 15 horsepower prohibited at all times. No camping on islands within Flathead Reservation. Motors over 10 horsepower prohibited above South Fork confluence. Catch-and-release cutthroat regulations for the entire river. Bull trout fishing closed on entire river.
For more information: Flathead Raft Company, Polson; Montana Fish, Wildlife and Parks, Kalispell; Confederated Salish and Kootenai Tribes, Pablo; Ronan Sports and Western, Ronan.

The Paddling

If Huck Finn had run away to Montana, he might have made the main branch of the Flathead his home. It's a big, broad, peaceful river—the perfect spot to lay back in a

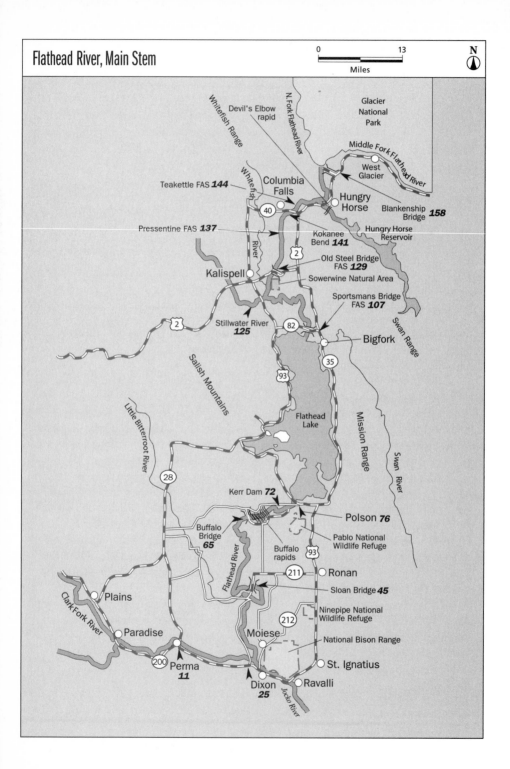

Flathead River, Main Stem

0   13
Miles

N

Whitefish Range

N. Fork Flathead River

Devil's Elbow rapid

Glacier National Park

Middle Fork Flathead River

West Glacier

Teakettle FAS **144**

Whitefish River

Columbia Falls

40

Hungry Horse

Blankenship Bridge **158**

Pressentine FAS **137**

Kokanee Bend **141**

Hungry Horse Reservoir

2

Old Steel Bridge FAS **129**

Kalispell

Sowerwine Natural Area

Sportsmans Bridge FAS **107**

Swan Range

Stillwater River **125**

82

Bigfork

2

35

93

Salish Mountains

Flathead Lake

Mission Range

Swan River

Little Bitterroot River

28

Kerr Dam **72**

Polson **76**

Buffalo Bridge **65**

Flathead River

Buffalo rapids

Pablo National Wildlife Refuge

93

211

Ronan

Sloan Bridge **45**

Clark Fork River

Plains

Ninepipe National Wildlife Refuge

212

Paradise

National Bison Range

200

Perma **11**

Moiese

St. Ignatius

Dixon **25**

Ravalli

Jocko River

Canada geese on the Flathead River attract hunters in fall.

raft or canoe and dream away a summer afternoon. Although its three magnificent forks often get more attention, the main Flathead offers scenic floats with good access that are suitable for beginners.

Floating on the main stem of the Flathead begins near Blankenship Bridge where the North and Middle Forks join. Watch for a rapid known as the Devil's Elbow just downstream from here. The South Fork enters a few miles downstream, just east of Columbia Falls, and there are also a few small rapids in this area.

Fluctuations in water levels caused by releases from Hungry Horse Dam (on the South Fork a few miles upriver from the mouth) create one of the main river's hazards. The water can rise 2 to 3 feet in a short period of time, which speeds up

Key Access Points along the Flathead River, Main Stem

Access Pont (River Mile)	Next Access Point	Access Pont (River Mile)	Next Access Point
Blankenship Bridge (158)	14 miles	Polson Park (76)	4 miles
Teakettle FAS (144)	3 miles	Kerr Dam (72)	7 miles
Kokanee Bend FAS (141)	4 miles	Buffalo Bridge (65)	20 miles
Pressentine FAS (137)	8 miles	Sloan Bridge (45)	20 miles
Old Steel Bridge FAS (129)	22 miles	Dixon (25)	14 miles
Sportsmans Bridge FAS (107)	31 miles	Perma (11)	none

the current significantly. Otherwise the river can be floated easily all the way to Flathead Lake.

Below where the South Fork enters, the main stem of the Flathead can be navigated by practiced beginners in a canoe or raft. It's popular with local residents. The river is particularly intriguing east of Kalispell, where it meanders through swampy lowlands. Here the river channels repeatedly and creates many islands. Old river channels have formed backwaters and oxbows that can teem with waterfowl and beaver. Watch for osprey nests and great blue heron rookeries on secluded islands.

The section of river from Pressentine to Old Steel Bridge is popular with anglers and floaters. Cutthroat and lake whitefish are the primary catch. Immediately upstream from Flathead Lake, the river gets used by floaters, anglers, motorboaters, and even water-skiers.

Below Flathead Lake, easy floating resumes at Buffalo Bridge, which spans the river about 10 miles downstream from Kerr Dam. Most casual floaters avoid the section between Kerr Dam and Buffalo Bridge because of the formidable Buffalo Rapids, which have some big-time whitewater that's suitable for good intermediates and experts only.

BUFFALO RAPIDS–KERR DAM TO BUFFALO BRIDGE While most of the main stem Flathead flows calm and flat, the 6-mile section south of Polson, known as Buffalo Rapids, is a definite exception.

The starting point for a Buffalo Rapids trip is immediately below Kerr Dam Road, only a short distance from where the river exits Flathead Lake. This section lies completely within the Flathead Indian Reservation, and tribal recreational permits are required. (Call the Confederated Salish and Kootenai Tribes at the number listed in appendix A.) The takeout is 7 miles downstream at Buffalo Bridge.

Fluctuating water levels from Kerr Dam can complicate a Buffalo Rapids outing. While summer flows average about 10,000 to 13,000 cfs, they sometimes get as low as 3,200 cfs or as high as 25,000 cfs. Peak flows during spring runoff can reach 60,000 cfs.

Surprisingly enough, the most difficult conditions do not occur at peak flows. In fact, at flows over 20,000 cfs many of the rapids wash out; at 30,000 cfs most of the big waves disappear and are replaced by wicked currents and whirlpools. A flip at high flows, even with a life jacket, can be a dangerous experience. The best whitewater conditions occur at flows between about 10,000 and 18,000 cfs, although some of the rapids get more difficult as the flow drops below 10,000.

The whitewater between Kerr Dam and Buffalo Bridge consists of four major rapids separated by stretches of minor whitewater. The first rapid, known as the Ledge, occurs about 1 mile downstream where the river takes a big bend. A horizontal band of rock crosses the river and creates a small drop with some holes and waves. While the Ledge washes out at flows much over 15,000 cfs, at low flows (3,000 to 6,000 cfs) it can be the most difficult rapid.

Next, about 0.5 mile downstream, comes Pinball, where numerous large rocks create a hazard. At very low flows it's a rock-dodging course, and you may find yourself careening from one rock to another. At more normal flows the rocks disappear and some big waves develop, as well as at least one tricky hole. This rapid can wash out at high flows.

Another 0.25 mile downstream comes Eagle Wave Rapid, the longest continuous white-water in the entire run and arguably the most interesting. At low flows it's a technical rapid with lots of rocks and fast channels. At higher flows a long set of standing waves creates great roller-coaster fun.

The last of the four major rapids is Buffalo Rapids itself, generally considered the most difficult. It's a long S-turn, with the water first sweeping left and then right. Buffalo Rapids is easily recognized because the river narrows markedly and the cliffs get higher. Be sure to scout if it's your first trip through. Look for an easy eddy where you can pull in on the left side of the river immediately above the rapid. You'll find a good path up to the cliffs for an excellent view of the river.

Watch for two major obstacles—a diagonal wave and a big rock in a narrow spot. Buffalo Rapids is ideal at about 15,000 cfs. At this flow, a huge wave forms in the bottom part of the run. Many rafters make the big climb up this wall of water, stall out in the vertical position, and flip over. The obvious line through Buffalo runs down the left channel, and almost everyone runs it that way. It's much more hazardous on the right. After Buffalo it's mostly flatwater before hitting the takeout at Buffalo Bridge.

While the Buffalo Rapids aren't particularly difficult (strong intermediates will do fine) they can be hazardous because of the high water volume and strong currents. The rapids are Class II and Class III, with Buffalo a difficult Class III at flows over 9,000 cfs. You can get information on water levels by calling the office at Kerr Dam. Be aware that these are current flows, not forecasts, and actual levels can vary significantly between morning and evening.

Floater use of Buffalo Rapids has increased markedly during the past two decades. According to recreation officials with the Confederated Salish and Kootenai Tribes, peak days may see as many as 200 people on the river. For those interested in commercial trips, the Flathead Raft Company generally runs two trips per day, June through Labor Day. (See appendix A for the company's phone number.)

Below Buffalo Bridge, the Flathead flows tranquilly for 65 miles before joining the Clark Fork River near Paradise. This extremely scenic section of river rolls by steep cliffs and unusual badlands. Abundant wildflowers and occasional abandoned homesteads accentuate the broad vistas along this isolated and undisturbed portion. The clear, aquamarine waters add a dimension to a trip quite unlike any other in western Montana.

Bird-watchers enjoy the great variety of avian life that darts and hops along the river; one group of floaters spotted more than seventy species during a two-day trip. During migration it's possible to see more than one hundred species. Raptors are particularly prevalent as the high cliffs provide excellent habitat. At least three breeding pairs of bald eagles nest along the lower river. Many species of waterfowl nest along the river, and concentrations of several thousand geese are not uncommon in early winter.

Motorboats are prohibited on the entire lower Flathead during the waterfowl-nesting season (March 15 through June 30). Motors larger than 15 horsepower are prohibited at all times.

The lower Flathead has the dubious distinction of being one of the worst trout-fishing streams in western Montana. Fisheries studies have discovered an average of only fifteen trout per mile in most segments. Irregular fluctuations of Kerr Dam hurt insect productivity and make some spawning habitat inaccessible. Glacial silts in the river are also thought to contribute to poor fish productivity. Be sure to check the tribal fishing regulations, as this section is catch-and-release (catch them if you can!) trout fishing.

On the other hand, the lower Flathead has an outstanding and extraordinary northern pike fishery that, for some people, more than compensates for the trout scarcity. Fisheries biologists report that the average pike caught in the Flathead weighs about seven pounds, and that pike in the twenty-pound class are not at all unusual. The northerns were introduced at Lone Pine Reservoir about twenty years ago and then made their way to the Flathead via the Little Bitterroot River. The northerns usually can be found in shallow, weedy backwater areas of the river.

The lower Flathead has four major access points: Buffalo Bridge, Sloan Bridge, Dixon, and Perma. The 20-mile section between Buffalo Bridge and Sloan Bridge is one of the nicest. While this trip can be made in a day with an early start, some people prefer to go overnight and continue to Dixon, the next access point. A Flathead Indian Reservation camping stamp can be purchased at Ronan Sports and Western (406-676-3701) and other area sporting stores

The section of the river between Dixon and Perma receives little pressure from floaters but receives some use by motorboaters. The river above Sloan Bridge receives minimal motorboat use.

Although the lower Flathead has some frisky riffles, it's an easy float that beginners can enjoy. It's the kind of river where it's possible to play a guitar or eat a picnic lunch while watching the scenery pass by. But do keep an eye peeled for occasional rocks or obstructions.

Canoes are the craft of choice on a big river like this, as they can be paddled effectively in strong headwinds where rafts can be troublesome. Under normal conditions, however, almost any craft will do.

Keep in mind that most of the river flows through the Flathead Indian Reservation, and floaters need a tribal recreational use permit. Camping stamps are needed for overnight trips. Dam proposals have been made for at least six different sites on the lower Flathead. In the late 1970s the U.S. Army Corps of Engineers had several dams under active consideration. They have settled into quiescence in recent years, but dam proposals are like a fungus. You can't always be sure whether they're dead or alive, but it's impossible to kill them. Be vigilant!

11 North Fork Flathead River

The glacial-green waters of the North Fork flow through heavily forested terrain along the west border of Glacier National Park, occasionally providing spectacular glimpses of snowcapped peaks.

Vital statistics: 58 miles long from the Canadian border to its juncture with the Middle Fork near West Glacier.

Level of difficulty: Class I with occasional Class II for most of its length. A short section of whitewater between Big Creek and Glacier Rim.

Flow: Annual mean flow: 2,889 cfs near Glacier Rim Fishing Access Site. Usually good all year, but can get too low above Ford in dry years (below 2,000 cfs). Best conditions are usually from mid-July to mid-August. Don't try floating with flows over 25,500 cfs.

Hazards: Dangerous logjams, narrow channels, shallow riffles; cold, glacial water.

Where the crowd goes: Big Creek to Glacier Rim.

Avoiding the scene: Polebridge to Big Creek.

Inside tip: Go overnight and howl with the wolves.

Maps: BLM: #9 (Whitefish Range), #10 (Kalispell)

USFS: Flathead

Flathead National Forest and Glacier Natural History Association: 3 Forks of the Flathead River

USGS: Kalispell, MT; Glacier National Park

Montana Afloat: #5 (The Flathead River: North Fork)

River rules: Entire river closed to bull trout fishing. Catch-and-release for cutthroats. Mouth of Big Creek closed to fishing June 1 through August 31. Campers beware: The park boundary runs down the middle of the river, and special permits are required to camp within the park.

For more information: Montana Raft Company, West Glacier; Glacier Raft Company, West Glacier; Flathead National Forest, Hungry Horse; Montana Fish, Wildlife and Parks, Kalispell.

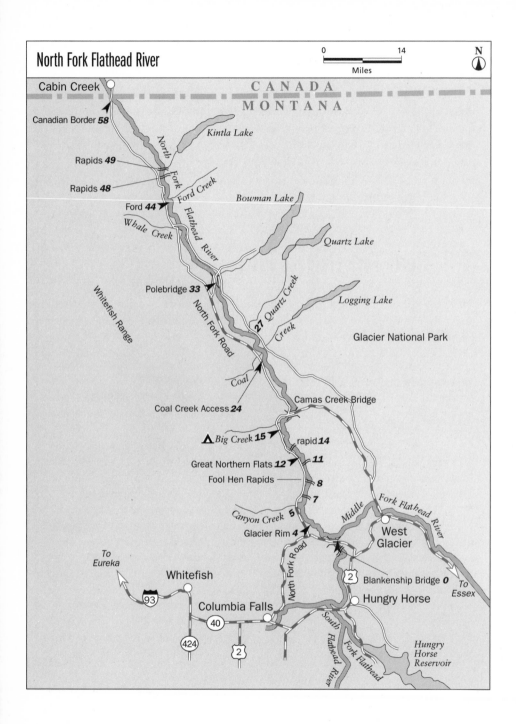

The Paddling

Born of glacial torrents, the North Fork of the Flathead flows wild and pure out of Canada and then rushes southward 58 miles through Montana, forming the western boundary of Glacier National Park. This beautiful, limpid-green river joins the Middle Fork of the Flathead just below Blankenship Bridge, near West Glacier, to form the main trunk of the Flathead. The entire length of the North Fork is a designated segment of the National Wild and Scenic Rivers System. The entire drainage is an elegant blend of towering mountains, verdant forests, and sparkling waters.

In 1892 a steamboat attempted to ascend the North Fork. An enterprising man by the name of James Talbot conceived this ill-fated venture. Talbot, an early-day boomer, learned of the coal deposits along the North Fork and envisioned this coal could fuel the construction of a railroad, which would stimulate the growth of his town of Columbia Falls and fatten his wallet at the same time.

Talbot built a 75-foot steamship, named it *The Oakes*, and in May of 1892 attempted the swollen North Fork. After several days of hard work, the crew was about 10 miles upriver. Somewhere in the vicinity of what we know today as Fool Hen Rapids the steamer *Oakes* took on too much water and sank. Though no crewmembers were lost, they all had to traverse difficult terrain to make their way back to Columbia Falls.

While steamships no longer try the North Fork, an armada of rafters and canoeists challenge it each year. Considering the North Fork's remote setting, access is excellent. Although an unpaved road parallels the river for its entire distance in Montana, it rarely can be seen. The North Fork Road, which runs along the west side of the river, has long been a focal point of controversy. Some folks want the road improved to promote tourism and logging. Conservationists and most local residents want it left the way it is—bumpy, narrow, and dusty. So far the latter group has prevailed.

A road on the east side of the river in Glacier National Park also parallels the river for much of its length and offers occasional access. Called the "inside" North Fork Road, it leads to Kintla Lake and offers limited river access between Polebridge and the lake.

Most floaters, however, launch from the west side of the river. Developed river access points occur at fairly regular intervals, and there are some undeveloped launch sites off the road.

Key Access Points along North Fork Flathead River

Access Point (River Mile)	Next Access Point	Access Point (River Mile)	Next Access Point
Canadian Border (58)	14 miles	Big Creek (15)	3 miles
Ford (44)	11 miles	Great Northern Flats (12)	8 miles
Polebridge (33)	9 miles	Glacier Rim (4)	4 miles
Coal Creek (24)	9 miles	Blankenship Bridge (0)	none

The Flathead's North Fork forms the west boundary of Glacier National Park.

Floating in Montana begins at the Canadian border river access and continues for the North Fork's entire distance in Montana. From the Canadian border to Polebridge, numerous logjams and fast currents provide serious hazards, particularly when the water is high. While the river is not technically difficult, the high wood content means mistakes can be dangerous. Because the nearby mountains are so high, run-off sometimes extends well into July. Watch for some large standing waves near the mouth of Kintla Creek. Intermediate rafters and canoeists can handle the section from the border to Polebridge.

The easiest section of the river lies between Polebridge and Big Creek. Beginners can handle it when the water is low and weather conditions are favorable, but they should stay clear during higher flows. The North Fork has extremely cold water, and early-season spills can be very dangerous. Again, watch carefully for logjams and narrow channels. Be wary of shallow riffles where the current is fast. You may tip your canoe if you aren't parallel to the current. Be prepared to jump out and walk your canoe through shallow spots if you get hung up.

The most challenging section of the North Fork lies between Big Creek and the Glacier Rim river access. It's suitable for intermediates in rafts or canoes at moderate flows. Deep runs and pools are interrupted by four significant rapids, the first about 1 mile below Big Creek, the second about 4 miles downstream (a small Class III). About 3 miles before the takeout at Glacier Rim are the Fool Hen Rapids, which actually are two Class III rapids less than a mile apart. Big standing waves usually line up below each of the rapids.

Spring runoff on the North Fork typically starts in late May and runs through late June. Best conditions are usually from about mid-July to mid-August. After mid-August, particularly during dry years, the river from the Canadian border to Ford Station can get really scratchy and may be too low to float. From Ford downriver, the North Fork is usually floatable unless it's frozen. Fall trips can be outstanding when there's enough water. Get up-to-date information by calling the Forest Service's Hungry Horse Ranger District at the phone number listed in appendix A.

Fishing on the North Fork is often mediocre, but it's unpredictable. Most of the fish in the river are migratory, so it's a matter of being in the right place at the right time. The North Fork is one of the few remaining rivers in Montana that support a native fishery. The primary species are westslope cutthroat and bull trout (also known as Dolly Varden). Dolly Varden was a character in a Dickens novel distinguished by her gaudy clothes. A member of the char family, this beautifully colored fish lives up to its name. Once native to many Montana rivers, healthy populations remain in only a few of the state's rivers. Westslope cutthroats are listed as a threatened species.

Because the North Fork is a glacial stream, it doesn't have the nutrients that make southwestern Montana trout streams so productive. As a result, there are fewer fish, and they grow more slowly. Moreover, some call the cutthroat trout the most gullible fish that swims, making them vulnerable to overfishing. The North Fork is a great place to practice catch-and-release fishing, especially for larger fish. All bull trout must be released. Be sure to check the regulations.

The North Fork's proximity to Glacier National Park makes it an excellent place to spot wild critters of all kinds. Bald eagles and ospreys are common, as are moose, which prefer the willow bottoms. It's a great river to spot river otters, and floaters sometimes even see grizzly bears and wolves.

While the North Fork currently runs clean and pure, several threats make its future cloudy. High-grade coal underlies much of the river's headwaters in Canada, and a coal company has been studying the feasibility of open-pit mining near Cabin Creek, a tributary of the North Fork just 8 miles over the border.

If possible coal development isn't enough, much of the surrounding Flathead National Forest has been explored for oil and gas development. But the North Fork's most persistent and pervasive problem is creeping subdivision, as more and more people want to build their houses or cabins near this pristine river.

A group of citizens known as the North Fork Preservation Association is the local watchdog group, and they can always use assistance—either writing letters or sending cash. If you'd like to give something back to the North Fork, the association's address is listed in appendix B.

12 Middle Fork Flathead River

An extremely challenging and remote whitewater stream, the Middle Fork roars through the Bob Marshall Wilderness and forms the southern border of Glacier National Park.

Vital statistics: 90 miles long from the confluence of Strawberry and Bowl Creeks in the Bob Marshall Wilderness to its juncture with the North Fork near West Glacier.

Level of difficulty: Extremely difficult whitewater in the wilderness section, with Class IV rapids or better at peak flows. Experts only. Class II, III, and IV rapids outside the wilderness.

Flow: Annual mean flow: 2,879 cfs near West Glacier. Wilderness section typically too low by late July. The river can be floated all year outside the wilderness. Check the gauge on the West Glacier bridge: Floating is possible when the flows are between 1 and 8 feet.

Hazards: Big rocks, dangerous snags, deep holes. Cold water and cold air can create hypothermic conditions even in summer.

Where the crowd goes: Moccasin Creek to West Glacier.

Avoiding the scene: The portion within the wilderness.

Inside tip: The Glacier Raft Company provides excellent raft trips at a fair price on the moderate whitewater section near West Glacier. This incredibly scenic float makes a great side trip when visiting Glacier National Park and is sure to please out-of-town visitors.

Maps: BLM: #9 (Whitefish Range), #10 (Kalispell), #17 (Saint Mary), #18 (Hungry Horse Reservoir)

USFS: Flathead, Bob Marshall Complex Topographic Map

USGS: Cutbank, MT; Kalispell, MT; Glacier National Park, MT

Flathead National Forest and Glacier Natural History Association: 3 Forks of the Flathead River Floating Guide.

River rules: Motors limited to recreation section (downstream from Bear Creek). Maximum size 10 horsepower. Special-use permits for outfitters only. Registration for wilderness floats at Schafer Meadows. Check for special fishing regulations. Park boundary is ordinary high-water mark on park side of river.

For more information: Montana Raft Company, West Glacier; Glacier Raft Company, West Glacier; Great Northern Whitewater, West Glacier; Flathead National Forest, Hungry Horse.

The Paddling

Those who have floated the Middle Fork of the Flathead know why it's called Montana's wildest river. Numerous large boulders have settled in the bottom of this heavily glaciated valley, which drops an average 35 feet per mile as it plunges out of one of the largest expanses of wilderness in the lower forty-eight states. Downed trees sometimes block the river, creating serious hazards for floaters but excellent habitat for fish. Throw in the high water volumes during runoff, and the difficulty of getting help if there's trouble, and it's plain why the Middle Fork is not a stream for the fainthearted.

A designated component of the National Wild and Scenic Rivers System for its entire length, the tumultuous Middle Fork gets its start in the untrammeled

The Middle Fork of the Flathead has been called Montana's wildest river.

peaks of the Bob Marshall Wilderness. As Dale Burk explains in his book *Great Bear, Wild River:*

> "The Middle Fork of the Flathead begins hard against the Continental Divide in the steep, highly erosive slopes of mountains where a glacier once rode the earth. . . . It is set amidst startlingly scenic mountains, its channel often literally carved through the sedimentary rock cliffs that sweep straight upward onto slopes so steep they are difficult for a man to hike upon."

Burk's book chronicles the bitter battle to establish the Great Bear Wilderness. The Great Bear, named for the grizzlies that inhabit the area, became a designated wilderness in 1978. This 285,000-acre area encompasses nearly 50 miles of the Middle Fork.

As might be expected, access to the uppermost sections of the Middle Fork is difficult. The options are to pack in with horses or fly in to the airstrip at Schafer Meadows. A pack trail parallels the river for most of its wilderness flow.

This starting point is located about 27 miles upstream from Bear Creek, where the river first meets civilization. From this point downstream (about 46 miles), the river parallels U.S. Highway 2.

Middle Fork Flathead River

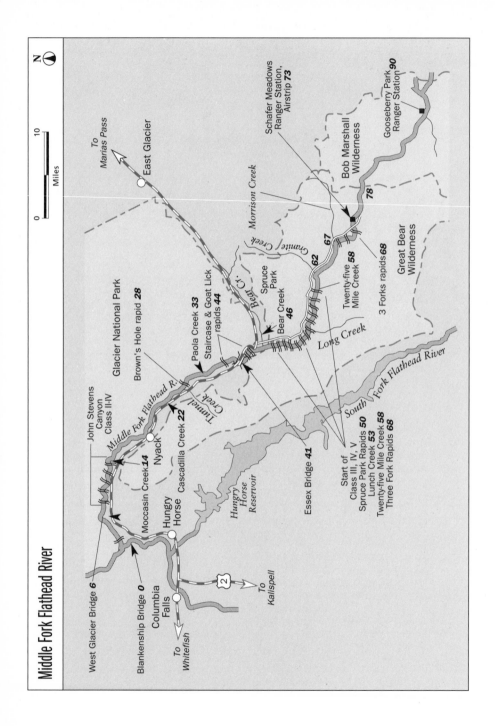

N

0   10
Miles

To Marias Pass

East Glacier

Glacier National Park

John Stevens Canyon Class II-IV

Brown's Hole rapid **28**

Paola Creek **33**

Staircase & Goat Lick rapids **44**

Bear Cr.

Spruce Park

Bear Creek **46**

Granite Creek

Morrison Creek

67

62

Schafer Meadows Ranger Station, Airstrip **73**

Bob Marshall Wilderness

78

Gooseberry Park Ranger Station **90**

Twenty-five Mile Creek **58**

3 Forks rapids **68**

Great Bear Wilderness

West Glacier Bridge **6**

Moccasin Creek **14**

Nyack

Middle Fork Flathead R.

Cascadilla Creek **22**

Tunnel Creek

Long Creek

South Fork Flathead River

Blankenship Bridge **0**

Columbia Falls

Hungry Horse

Hungry Horse Reservoir

2

To Whitefish

To Kalispell

Essex Bridge **41**

Start of Class III, IV, V

Spruce Park Rapids **50**

Lunch Creek **53**

Twenty-five Mile Creek **58**

Three Fork Rapids **68**

Key Access Points along Middle Fork Flathead River

Access Point (River Mile)	Next Access Point	Access Point (River Mile)	Next Access Point
Schafer Meadows (73)	27 miles	Cascadilla Creek (22)	8 miles
Bear Creek (46)	5 miles	Moccasin Creek (14)	8 miles
Essex Bridge (41)	8 miles	West Glacier (6)	6 miles
Paola Creek (33)	11 miles	Blankenship Bridge (0)	none

Most people fly in, which provides an interesting river perspective. From the air the Middle Fork looks like a frothing thread of water, liberally sprinkled with large boulders and occasional logjams.

To avoid human "logjams," the Forest Service has placed restrictions on the number of commercial outfitters who can operate on the river, but it has not restricted private floaters. The Forest Service limits party size to ten people both for commercial and noncommercial groups.

Although flows average about 1,000 cubic feet of water per second (measured at West Glacier), peak flows can exceed ten times that amount. While the river typically carries about 700 cfs of water in February, flows increase dramatically when the snow melts, sometimes climbing to more than 11,000 cfs at the peak of runoff in early June. The Middle Fork is unfloatable during these peak discharges. Even professional outfitters don't go.

The optimum floating period on the wilderness portion of the Middle Fork is usually from early June through mid-July. Air temperatures dictate the rate of runoff. Keep in mind, however, that even on warm days, water temperatures will be quite low—usually around 40 degrees. Rainstorms, combined with the low water temperatures in the river, make hypothermia a real threat on early-season floats.

In a normal year, flows in the upper river drop sharply in mid-July, and floating can become difficult. In low-water conditions, each rapid becomes a maze of exposed rocks that can tear up rafts. Check river conditions with the Forest Service's Hungry Horse Ranger District at Hungry Horse or on the USGS Web site.

When the river is ripping, it's easy to float from Schafer Meadows to Bear Creek in a day. Most floaters, however, choose to take a couple of days so they can camp and have time to explore the Great Bear Wilderness. While it's possible to get out at Bear Creek, the Essex Bridge is the usual take-out spot. With these few extra miles, floaters not only catch a couple more good rapids but also get to visit the famous goat lick on the edge of Glacier National Park.

The goat lick is a slumping cliff on the north side of the river where mountain goats come down from the crags to lick exposed mineral salts. It's one of the few places in North America where it's possible to see wild goats next to a wild river. If you've managed to keep your camera dry, it's an excellent place to take pictures. Just don't approach the goats too closely.

The trip through the wilderness section of the Middle Fork can be run by intermediates at lower flows but only by experts when it's high. The rapids change from year to year as boulders tumble into the river and trees lodge in different places. The most difficult rapids lie in a 3-mile canyon below Spruce Park. (For a complete description, see the "River Wild" sidebar.)

The remoteness of the upper Middle Fork makes it doubly dangerous. Those who haven't run many rivers as technically difficult as the Middle Fork may want to consider hiring an outfitter. The Hungry Horse Ranger District can provide a list of reputable ones.

Middle Fork float trips require considerable skill and quality equipment. A durable raft (a self-bailer would be an excellent choice) with a rowing platform is the standard. For safety purposes, it's best to have two or three rafts per party. Be sure to take along extra paddles or oars, as they can be snapped off on cliff walls or submerged logs. Wetsuits or rain gear is a necessity. This is one river where it's not necessary to remind people to wear life jackets. You may wish you had two.

Because the number of good campsites along the river is limited, this river corridor has potential for overuse. Tread lightly, and pack everything out. To avoid problems with grizzly bears, hang food and other bear attractants out of their reach and keep a clean campsite. Consult *Bear Aware* by Bill Schneider (Falcon, 2004) and *Leave No Trace: Minimum Impact Outdoor Recreation* by Will Harmon (Falcon, 1997) for advice on camping safely and responsibly in bear country.

The nonwilderness section of the Middle Fork receives heavy summertime use, much of it from Glacier National Park visitors. The tourists usually get their money's worth. Moose, deer, bears, and a host of smaller mammals and birds often are seen near the river. Cutthroat trout, bull trout, and whitefish—all native fish—swim the waters and occasionally fall prey to artificial flies or wobbling spoons.

The Middle Fork is one of Montana's best-protected rivers. It flows through the wilderness for half its length, and it forms the southern border of Glacier National Park for the other half. The biggest problem this river faces is potential overuse, but the Forest Service so far has done an excellent job of managing people problems.

RIVER WILD
The wilderness section of the Middle Fork has some challenging rapids, as does the more accessible portion of the river that runs immediately adjacent to Glacier National Park.

Soaking rains may accompany early-season Middle Fork trips, and without a wetsuit or quality rain gear, hypothermia is possible. This can cause serious errors in judgment, such as not scouting difficult rapids. Be prepared for cold temperatures and adverse weather.

Major rapids on the Middle Fork begin a couple of miles below Schafer Meadows, with a group known as the Three Fork series. The Forest Service rates them Class IV at high flows and Class III at normal flows. These three rapids occur in a 1-mile stretch upstream from Morrison Creek. You can breathe easier for the next 10 miles after Morrison Creek, until you pass Twenty-five Mile Creek. Below here, for the next 7 miles, is the most difficult water the Middle Fork offers. The toughest rapids are the Spruce Park Rapids, a set of three sharp drops that start just downstream from the Spruce Park guard station. The rapids have huge waves, big rocks, and turbulence capable of flipping a raft. The Forest Service rates them Class V at peak flows, but under more normal conditions they are Class IV. You'll want to check these out carefully before going through, but the rugged terrain and lack of eddies to pull out makes scouting difficult.

After Spruce Park there are no more difficult rapids before the Middle Fork meets U.S. Highway 2 near Bear Creek. Just downstream from Bear Creek, however, are two more Class III rapids known as Staircase and Goat Lick. They are close to the place along the river where exposed natural salts attract mountain goats. The Isaak Walton Lodge is nearby also.

Between Essex Bridge and Moccasin Creek, expect mostly Class II water. Watch for a drop called Brown's Hole, about 1 mile below Paola Creek, that's difficult at high water. Expert and strong intermediate canoeists can handle this strikingly beautiful section of river except at peak flows. Watch for snags and dangerous logjams. If you don't have a spray skirt, be prepared to bail.

The Middle Fork's last gasp happens between Moccasin Creek and West Glacier in the 8-mile-long John Stevens Canyon. Cliff walls restrict the river to a narrow channel as it descends over rock ledges. It drops about 35 feet per mile as it dashes through the canyon. Expect to encounter fairly continuous whitewater for 2 to 3 miles through the middle of the canyon, suitable for intermediate and better rafters and kayakers, depending on water levels.

For those who like to know the names, here's a rundown of rapids for the John Stevens Canyon: The first two, Tunnel and Bonecrusher, are pretty mild and get you ready for the toughest rapid, known as Jaws. Next comes Narrows, then Repeater, then C.B.T.; shortly before West Glacier is Pumphouse. Most of the rapids are Class II or III, but the Forest Service rates Jaws as Class IV at peak flows.

From West Glacier to the Blankenship Bridge is a good half-day float for beginners in rafts or canoes.

13 South Fork Flathead River

The South Fork is a fairy-tale wilderness river that flows through the heart of the Bob Marshall Wilderness, with crystal-clear waters, native cutthroat trout, and an occasional grizzly bear.

Vital statistics: 100 miles long (including 35 reservoir miles) from the confluence of Danaher and Youngs Creeks to the Flathead River at Hungry Horse.

Level of difficulty: The river is predominately Class I but is punctuated by some difficult rapids. The extremely remote Meadow Creek Gorge has Class III and IV rapids (Class V at peak flows) and should only be attempted by experts. Watch for a short set of Class III and IV rapids below Hungry Horse Dam.

Flow: Annual mean flow: 2,310 cfs near Twin Creek. Not recommended at high flows (above 5,500 cfs). Few people risk the South Fork during runoff, which usually peaks in mid-June. July is prime time. In dry years it usually gets too low by early August. For floats starting at Youngs Creek, 2,000 cfs is minimum; 750 cfs is minimum for floats beginning at Big Salmon Creek.

Hazards: Logjams and shallow riffles in the upper section, major rapids and narrow restrictions in the middle section. Hang your food at campsites, away from bears, porcupines, and squirrels.

Where the crowd goes: Difficult access limits use, but many outfitters take clients from Youngs Creek to the takeout above Meadow Creek Gorge.

Avoiding the scene: Few people float the gorge (for good reason).

Inside tip: Harrison Creek to Spotted Bear (via the Cedar Flats access) is a great one-day trip.

Maps: BLM: #10 (Kalispell), #18 (Hungry Horse Reservoir), #19 (Swan Peak)
USFS: Flathead, Bob Marshall Complex
USGS: Choteau, MT; Cut Bank, MT; Kalispell, MT
Glacier Natural History Association: 3 Forks of the Flathead River Floating Guide

River rules: No motors, special fishing regulations.

For more information: Flathead National Forest, Hungry Horse; Spotted Bear Ranger Station, on the river.

The Paddling

Nature writer Edwin Way Teale once wrote, "To the lost man, to the pioneer penetrating a new country, to the naturalist who wishes to see the wild land at its wildest, the advice is always the same—follow a river. The river is the original forest highway. It is nature's own Wilderness Road."

So it is with the South Fork of the Flathead River, the main travel route through Montana's Bob Marshall Wilderness. The South Fork is Montana's most pristine and inaccessible river, a designated component of the National Wild and Scenic Rivers System for nearly its entire length.

Those wishing to float the wilderness portion of the South Fork must either hike or ride horses a considerable distance before they hit the water. Most people approach

A very narrow restriction in the Meadow Creek Gorge—this is the entire river!

the river via Holland Lake and Gordon Creek, a distance of about 27 miles. Others pack in over Pyramid Pass and reach the South Fork via Youngs Creek, which is slightly farther. The usual starting point is Big Prairie, as the river is often too low to float after mid-July above this point.

The South Fork offers what may be the best native cutthroat fishery in the state. Special regulations designed to protect large fish have resulted in large numbers in the 12- to 18-inch range. Moreover, cutthroats are notoriously easy to catch.

The trip from Big Prairie to the South Fork access just downstream from Spotted Bear Ranger Station covers about 45 miles and can easily be floated in four days. Because equipment must be packed such a long distance, most people make the trip in small rafts, allowing for two persons and about sixty pounds of gear per raft. Campsites are easy to find along the river.

From Big Prairie to Salmon Forks, a distance of about 14 miles, you can relax and enjoy the scenery, as there are few or no rapids. This upper section of the river may have logjams that completely block the river, however, so be prepared for portages. This upper section is often too low by mid-August or earlier in dry years, and it may be necessary to drag your raft across some riffles. Salmon Forks can generally be reached the first day.

The next section, between Salmon Forks and Black Bear Creek, is about 12 miles. Here the river increases in depth and begins to form more pools and riffles.

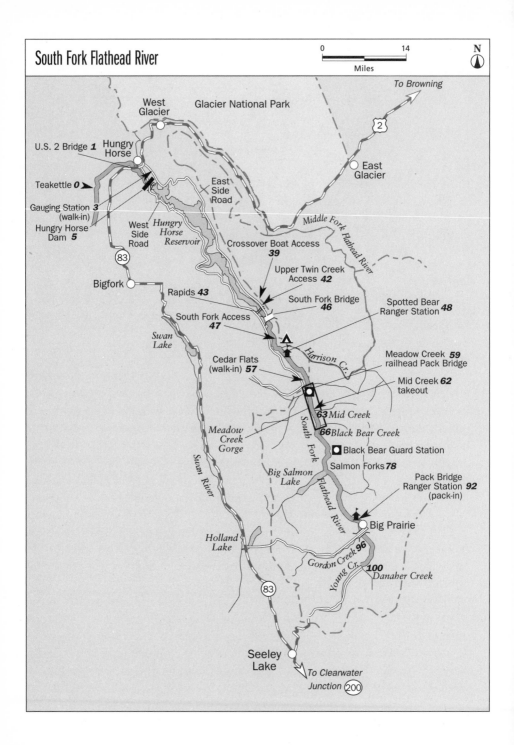

South Fork Flathead River

0   14
Miles

N

To Browning

Glacier National Park

West Glacier

U.S. 2 Bridge *1* Hungry Horse

Teakettle *0*

Gauging Station *3*
(walk-in)

Hungry Horse Dam *5*

West Side Road

East Side Road

Hungry Horse Reservoir

East Glacier

Middle Fork Flathead River

Crossover Boat Access *39*

Upper Twin Creek Access *42*

South Fork Bridge *46*

Spotted Bear Ranger Station *48*

Rapids *43*

South Fork Access *47*

Swan Lake

Harrison Cr.

Meadow Creek *59* railhead Pack Bridge

Cedar Flats (walk-in) *57*

Mid Creek *62* takeout

63 Mid Creek

Meadow Creek Gorge

66 Black Bear Creek

South Fork

Swan River

Big Salmon Lake

Black Bear Guard Station

Salmon Forks *78*

Pack Bridge Ranger Station *92* (pack-in)

Flathead River

Holland Lake

Big Prairie

Gordon Creek 96

Young Cr.

100

Danaher Creek

Bigfork

83

83

Seeley Lake

To Clearwater Junction 200

Key Access Points along South Fork Flathead River

Access Point (River Mile)	Next Access Point	Access Point (River Mile)	Next Access Point
Big Prairie (pack-in) (92)	30 miles	Upper Twin Creek Access (42)	3 miles
Mid Creek Takeout (pack-in) (62)	5 miles	Crossover Boat Access on	
Cedar Flats (walk-in) (57)	10 miles	Hungry Horse Reservoir (39)	none
South Fork Access		Gauging Station (3)	5 miles
(primitive access) (47)	5 miles	Teakettle FAS (2 miles on the main Flathead)	

The South Fork's water is extraordinarily clear and pure, and the bottom is dotted with brick-red, chalk-white, and aqua-green rocks. The water is so clear that, with polarized sunglasses, it's often possible to see trout coming to your fly well in advance of the strike. While the river speeds up a bit, it's still not very difficult. What's so remarkable about the South Fork isn't that it's so unusually spectacular but that it's so wild and untrammeled. The South Fork looks much like many other broad western Montana valleys, with one exception—it has no roads.

Floaters typically hit the tough part of the South Fork on the third day. While it's only about 9 river miles from Black Bear Creek to Harrison Creek, allow an entire day for this spectacular section. Look for a few rapids right below Black Bear Creek, but the real hazards begin in a narrow canyon just downstream from where Mid Creek pours into the South Fork. A large Forest Service sign just above this point warns boaters that this is the last safe takeout if you intend to portage around the downstream gorge. In the course of the next 2 miles below the sign, the river squeezes into restrictions so narrow in two separate places that a raft cannot pass through. At one of these points, it's possible to stand with one foot on each side of the river and watch the river flow between your legs.

Less than 1 mile below the second major restriction comes the incredible Meadow Creek Gorge. Be prepared for a spectacular entry. Just above the gorge, there's a tricky little rapid that shoots you around a blind corner, under the Meadow Creek pack bridge, and into the gorge. It's a real thrill—the river is too fast and the cliff walls too steep to permit any scouting of what's coming. Instead you blast into the gorge praying there aren't any serious obstacles or obstructions.

From a sheer geologic perspective, the gorge is the most spectacular part of the trip. Canyon walls rise up nearly 150 feet, as the gorge itself is but a narrow cleft, a ribbon of water in an otherwise solid mass of rock. Often less than 15 feet wide, it's like being in a labyrinth; the canyon twists and turns, and it's impossible to see what lies around the corner. It's quite dark in the bottom of the canyon and eerily quiet except for one place where a waterfall pounds down from above. While the current in the mile-long gorge is rather swift, it's smooth and there aren't permanent hazards. While winding around the curves, however, one can't help but be apprehensive about the possibility of a logjam in this narrow chasm. It's often possible to look up and see logs that completely bridge the canyon. When in the gorge (and in other narrow spots on the river), you'll want to have a stout stick or a rugged canoe paddle handy to keep your boat from bouncing off cliff walls. It's such a narrow gorge that standard raft oars on a frame are almost useless.

Immediately past the gorge begins some of the South Fork's most difficult and dangerous whitewater. Large rocks combined with swift current make passage rather technical, and scouting is recommended. The whitewater doesn't last very long, however. By the time Harrison Creek enters, the difficult water is behind you.

From Harrison Creek to Spotted Bear, the river is also wild and beautiful and receives only modest use. While the upper section of the river receives heavy outfitter pressure, almost no outfitters take clients through the gorge. Consequently the river below Mid Creek receives much less boat traffic. The road on the east side of Hungry Horse Reservoir is the quickest route to Spotted Bear, although it is dirt for its entirety. It's a ninety-minute drive from Hungry Horse to Cedar Flats. The only access points are the Meadow Creek airstrip or the Cedar Flats river access, off the Meadow Creek Road (Forest Road 2826). The Cedar Flats access involves a steep, 400-yard hike down a narrow trail to the river, but it is possible to wrestle a boat down. It's about a four-hour float from Cedar Flats to the South Fork access—short but spectacular. From Spotted Bear downstream to where Hungry Horse Reservoir impounds the river, there's easy public access on both sides of the road.

While floating on the South Fork is only moderately difficult, its extreme isolation makes it far too risky for beginners. Errors here can mean serious discomfort, even death. Intermediates could make the trip if they go when the water is low and they portage around Meadow Creek Gorge (about 4 miles by trail—it's best to make arrangements with an outfitter).

Only experts should attempt the hazardous float between Mid and Harrison Creeks. While the gorge itself is not that dangerous if one portages the narrow restrictions, the hazard level is high and there's little margin for error if you make a mistake. Anyone floating below the warning sign should get out and scout each dangerous point. Except at the highest flows, it's possible to get out and scout except where the river rushes under the Meadow Creek pack bridge. It's easy to hear the roar of the obstructions well in advance. At the two restrictions where portages are mandatory, the routes are obvious along the canyon walls. The first one is short and the second one a few hundred yards.

No official access exists on the 5 miles of the South Fork that flows below Hungry Horse Reservoir. An unofficial access point exists about 3 miles north of U.S. Highway 2. This section of river has Class III whitewater and fluctuates significantly based on dam releases. Use caution; several people have drowned in this section after floating mishaps.

14 Gallatin River

Originating in Yellowstone National Park, the alpine-surrounded Gallatin River provides great whitewater and good fishing as it courses through one of the most scenic valleys in Montana. The Gallatin River actually consists of two forks, the East Gallatin and the West Gallatin Rivers. Because the West Gallatin is substantially larger, it's generally recognized as the main-stem river. While both branches are floatable, they differ sharply in character.

Vital statistics: 100 miles long from the Wyoming border to the Missouri River near Three Forks. The East Gallatin River, a major tributary of the Gallatin, is also floatable for about 20 miles from Bozeman to its confluence with the main stem near Manhattan.

Level of difficulty: A difficult whitewater stream with Class II, III, and IV rapids in the upper 40 miles. Very technical; experts only at high flows.

Flow: Annual mean flow: 810 cfs near Gallatin Gateway. Often too low by late July. On the lower river (measured at Gallatin Gateway), 500 cfs is a minimum flow and 2,500 cfs is a maximum flow. For the Mad Mile, 8,000 cfs should be maximum for whitewater enthusiasts.

Hazards: Large rocks, tricky currents, large waves, diversion dams, and logjams on the Gallatin. Barbed-wire fences, sharp bends, low water, and narrow brushy channels on the East Gallatin.

Where the crowd goes: Big Sky to Squaw Creek.

Avoiding the scene: Shed's Bridge Fishing Access Site to Missouri Headwaters State Park.

Inside tip: Great fall duck hunting from Logan to Trident. A birder's paradise.

Maps: BLM: #43 (Bozeman), #44 (Ennis)
USFS: Gallatin
USGS: Bozeman, MT
Montana Afloat: #11 (The Gallatin River)

River rules: No fishing from boats from Yellowstone National Park to the confluence with East Gallatin.

For more information: Yellowstone Raft Company, Big Sky; Montana Fish, Wildlife and Parks, Bozeman.

The Paddling

The Gallatin River springs from the snow-clad peaks of the Madison and Gallatin Mountain ranges and courses for more than 90 miles before joining the Madison and Jefferson Rivers at Three Forks. The Gallatin comes close to being an alpine stream as it spills through the scenic Gallatin Canyon, where frequent rapids alternate with deep, green pools alive with trout.

The upper 40 miles of the Gallatin River contain some of Montana's very finest whitewater with an abundance of technical rapids, tight turns, big rocks, and large waves. While much of Montana's whitewater consists of large drops separated by long stretches of flatwater, the Gallatin distinguishes itself with its quantity of whitewater as well as its quality. Some stretches have nearly continuous action. Almost all the Gallatin's whitewater is easily accessible, as the river flows mostly through public land and

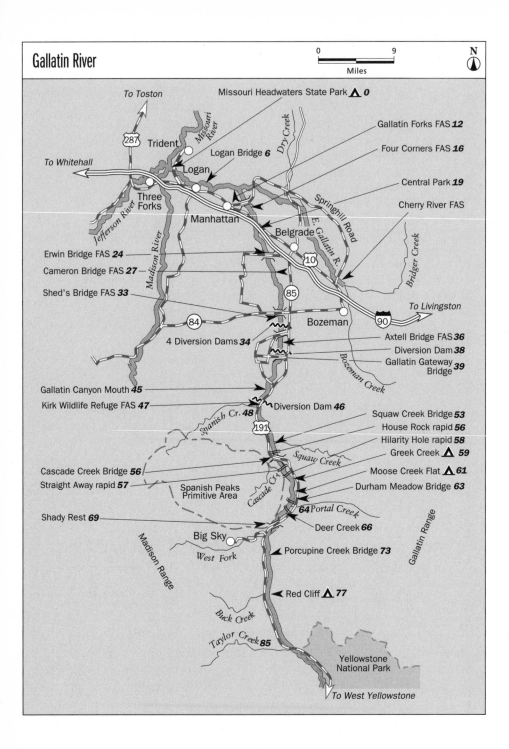

Gallatin River

0   9
Miles

N

To Toston

Missouri Headwaters State Park ⛺ *0*

Gallatin Forks FAS *12*

Four Corners FAS *16*

Central Park *19*

Cherry River FAS

Trident

287

Logan Bridge *6*

To Whitehall

Logan

Three Forks

Manhattan

Missouri River

Dry Creek

Springhill Road

Belgrade

E. Gallatin R.

Bridger Creek

Jefferson River

Erwin Bridge FAS *24*

Cameron Bridge FAS *27*

Shed's Bridge FAS *33*

Madison River

10

85

To Livingston

90

Bozeman

84

4 Diversion Dams *34*

Axtell Bridge FAS *36*
Diversion Dam *38*
Gallatin Gateway *39*
Bridge

Bozeman Creek

Gallatin Canyon Mouth *45*

Kirk Wildlife Refuge FAS *47*

Diversion Dam *46*

Spanish Cr. *48*

191

Squaw Creek Bridge *53*
House Rock rapid *56*
Hilarity Hole rapid *58*
Greek Creek ⛺ *59*
Moose Creek Flat ⛺ *61*
Durham Meadow Bridge *63*

Squaw Creek

Cascade Creek Bridge *56*

Straight Away rapid *57*

Spanish Peaks
Primitive Area

Cascade Cr.

64 Portal Creek

Deer Creek *66*

Gallatin Range

Shady Rest *69*

Madison Range

Big Sky

West Fork

Porcupine Creek Bridge *73*

Red Cliff ⛺ *77*

Buck Creek

Taylor Creek *85*

Yellowstone
National Park

To West Yellowstone

Key Access Points along the Gallatin River

Access Point (River Mile)	Next Access Point	Access Point (River Mile)	Next Access Point
Red Cliff (77)	4 miles	Axtell Bridge FAS (36)	3 miles
Porcupine Creek Bridge (73)	4 miles	Shed's Bridge FAS (33)	6 miles
Shady Rest (69)	3 miles	Cameron Bridge FAS (27)	3 miles
Deer Creek (66)	3 miles	Erwin Bridge FAS (24)	5 miles
Durham Meadow Bridge (63)	2 miles	Central Park (19)	3 miles
Moose Creek Flat (61)	2 miles	Four Corners FAS (16)	4 miles
Greek Creek (59)	3 miles	Gallatin Forks FAS (12)	6 miles
Cascade Creek Bridge (56)	3 miles	Logan Bridge (6)	6 miles
Squaw Creek Bridge (53)	6 miles	Missouri River Headwaters	
Kirk Wildlife Refuge FAS (47)	2 miles	State Park (0)	none
Gallatin Canyon Mouth (45)	9 miles		

generally runs close to U.S. Highway 191. Even though the Gallatin is a small river, it can sustain good boating well into summer.

The Indians knew this area as "the valley of the flowers." Despite ever-increasing development, it remains one of Montana's loveliest valleys.

Lewis and Clark named the river for President Thomas Jefferson's secretary of the treasury, Albert Gallatin. Captain William Clark explored the Gallatin Valley in July 1806 on his return trip from the Pacific. He wrote in his journal:

"I saw Elk, Deer and Antelope, and great deal of old signs of buffalo. Their roads is in every direction . . . emence quantities of beaver on this Fork . . . and their dams very much impede the navigation of it."

Had Captain Clark proceeded farther upstream, he would have discovered some challenging rapids that would have tested the Corps of Discovery's buffalo-skin boats. Modern-day explorers, however, find the whitewater much to their liking.

After its start in Yellowstone National Park, the Gallatin dashes its way through beautiful forested country, providing good fishing and excellent whitewater boating along the way. Access is good, and public land touches the river in many locations.

The sinuous East Gallatin winds through open meadows and agricultural country. With its brushy banks, deep holes, and sometimes silty bottom, it resembles the Beaverhead, only smaller. Its high nutrients make for a good fishery, but access is difficult and fences are common.

Floating on the East Gallatin is usually possible except in dry years. With normal flows, floating is possible as high as the Cherry River Fishing Access Site in Bozeman. This winding upper section can be handled by intermediate canoeists and rafters. Practiced beginners can give it a try below Dry Creek, although the sharp bends and occasional brush piles necessitate constant maneuvering. Because the river is occasionally blocked by barbed-wire fences and is so narrow and winding, it's rather

A calm stretch of the main stem of the Gallatin River.

difficult to float, but some people do because there is no way to get to the river—it's all private land.

County road bridges provide the primary access for East Gallatin float trips, and they occur at fairly regular intervals. Most of the river receives only moderate floating pressure.

The main-stem Gallatin is a river for experienced floaters. From Taylor Creek to the West Fork, intermediate canoeists and rafters can test their skills. During peak flows, however, canoeists will have problems with high waves. Below the West Fork, the Gallatin is extremely challenging all the way to Squaw Creek, and only experts or solid intermediates should try it. The most difficult section runs for 2 miles directly below the highway bridge at Cascade Creek. Large rocks in the river spawn tricky currents and frothing water.

The often-photographed House Rock Rapid, the most formidable of all, are visible from the highway, and crowds often gather to watch the intrepid boaters. At peak flows, only experienced floaters with high-flotation life jackets, helmets, and wet suits should try this stretch.

BIG FUN ON THE GALLATIN

The upper 40 miles of the Gallatin River contain some of Montana's very finest whitewater, with an abundance of technical rapids, tight turns, big rocks, and large waves. Some stretches have near-continuous action, and almost all the Gallatin's whitewater is easily accessible. The river flows mostly through public land and generally runs close to U.S. Highway 191. Most of the whitewater fun takes place in May and June; the water generally gets low by mid-July.

The action starts right where the Gallatin leaves Yellowstone National Park near Taylor Creek (boating is not permitted inside the park boundary). From the park boundary to Big Sky (where the West Fork enters), intermediate rafters and strong intermediate canoeists will have fun. The river is broad and shallow with tight turns. It's a Class II run with some big waves. A favorite run is from Red Cliff to Big Sky, a distance of about 8 miles. The river above Red Cliff doesn't get much floating use. It's typically too low for boats by mid-July. Watch for downed trees.

As the Gallatin churns downstream, it grows increasingly difficult. Big Sky to Greek Creek features tight turns and challenging rapids as the river picks up volume. There's a particularly challenging spot near where Portal Creek spills in. Intermediate rafters can handle it, but it's on the margin for canoeists. It's mostly Class II, but Portal Creek is a difficult Class III.

The real heavy-duty Gallatin whitewater lies between Greek Creek and the Squaw Creek Bridge. Not long after Greek Creek, the canyon narrows and the river changes. The turns get tighter, the river grows rockier, and the whitewater becomes more continuous. It gets hard to find eddies where it's easy to pull out and bail or take a break. Between Greek Creek and the Cascade Creek Bridge (also known as the 35-mile-per-hour bridge) lie several tricky rapids, including a wicked bend known as Screaming Left Turn and a tricky keeper called Hilarity Hole. While the rapids can be intense (this section rates a solid Class III), the most difficult whitewater comes between Cascade Creek and the Squaw Creek Bridge. At high flows this final 3 miles is for experts only, so don't miss the takeout at Cascade Creek (on the left side of the river, opposite the highway) if you're not up to the run.

Below the Cascade Creek Bridge the whitewater is nearly continuous, with big rocks and big water in the narrowly constricted river. This section contains the Gallatin's most famous and most photographed whitewater, House Rock Rapid. Immediately downstream lie a boulder field and a swift section known as the Mad Mile. Again, this section is for properly equipped experts, running in groups. Super-expert canoeists have run this section in recent years, but it requires a great deal of flotation and really exceptional skills. This section contains many Class III rapids and a couple of Class IVs.

A Gallatin River landmark, House Rock is visible from US 191.

The last section of good whitewater lies between Squaw Creek and the bridge at the mouth of the Gallatin Canyon. This popular section has some Class III water. Watch for a dangerous diversion dam about 1 mile before the takeout.

Although the Gallatin loses its whitewater below the mouth of the Gallatin Canyon, it remains difficult until it reaches the East Gallatin near Manhattan. The river frequently channels and has numerous logjams that sometimes completely block the river. Combine that with occasional diversion dams (especially in the area immediately below Axtell Bridge), and it all adds up to frustrating floating. Rafters are smart to pass up this section. Only expert canoeists or kayakers should try it during runoff. Afterward, intermediates can handle it if there's enough water. Irrigation dewatering may deter summer floating in some sections.

Biologists report trout numbers as high as 3,000 fish per mile on the upper Gallatin. While the river isn't renowned for huge trout, there are some nice browns below Erwin Bridge. Anglers should be aware that the entire West Gallatin—from Yellowstone National Park to its confluence with the East Gallatin—is closed to fishing from boats. The Montana Fish and Game Commission established this closure to alleviate conflict between floaters and bank anglers. Because the Gallatin is classified as a navigable river, it remains open to floaters who are not fishing.

The two forks of the Gallatin join about 2 miles north of Manhattan (at Gallatin Forks Fishing Access Site) and provide easy floating, suitable for beginners, for about the next 6 miles downstream to Logan Bridge. Between Logan and Trident (another 6 miles downstream) occasional logjams and sharp bends increase the hazard level. Like the last few miles of the Jefferson and Madison Rivers, the last segment of the Gallatin is alive with wildlife, including waterfowl, deer, and an occasional moose.

The Gallatin River has begun to feel some of the impacts of man-caused pollution. A federal report issued in the 1980s identified four problems:

- Logging and construction activities in geologically fragile areas are causing siltation in both forks through their tributaries.
- Brush removal and overgrazing are also causing sedimentation and erosion.
- Increasing numbers of septic systems, a result of rural subdivision, are polluting groundwater in some areas.
- Urban runoff, as well as discharges from Bozeman's sewage treatment facility, is hurting water quality in the East Gallatin.

Those who care about the Gallatin should take the time to get involved.

15 Jefferson River

Once traversed for its entire distance by the Lewis and Clark Expedition, the Jefferson meanders peaceably through thick cottonwood bottoms while providing good fishing and excellent wildlife viewing.

Vital statistics: 83 river miles long from the confluence of the Big Hole and Beaverhead Rivers to its juncture with the Madison and Gallatin Rivers to form the Missouri River near Three Forks.

Level of difficulty: Class I, suitable for practiced beginners its entire length.

Flow: Annual mean flow: 1,979 cfs near Three Forks. Usually floatable all year but sometimes suffers summertime dewatering below Silver Star. Don't float the Jefferson with flows over 12,000 cfs (Twin Bridges gauge).

Hazards: Logjams, protruding trees, and narrow channels. Dangerous diversion dams.

Where the crowd goes: From Twin Bridges on the Beaverhead River to Kountz Bridge.

Avoiding the scene: Downstream from Cardwell.

Inside tip: Driving down Interstate 90 with your boat? Put in at Cardwell Fishing Access Site and take out anywhere along Highway 2.

Maps: BLM: #33 (Butte South), #43 (Bozeman)
USFS: Beaverhead, Deerlodge
USGS: Dillon, MT; Bozeman, MT
Montana Afloat: #10 (The Jefferson River)

River rules: No boats over 10 horsepower.

For more information: Four Rivers Fishing Company, Twin Bridges; Frontier Anglers, Dillon; Montana Fish, Wildlife and Parks, Bozeman.

The Paddling

The Beaverhead and Big Hole Rivers merge near Twin Bridges to form the Jefferson, which then flows generally northeast for more than 80 miles. The river winds and braids repeatedly through mostly arid benchland and irrigated farmland, encompassing a wide band of thick, brushy river bottom.

Key Access Points along the Jefferson River

Access Point (River Mile)	Next Access Point	Access Point (River Mile)	Next Access Point
Jesen Park, Twin Bridges (80)	14 miles	Cardwell Bridge FAS (39)	9 miles
Hell's Canyon FAS (76)	3 miles	Limespur FAS (30)	6 miles
Silver Star FAS (73)	10 miles	Sappington Bridge FAS (24)	8 miles
Parson's Bridge (63)	7 miles	Williams Bridge FAS (16)	7 miles
Parrot Castle FAS (56)	7 miles	Drouillard FAS (9)	9 miles
Kountz Bridge FAS (49)	6 miles	Missouri River Headwaters State Park (0)	none
Mayflower Bridge FAS (43)	4 miles		

Jefferson River

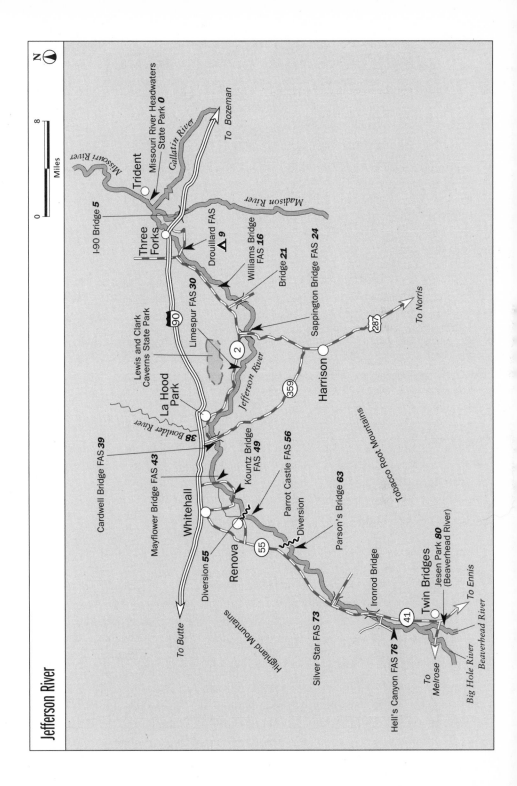

The Jefferson gets less traffic than other nearby streams.

For those who like to drift back in history as they float down rivers, the Jefferson offers a gold mine of river lore. Not only did Lewis and Clark travel its entire length, but famous mountain man John Colter also made his legendary run along the Jefferson's brushy banks.

In the spring of 1808, Colter and a companion were each paddling a canoe down the Jefferson when they were accosted by Blackfeet Indians, a tribe vigorously resisting the invasion of the white man. The Indians motioned for them to come to shore. Colter's companion balked, which was a fatal mistake. He was killed on the spot, and Colter was captured.

Since Colter's scalp would be a substantial prize, the Indians decided it should go to the fleetest brave. Colter was stripped of his clothes and shoes and given a chance to run for his life. When the chief inquired about the white man's speed, the clever Colter responded he was a poor runner. The Blackfeet gave Colter a head start, all the speedy fur trapper needed. He ran about 5 miles before diving into the Jefferson and finding a hiding spot under a logjam. Although the Indians searched the river extensively, they failed to find the well-hidden mountain man.

Colter's ordeal, however, had only begun. When night fell he began the long trek to nearest civilization—a fort at the mouth of the Bighorn River, 250 miles distant. Even though he had neither food nor clothing, Colter reportedly covered the distance in eleven days, losing so much weight that his friends didn't recognize him when he appeared at the fort.

Captain Lewis's August 2, 1805, description of the Jefferson River and its valley remains quite accurate today. His journal reads:

> "we found the current very rapid waist deep and about 90 yds. wide. bottom smooth pebble with a small mixture of coarse gravel . . . The valley along which we passed today, and through which the river winds it's meandering course is from 6 to 8 miles wide and consists of a beautiful level plain with but little timber, and that confined to the verge of the river; the land is tolerably fertile, and is either black or dark yellow loam, covered with grass from 9 inches to 2 feet high. the plain ascends gradually on either side of the river to the bases of two ranges of high mountains. the tops of these mountains are yet covered partially with snow, while we in the valley are nearly suffocated with the intense heat of the mid-day sun; the nights are so cold that two blankets are not more than sufficient covering."

The Corps of Discovery had an arduous journey as they lined their boats up the brushy Jefferson. Hot weather, mosquitoes, and slippery rocks plagued the crew. Today modern explorers encounter some of the same problems. Captain Lewis even got lost on the Jefferson and was forced to spend the evening on an island. During his restless night, he heard a large splash, which he feared was the dreaded "white" bear, the grizzly. River rats no longer have to deal with Old Griz on the Jefferson, but present-day explorers will be pleased to find parts of the Jefferson much as Lewis and Clark saw it. The picturesque Tobacco Root Mountains (still largely roadless) rise to the east, while the more rounded Highland Mountains enliven the view on the west side. Most of the river bottom remains undeveloped, although cattle have replaced the elk Lewis and Clark saw.

Water quality is the biggest change since frontier days, and it's the biggest drawback to a Jefferson float. Irrigation runoff and grazing practices create turbidity that often clouds the river. Although the Jefferson is usually clear in late summer and fall, rainstorms can muddy the river in short order. In addition, excessive nutrients in the water often foster rapid growth of algae in summer, creating a nuisance for anglers and swimmers. In late summer the river can be too low to float due to irrigation.

While fishing sometimes is excellent on the Jefferson, water clarity and water temperature are crucial components of a good fishery. Most anglers float the upper stretches and favor big wet flies or streamers. Browns inhabit the river (fewer than 800 per mile below Ironrod Bridge) along with a few rainbows (catch-and-release only) and whitefish.

With proper caution, the entire Jefferson can be floated by beginners. Much of the river is broad and slow moving, although the river sometimes channels and picks up speed. Logjams, protruding trees, and narrow channels are the major hazards.

In the upper sections, the river is quite removed from civilization. Occasional diversions and riprap, however, will remind you that man isn't far away. The diversions below Parson's Bridge and at the Parrot Castle Fishing Access Site are hazardous. Adequate in-stream flows to protect fish and wildlife are sorely needed.

Below Parrot Castle fishing access and the Renova Bridge, the river divides into two channels of nearly equal size for about 8 miles, forming a large island. This section of the river is particularly scenic as it sweeps by the Tobacco Roots. About 3 miles below Cardwell Fishing Access Site, the river enters a narrow canyon, as does the old highway, which parallels the river for the next several miles. As the river cuts through the canyon, it forms many deep pools as well as a few fast runs. Steep limestone walls and colorful rock formations make it an interesting section. The popular Lewis and Clark Caverns, which were never actually visited by Lewis and Clark, can be viewed from the river just a few miles below Cardwell.

As the river approaches Three Forks, it again becomes isolated. It braids into several channels as it winds through brushy, lowland habitat for its last few miles before helping to form the Missouri. The numerous channel changes and occasional downed trees make this the trickiest section. Still, beginners can handle it if the water isn't high.

The last few miles of the Jefferson are a great place for wildlife viewing. Ducks and geese nest in this area, and the brush is alive with whitetails. The area also has a few moose, so keep your eyes peeled for the king of the deer family.

The floating pressure the Jefferson receives is light and well distributed. Most floaters are anglers from Butte and surrounding communities. This river offers excellent potential for multiday float trips, and one could start on the Big Hole or Beaverhead and take a really extended trip right through the heart of Lewis and Clark country.

16 Judith River

This excellent canoeing stream flows through isolated breaks country that features white cliffs, deep coulees, and peculiar rock formations.

Vital statistics: 130 river miles from the confluence of the Middle and South Forks to the Missouri River.

Level of difficulty: Mostly Class I, except for a 1-mile Class II rapid beginning 1 mile upstream from the Highway 81 bridge. Suitable for intermediates in canoes or practiced beginners in rafts.

Flow: Annual mean flow: 60 cfs near Utica. Too low to float by mid-July except in wet years.

Hazards: Barbed wire (even some electric fences!), many rocks, ledges across the river, some snags, rattlesnakes.

Where the crowd goes: Nowhere. Most floating occurs between the Highway 81 bridge (east of Denton) and Anderson Bridge.

Avoiding the scene: Just show up.

Inside tip: In wet years a fall trip may be possible.

Maps: BLM: #51 (White Sulphur Springs), #58 (Winifred), #59 (Lewistown), #60 (Big Snowy Mountains)

USFS: Lewis & Clark (Jefferson Division)

USGS: White Sulphur, MT; Roundup, MT; Lewistown, MT

For more information: BLM, Lewistown.

The Paddling

The fast-flowing Judith River gets its start in the Little Belt Mountains and then courses through forests, badlands, and arid prairies for 130 miles before meeting the Missouri River not far from Judith Landing. This must have been the point in Lewis and Clark's journey where they got lonely for female companionship—Captain Clark named the Judith for Julia "Judy" Hancock (whom he later married), and not far upstream Captain Lewis named the Marias (Maria's River) after Maria Wood, a favorite cousin.

The Judith is a small stream floatable only early in the season or in wet years. It's largely unfloatable above Hobson, as beaver dams and fences create frequent barriers. Between Hobson and the Highway 81 bridge, occasional county bridges provide access. A 1-mile rock garden beginning 1 mile upstream from the Highway 81 bridge has some moderate rapids (Class II). Otherwise the river is mostly flat but swift-flowing water.

The small amount of floating that does occur on the Judith takes place mainly between the Highway 81 bridge and the Missouri River, where the river flows through a secluded canyon. This river has a surprisingly lively flow for a prairie stream, rushing down a rocky streambed with occasional ledges. Rugged terrain surrounds the river, including sandstone cliffs, clay banks, and slightly timbered hillsides. There aren't many trees, just occasional groves of cottonwoods and occasional buffalo berry bushes and willows. The river is extremely isolated, with only a handful of ranch houses near the river. We floated the Judith one October, and a rancher told us we were the first

The Judith meanders through isolated breaks country on its way to the Missouri.

floaters she had seen in thirty years. While this river sees a few floaters every year, it's very remote and you'll feel like an explorer. It's an outstanding river for canoeing, as it requires constant maneuvering. Wildlife viewing is great; expect to see deer, coyotes, eagles, and pheasants. The Judith has places with more wild asparagus than we've seen on any other Montana river.

The biggest problem with Judith River floats is the barbed-wire fences. They're very floater-unfriendly—some are even electrified! They are very hard to portage around; lifting them is the best bet. Lots of barbed wire translates into lots of cows, and the Judith has its share. Heavy cow use has rendered many potential campsites undesirable. Public land along the Judith is limited, however, so you may have to take what you can get.

Key Access Points along the Judith River

Access Point (River Mile)	Next Access Point	Access Point (River Mile)	Next Access Point
U.S. Highway 87 bridge (103)	8 miles	Danvers Bridge (67)	7 miles
Bridge (95)	6 miles	Highway 81 (Denton) bridge (60)	38 miles
Bridge (89)	7 miles	Anderson Bridge (22)	22 miles
Bridge (82)	15 miles	Judith Landing (0)	none

Judith River

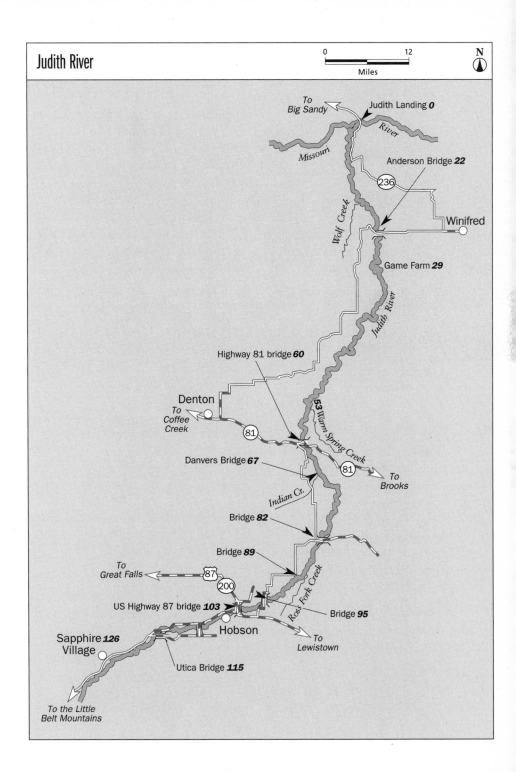

0   12
Miles

N

Judith Landing **0**

To Big Sandy

River

Missouri

Anderson Bridge **22**

236

Wolf Creek

Winifred

Game Farm **29**

Judith River

Highway 81 bridge **60**

53 Warm Spring Creek

Denton

To Coffee Creek

81

81

To Brooks

Danvers Bridge **67**

Indian Cr.

Bridge **82**

Bridge **89**

To Great Falls

87

200

Ross Fork Creek

US Highway 87 bridge **103**

Bridge **95**

Hobson

To Lewistown

Sapphire **126** Village

Utica Bridge **115**

To the Little Belt Mountains

In a normal year, floating on the Judith is possible until mid-July (it can pick up with fall rains). If you see lots of rocks above the surface and the water looks low just above the Highway 81 bridge, you should definitely not try the float between Danvers Bridge and the Highway 81 bridge. If you put in at the Highway 81 bridge, Warm Springs Creek, 6 miles downstream, provides a significant boost of water (at least 100 cubic feet per second). You'll also see a major game farm about 7 miles before Anderson Bridge on the east side of the river. Highway 81 bridge to Anderson Bridge is a two-day trip when days are long and the water is up. Add another day to go from Anderson Bridge to Judith Landing. While the Judith is almost all Class I water, this brisk-flowing river with its profusion of rocks will challenge inexperienced canoeists. Beginners in rafts should have no problems, but watch out for that barbed wire.

With a few less barbed-wire fences, a few less cows right next to the river, and some better public-land campsites, the Judith could provide a truly first-class river experience. The Bureau of Land Management studied the river for possible Wild and Scenic River status in the mid-1980s. If you take a trip on this river, you may wish to follow up by calling BLM in Lewistown (see appendix A) and urging it to get involved with protecting the Judith's considerable natural attributes.

17 Kootenai River

This big, clear river courses through heavily forested mountains, providing good fishing and excellent scenery along the way. Scenes from the movie *The River Wild* were filmed here.

Vital statistics: 100 miles in Montana (50 reservoir miles) from the Canadian border north of Eureka to the Idaho border. Second-largest river in Montana in water volume.

Level of difficulty: Mostly Class I, with a couple of difficult sections that are Class II and III. China Rapids and Kootenai Falls Gorge are Class IV and V, respectively.

Flow: Annual mean flow: 13,340 cfs at Leonia, Idaho. The river is dam controlled, and large fluctuations in volume are not uncommon. Floatable all year. Optimum floating between 7,000 and 11,000 cfs.

Hazards: Large waves, choppy water. Avoid Kootenai Falls. Experts only for Kootenai Falls Gorge, immediately below the falls for about 2 miles.

Where the crowd goes: Libby Dam to Libby.

Avoiding the scene: Troy to Leonia.

Inside tip: Float immediately below Libby Dam in the fall to watch eagles, as many as 160 in a single day.

Maps: BLM: #4 (Yaak River), #5 (Libby) USFS: Kootenai-Kaniksu East USGS: Kalispell, MT

River rules: Check for special fishing regulations.

For more information: Montana Fish, Wildlife and Parks, Kalispell; Kootenai National Forest, Libby; U.S. Army Corp of Engineers, Libby Dam; Kootenai Angler, Libby.

The Paddling

The Kootenai rises in British Columbia and flows southwest in a great loop through northwestern Montana. Its total length exceeds 480 miles, and it is the second-largest river in Montana in water volume. "Kootenai" (or "kutenai") is an Indian word meaning "deer robes." The first white man to navigate the Kootenai was David Thompson, who paddled a birch-bark canoe down the river in 1808 and later founded a settlement near Libby. The river has an interesting history. Steamboats traveled on it for a short time while the mining industry was booming.

Once known as Montana's "dream stream," the U.S. Army Corps of Engineers turned much of the Kootenai River into a nightmare. Prior to 1972 floaters could cruise for nearly 150 miles through rugged mountains and undisturbed river bottoms on a stream that may have had the best native cutthroat fishery in the country. Then came Libby Dam, which reduced floating on the Kootenai to less than 50 miles and turned the river into fluctuating, mud-lined Koocanusa Reservoir. Koocanusa is not an Indian name. The name borrows its first three letters from Kootenai, its next three from Canada, and its last three from USA.

Floating on the Kootenai starts below Libby Dam and continues to the Idaho border and beyond. Small aluminum boats, canoes, and rafts all work well. While most of the river is broad and swift flowing, occasional rapids and big standing waves require some caution. Jennings Rapid, just below the Fisher River, requires care. Because of the fluctuations in the amount of water discharged from Koocanusa Reservoir, river levels can rise sharply, by as much as 2 to 4 feet. Because of these fluctuations and occasional rapids, beginners should steer clear of the Kootenai above the falls.

About 10 miles below the Libby Bridge, as the river approaches Kootenai Falls, lies a long, difficult section of river known as China Rapids. As the story goes, the rapids got their name in the 1860s when a party of Chinese miners from British Columbia tried to raft down the river with a load of gold dust. They took the river rather than an overland route because they feared their fortune would be stolen by other miners. As the raft hit the rapids, however, the heavy gold shifted and the raft upended. Only one miner made it to shore to tell the story, and the river kept the gold.

All but expert canoeists (with or without gold) should portage around China Rapids (Class IV). Expert rafters and kayakers can try it, but be sure to scout first. Don't forget to check the flows before any Kootenai River trip.

The power line above Kootenai Falls marks a good take-out point for floaters. Don't worry about missing the power line; you'll see and hear the falls in plenty of time. Obviously floaters should be careful not to venture too close. Early settlers called it "Disaster Falls" for good reason. Kootenai Falls is the largest undammed falls in the state.

Immediately below the falls the river remains fast and turbulent for about 2 miles. Only experts in kayaks and large rafts should try it. Don't forget that the extreme water fluctuations caused by the dam make this section different each time. Each

Key Access Points along the Kootenai River

Access Point (River Point)	Next Access Point	Access Point (River Point)	Next Access Point
Alexander Creek Recreation Area (49)	1 mile	Bighorn Terrace (23)	9 miles
Dunn Creek Recreation Area (48)	1 mile	Troy Bridge (14)	8 miles
Blackwell Flats Recreation Area (47)	5 miles	Yaak River Campground (6)	6 miles
Osprey Landing (42)	9 miles	Leonia, Idaho (0)	none
Libby Bridge (33)	10 miles		

of the five major rapids (Class IV) in this 2-mile gorge should be inspected on foot before going through. Once committed to floating this gorge, the steep walls prevent turning back.

Below Troy, as the river leaves the highway, lies the last Montana vestige of the Kootenai as it once was. Although railroad tracks parallel the river, one still gets a feeling of isolation on this big river, particularly below where the Yaak River enters.

While the transparent Kootenai remains large and fast flowing, practiced beginners can handle this section. High waves create the biggest hazard, and they can swamp open canoes. Most of the choppy water can be skirted if paddlers are alert. The most serious high waves in the section below Troy are at the Yaak River confluence. If you're in a raft, they provide a real roller-coaster ride.

Access points are limited below Troy. Floaters can get out easily at Leonia, Idaho, just across the border, or continue to float all the way to Bonner's Ferry, 20 miles into Idaho.

The Kootenai has a substantial fishery, which produces large numbers of rainbow trout and whitefish. Both species of fish grow quickly; three-pound trout are quite common. The Kootenai has earned the reputation of being the best "big fish" fishery in northwestern Montana, and the state record rainbow trout—thirty-three pounds, one ounce—was caught in the Kootenai in the section immediately below the dam. Many believe the fish directly below the dam grow to such an enormous size by feeding on small perch that are chopped up in the dam's turbines. Although a good deal of fish habitat has been destroyed to accommodate the railroad, the Kootenai is still a very productive river, with great insect hatches throughout the summer and fall. Catch-and-release fishing from Libby Dam to Kootenai Falls for trout 13 to 18 inches has increased this size class remarkably.

In addition to trout, the unusual and rare white sturgeon resides in the Kootenai below the falls. These large fish, which can weigh more than one hundred pounds, are an endangered species. At the turn of the twentieth century, old-timers used to think it was great sport to dynamite these big fish at the large pool at the base of the falls. They floated out to the pool on rafts and dropped the charges into the water. During one such foray, a misplaced charge blew up the raft and all the anglers. Fishing with hook and line—as well as dynamite—is now prohibited for these disappearing behemoths.

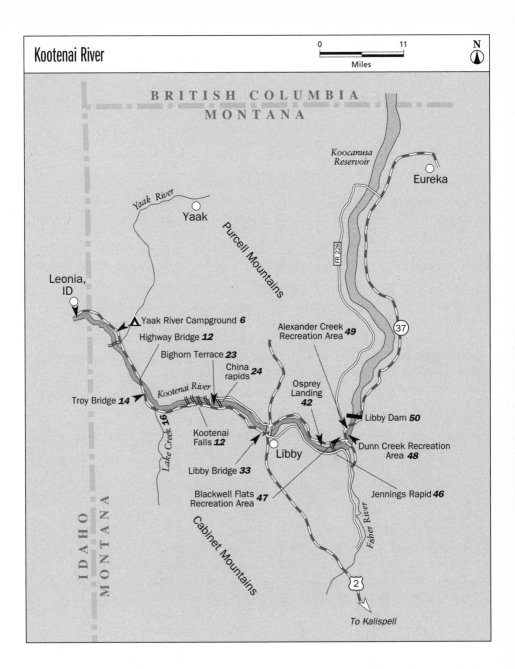

Kootenai River

0   11
Miles

N

BRITISH COLUMBIA
MONTANA

Koocanusa Reservoir

Eureka

Yaak River

Yaak

Purcell Mountains

FR 228

Leonia, ID

△ Yaak River Campground **6**

Highway Bridge **12**

Bighorn Terrace **23**

China rapids **24**

Alexander Creek Recreation Area **49**

Osprey Landing **42**

37

Troy Bridge **14**

Kootenai River

Libby Dam **50**

Lake Creek **16**

Kootenai Falls **12**

Libby

Dunn Creek Recreation Area **48**

Libby Bridge **33**

Jennings Rapid **46**

Blackwell Flats Recreation Area **47**

IDAHO
MONTANA

Fisher River

Cabinet Mountains

2

To Kalispell

Isolated portions of the Kootenai still contain abundant wildlife. The king of all anglers, the osprey, can often be seen diving for fish. Bighorn sheep live on the cliffs near the falls, and whitetails walk most of the thickets. The Kootenai is one of the few rivers in Montana where black bears are commonly sighted prowling along the river in late spring. Bald eagles concentrate along the river in winter, as do waterfowl.

Floating pressure on the Kootenai has increased with tales of great fishing. In comparison to southwestern Montana rivers, however, pressure is light and comes mostly from local people, as this neglected corner of the state is far from everywhere. Some people use motorboats on the river.

Trivia buffs will be interested to learn that the lowest point in Montana is where the Kootenai leaves the state near Leonia, Idaho. The elevation is 1,820 feet, substantially lower than most places in Montana.

18 Madison River

Montana's most famous fishing river, the rapid-flowing Madison cuts a beautiful swath through a broad valley, passing by lush meadows and broken timber.

Vital statistics: 133 miles long (including 23 reservoir miles) from the Wyoming border to its juncture with the Jefferson River to form the Missouri River near Three Forks.

Level of difficulty: All Class I except for two sections—below Quake Lake and Bear Trap Canyon—that have difficult rapids.

Flow: Annual mean flow: 1,753 cfs downstream from Ennis Lake. Usually floatable all year. In dry years, Varney to Ennis Lake can be marginal because the river braids extensively. Bear Trap Canyon may be unfloatable at peak flows (over 3,000 cfs). Minimum Bear Trap flows are 1,000 to 1,200 cfs. Below Ennis Lake, floating is best below 4,500 cfs.

Hazards: Fast water with frequent rocks in the upper river. Low bridges with debris around the pilings, logjams, snags, and a diversion dam below Varney. Bear Trap Canyon and the difficult water below Quake Lake.

Where the crowd goes: For anglers, Lyons Bridge to Ennis. For whitewater enthusiasts, the Bear Trap Canyon. For inner-tubers, Warm Springs to Greycliff.

Avoiding the scene: Ennis to Ennis Lake on the upper Madison (though it's all crowded in the summer). Greycliff to Headwaters State Park on the lower river.

Inside tip: Fish the often-neglected lower river in spring and fall when water temperatures are cool. Whirling disease has hurt fishing on the upper river, which is predominantly a rainbow fishery, but hasn't had a big impact on the lower river where brown trout are more common. Don't pass up fishing the side channels.

Maps: BLM: #43 (Bozeman), #44 (Ennis), #45 (Hebgen Lake); Bear Trap Canyon Wilderness Visitor's Guide

USFS: Gallatin (West), Beaverhead Interagency Travel Plan (East)

USGS: Ashton, ID; Bozeman, MT

River rules: No motors over 10 horsepower anywhere. No motors in Bear Trap Canyon. No floating in Yellowstone National Park. Quake Lake to Lyons Bridge and Ennis Bridge to Ennis Lake are closed to fishing from boats. Check ever-changing fishing regulations. No float camping. Fire pans and self-registration required in Bear Trap Canyon.

For more information: Yellowstone Raft Company, Big Sky; Madison River Fishing Company, Ennis; The Tackle Shop, Ennis; Montana Fish, Wildlife and Parks, Bozeman; BLM, Dillon.

The fabled Madison delivers again.

The Paddling

Anyone who reads outdoor magazines knows that for many Americans, trout fishing is synonymous with Joe and his pal driving out from New Jersey to catch hook-jawed brown trout on Montana's Madison River. It's the fisherman's equivalent of a trip to Mecca. The folklore lives on, and the beautiful Madison is probably Montana's most famous river.

The Madison River's popularity is well founded. Originating from pristine sources high in Yellowstone National Park, the Madison flows gin-clear and undisturbed through lush meadows and broken timber. Within the park, elk and bison graze along the shores, and trumpeter swans dip their graceful necks underwater to reach vegetation. It's a "Peaceable Kingdom" setting. The only downside is that the park gets extremely crowded in summer. As mentioned above, floating the Madison within the boundaries of the national park is prohibited.

Key Access Points along the Madison River

Access Point (River Mile)	Next Access Point	Access Point (River Mile)	Next Access Point
Raynolds Pass FAS (98)	9 miles	Madison Dam (40)	1 mile
Lyons Bridge FAS (89)	10 miles	Powerhouse (39)	8 miles
South Madison (79)	4 miles	Warm Springs (31)	7miles
West Madison (75)	3 miles	Black's Ford FAS (24)	4 miles
McAtee Bridge FAS (72)	12 miles	Greycliff FAS (20)	9 miles
Varney Bridge FAS (60)	6 miles	Cobblestone FAS (11) walk-in	7 miles
Eight Mile Ford FAS (54)	1 mile	Milwaukee FAS (4)	1 mile
Burnt Tree Hole FAS (53)	2 miles	Blackbird FAS (3)	3 miles
Ennis FAS (51)	2 miles	Missouri River Headwaters State Park (0)	none
Valley Garden FAS (49)	9 miles		

Two dams and a natural lake check the flow of the river outside Yellowstone National Park. First comes Hebgen Dam, which backs up the Madison to within 2 miles of the park boundary. A few miles below Hebgen Dam comes Quake Lake, a small lake formed by a major earthquake and subsequent landslide in 1959. Then, some 60 miles downstream, lies the Madison Dam, a small hydropower project built around the turn of the twentieth century. The Madison Dam forms Ennis Reservoir and marks the artificial distinction between the upper and lower river.

Floating on the upper Madison usually begins about 4 miles downstream from Quake Lake at Raynolds Pass Fishing Access. The 4-mile section immediately below Quake Lake is extremely dangerous because of fast water, big drops, and sharp, jagged rocks. The sharp rocks are remnants of the 1959 earthquake, and even thrill-seekers tend to avoid this whitewater. It should be good floating in a few hundred years— once the fast-flowing waters round off these sharp edges.

Most of the 40-mile stretch between Quake Lake and Varney Bridge flows swiftly but at a very uniform depth. The river gushes in a wide, shallow channel averaging about 3 or 4 feet deep and resembles a long, continuous riffle. Occasional large boulders present the only hazard for floaters. The cannonball-size rocks that blanket the bottom of the river have a slick coating of algae that results in treacherous footing. Practiced beginners in rafts or canoes can handle this section, but watch out for those rocks!

The river winds through highly scenic country, with the lofty Madison Range to the east and the sage-covered foothills of the Gravelly Mountains to the west. Access is excellent, and much of the land bordering the river is publicly owned. There are numerous picnic areas, campgrounds, and fishing access sites.

The section of river from Varney Bridge to Ennis Lake braids into several channels where logjams and downed trees are common. Beginners should stay clear. Low summer flows may require floaters to drag their crafts over sandbars. The section of

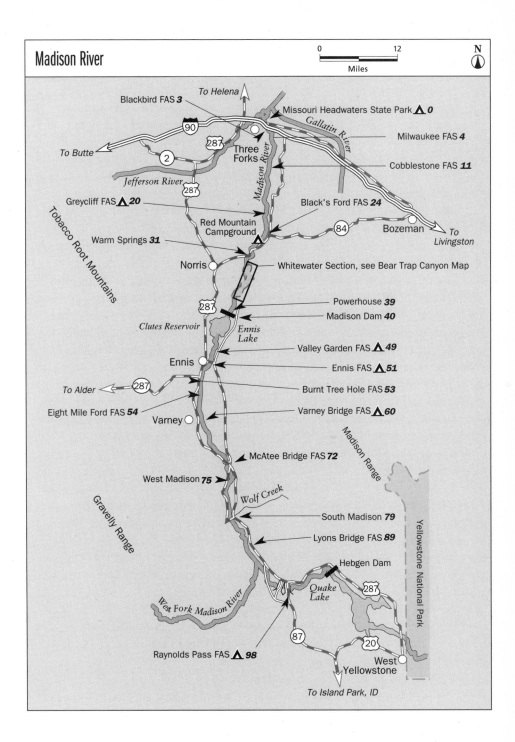

Madison River

0   12
Miles

N

To Helena

Blackbird FAS *3*

Missouri Headwaters State Park ▲ *0*

Gallatin River

90

287

Milwaukee FAS *4*

Three Forks

To Butte

2

Cobblestone FAS *11*

Jefferson River

287

Madison River

Greycliff FAS ▲ *20*

Black's Ford FAS *24*

Warm Springs *31*

Red Mountain Campground ▲

84

Bozeman

To Livingston

Tobacco Root Mountains

Norris

Whitewater Section, see Bear Trap Canyon Map

287

Powerhouse *39*

Madison Dam *40*

Clutes Reservoir

Ennis Lake

Valley Garden FAS ▲ *49*

Ennis

Ennis FAS ▲ *51*

To Alder

287

Burnt Tree Hole FAS *53*

Eight Mile Ford FAS *54*

Varney

Varney Bridge FAS ▲ *60*

McAtee Bridge FAS *72*

West Madison *75*

Gravelly Range

Wolf Creek

South Madison *79*

Lyons Bridge FAS *89*

Madison Range

Hebgen Dam

287

Quake Lake

Yellowstone National Park

West Fork Madison River

Raynolds Pass FAS ▲ *98*

87

20

West Yellowstone

To Island Park, ID

river from Ennis Bridge to the lake is an excellent area to view wildlife. Look for deer, moose, mink, and beaver, as well as raptors and shorebirds. Several great blue heron rookeries can be found as well. Keep in mind that fishing from a boat in this section is prohibited, although floating is fine.

Floating pressure on the upper river is quite high. Recreational studies reveal a 500 percent increase in angler pressure over the past three decades. The upper river now supports over 60,000 anglers annually. Dozens of professional outfitters offer guide service on this upper section, and it's very popular with tourists and out-of-state anglers. The large number of floaters has created a conflict between float anglers and bank anglers, and that's why some sections have been closed to fishing from boats.

The upper Madison has received a great deal of national attention in recent years because of whirling disease, an infectious fish microbe that in the early to mid-1990s reduced rainbow trout populations by as much as 90 percent. Be sure to check current fishing regulations.

The lower Madison (below Ennis Lake) isn't nearly as popular as the upper section. While this part of the river was once one of the most productive trout streams in Montana, thermal problems have affected the fishery.

Fisheries biologists have learned that during the hot summer months, Ennis Lake acts as a giant solar collector, and its water temperature sometimes gets as high as 85 degrees. Since the lake has filled in with silt and become very shallow, it has no thermocline (a natural dividing point between warm and cold water). All the lake water gets warm, then flows over the dam and heats up the river downstream. Since trout do best with cold water temperatures, their growth rates have been dramatically affected below Ennis Dam. Fish numbers remain fairly good (more than 3,000 fish per mile) until the Greycliff Fishing Access Site. In addition, plant and insect life has changed.

While all this is of grave concern to trout anglers, swimmers and inner-tubers certainly don't mind the warm water temperatures. Consequently, during the heat of summer, the lower river near Highway 84 has become a popular recreation site.

Floating on the lower river can begin right below the dam, although not for everyone. Below the dam lies the rugged, inaccessible Bear Trap Canyon, which has some outstanding rapids. The Bureau of Land Management currently manages this 9-mile section of the river, known as the Bear Trap Canyon Recreation Area. It encompasses 36,700 acres and is a designated wilderness.

The Bear Trap has a few hazards other than tough whitewater. Rattlesnakes inhabit the canyon, and if you believe all the stories, they're more common here than earthworms. Ticks are numerous in spring. Poison ivy awaits you. Still want to go? Grizzly bears occasionally make an appearance as well.

The BLM has published an excellent map of the river and the Bear Trap Canyon. The *Bear Trap Canyon Wilderness Visitor's Guide* has an excellent topographic map as well as photos of the approaches to the four major rapids. It's available free of charge by writing to the Bureau of Land Management at the address in appendix A.

After the Madison exits Bear Trap Canyon, it's pretty tame. Once the river leaves Highway 84, access is limited and the river is more remote. Access points at Greycliff, Cobblestone (no boat ramp, walk-in access only), and Three Forks occur in about equal intervals in the 24-mile section from the Highway 84 bridge to the headwaters of the Missouri.

The lower sections of the Madison are quite isolated and can have excellent fishing in spring and fall. Hundred-foot gray cliffs tower over the river, and many vantage points offer spectacular views of the Spanish Peaks. Because of high winds that stir up mud in Ennis Lake, the lower Madison sometimes gets dirty even at non-runoff times.

THE BEAR TRAP

The 1,500-foot-high cliffs above the Madison River serve as a backdrop for one of Montana's most scenic whitewater trips—the run through Bear Trap Canyon Wilderness. The Bear Trap offers excitement for experts in large rafts or kayaks. Small rafts or open canoes should stay away.

The canyon starts at the outlet to Ennis Lake and continues until Highway 84 meets the river, slightly less than 10 miles downstream. A narrow dirt road, a hazard in itself, leads to the put-in. The take-out point is BLM's Warm Springs Access.

Although dams regulate flows on the Madison, neither Ennis nor Hebgen Lake is a storage reservoir. So when there's a high influx of water, it gets passed downriver. Flows vary from 900 to 10,000 cubic feet per second (cfs) based on the season. Optimal flow for floating activities is about 1,500 to 2,200 cfs. The Bear Trap Canyon gets exceedingly dangerous when flows hit 4,000 to 5,000 cfs. Look for a riverflow sign about 200 yards upstream from the powerhouse. It displays current water levels and is updated daily.

Intense rapids with considerable stretches of easy water in between characterize the Bear Trap Canyon. There are four primary rapids, and all have unmarked portage routes for those not along for the thrills. The first whitewater is Double Drop Rapids, which you'll miss if you put in too close to the powerhouse. The next major whitewater, White Horse Rapids, lies about 2 miles downstream. It's a long set of big waves.

After White Horse comes the most difficult and dangerous rapids in the Bear Trap, the Kitchen Sink—Class IV even at low flows and Class V when the water is up. It's a tricky, dangerous piece of whitewater that people without the proper skills shouldn't attempt. It has large waves, big drops, lots of rocks, and two turns. A wave that lurches back over a large rock—which some people think looks like a drain at the bottom of a sink—gives this rapid its name. According

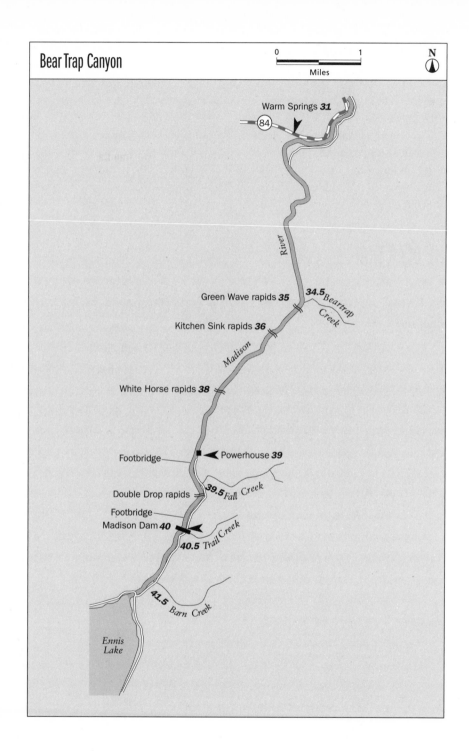

Bear Trap Canyon

0   1
Miles

N

Warm Springs **31**

84

34.5 Beartrap Creek

Green Wave rapids **35**

Kitchen Sink rapids **36**

Madison

White Horse rapids **38**

River

Footbridge —————— ◄ Powerhouse **39**

Double Drop rapids **39.5** Fall Creek

Footbridge
Madison Dam **40**

40.5 Trail Creek

41.5 Barn Creek

Ennis
Lake

to BLM, at least eight people have lost their life here in the last twenty years. At peak flows it's a life-threatening Class V. The remoteness of this rapid accentuates the danger. It's almost exactly in the middle of the canyon.

The last major whitewater is known either as Green Wave Rapids or The Dumplings. Some creative mind decided that this series of huge rocks in the river looks like dumplings floating in a bowl of chicken broth. These rapids are about 4 miles before the takeout.

Quality equipment is important on a tough run like the Bear Trap Canyon, but experience and judgment are just as critical. Only strong intermediates or better should try the Bear Trap at normal flows, and only experts should attempt it at high water. This isn't the place for flimsy rafts and horse-collar life jackets. Several outfitters run trips in the Bear Trap Canyon if you want to check the river out with experienced people first.

Since fishing is the main attraction on the Madison, it's only fair to tell why. Fisheries biologists, who survey the river regularly, report that sections of the river contain as many as 2,000 brown trout per mile. These fish are wild—they're not raised in a hatchery—and average about a pound each. And while whirling disease has hit rainbow trout hard (down from 3,000 per mile to about 500 per mile), it has had only minimal impacts on brown trout. For those who think big, biologists occasionally capture fish in the five- to seven-pound range when doing fish surveys.

The Madison salmon fly hatch usually occurs on the upper river in late June. During this time, incredible numbers of large stoneflies buzz through the air like miniature helicopters, and the fish go wild. So do the anglers, and the river gets so thoroughly flailed that there's foam all the way to Three Forks.

19 Marias River

The isolated Marias River originates east of Glacier National Park and features spectacular badlands and sandstone cliffs reminiscent of the Missouri River.

Vital statistics: 171 miles (26 reservoir miles) from the confluence of Two Medicine River and Cut Bank Creek to its juncture with the Missouri River near Loma.

Level of difficulty: Class I, suitable for beginners its entire length.

Flow: Annual mean flow: 915 cfs near Chester. Bureau of Reclamation tries to maintain a minimum flow of 500 cfs from Tiber Dam. Too low to float below 500 cfs. Optimum flows are 700 to 1,500 cfs below Tiber Dam. Typically gets too low for floating in summer above Tiber Reservoir in dry years.

Hazards: Extreme temperatures, mosquitoes, rattlesnakes, unpaved roads that become impassible after rainstorms.

Where the crowd goes: Highway 223 bridge to Loma.

Avoiding the scene: Above Tiber Reservoir.

Inside tip: A great river for conceiving children. Our oldest son's middle name is Marias.

Maps: BLM: #28 (Valier), #38 (Conrad), #48 (Lonesome Lake), #49 (Fort Benton)
USGS: Cut Bank, MT; Shelby, MT; Great Falls, MT

River rules: No hunting on the Brinkman Game Preserve, a state wildlife refuge that borders the river for 10 miles immediately below the Highway 223 bridge.

For more information: Bureau of Land Management, Havre; Montana Fish, Wildlife and Parks, Great Falls; Coyotes Den Sports, Chester; Bureau of Reclamation, Tiber Dam.

The Paddling

Known to the Indians as "the river that scolds at all others," the slow-moving but scenic Marias River is one of Montana's finest floatable streams. While its headwaters actually originate near Glacier National Park, the river begins about 12 miles south of the town of Cut Bank, where Cut Bank Creek and Two Medicine River join. While floating is possible from this point down to Tiber Reservoir, access is restricted, and this section receives little pressure. Most floaters go below the reservoir, where fishing is better and the scenery more appealing.

The Marias has a rich historical background. Lewis and Clark camped at the river's mouth, near the present-day site of Loma, on June 3, 1805. Captain Lewis named the river Maria's River in honor of his cousin, Miss Maria Wood. Obviously not much of a lady's man, Lewis later apologized in his journal for naming such a silt-laden, unromantic river in honor of his beloved cousin. Historians later dropped the apostrophe.

Lewis and Clark had to make a critical decision when they reached the mouth of the Marias. The explorers were unsure which branch was the main fork of the Missouri. The Marias most resembles the part of the Missouri the crew had already

Sandstone cliffs, rock pedestals, and badlands make the Marias look like a miniature Missouri River.

traversed, as it is slow and turbid. The other fork—which we now recognize as the main-stem Missouri—flowed clear and seemed to lead to the mountains. Almost all the crew thought the Marias was the main fork of the Missouri. Lewis and Clark, however, thought differently. After several days of careful deliberation, they made the correct decision.

What if Lewis and Clark had proceeded up the Marias instead of the Missouri? They might have been forced to retrace their path, losing valuable time that could have meant a late, dangerous trip across the mountains in November. On the other hand, they might have found Marias Pass near Glacier National Park, the lowest and least formidable path across the Continental Divide.

The beauty of the rolling prairies that surround the Marias captivated both Lewis and Clark. Lewis wrote in his journal:

"[The river] passes through a rich fertile and one of the most beautifully picturesque countries that I ever beheld, through the wide expanse of which innumerable herds of living anamals are seen, it's borders garnished with one continued garden of roses, while it's lofty and open forrests are the habitation of miriads of the feathered tribes who salute the ear of the passing traveler with their wild and simple, yet sweet and cheerfull melody."

No less ecstatic, Captain Clark reported:

Key Access Points along the Marias River

Access Point (River Mile)	Next Access Point	Access Point (River Mile)	Next Access Point
Bridge (171)	28 miles	Pugsley Bridge (75)	6 miles
Shelby Golf Course (143)	2 miles	Moffat Bridge (69)	10 miles
Old Highway 91 bridge (141)	24 miles	Highway 223 bridge (59)	58 miles
Highway 417 bridge (117)	37 miles	Loma Bridge FAS (1)	none
Sanford Campground (80)	5 miles		

"[T]he country in every derection around us was one vast plain in which innumerable herds of Buffalow were seen attended by their shepperds, the wolves; the solatary antelope which now had their young were distributed over it's face; some herds of Elk were also seen; the verdue perfectly cloathed the ground, the weather was pleasant and fair."

Between Tiber Reservoir and the Missouri River, the Marias flows past towering sandstone cliffs and fascinating badlands formations. Thick cottonwood groves often line the river. It's like a mini Missouri River, but the scenery is up-close and personal.

Like the nearby Missouri, the Marias is slow moving and muddy, except for the approximately 15-mile section immediately below the dam, where the water is clearer and colder. There's decent trout fishing in the section, especially for large fish. The fishery is now improving because the Bureau of Reclamation has changed the flow regimen from Tiber Reservoir to more closely mimic natural runoff.

There's good access to the river right below the dam, and two county roads and a state highway cross the river in the next 20 miles. After the Highway 223 bridge, the river remains quite isolated for the rest of its course. Beginners can handle the Marias. Although the dam can cause water fluctuations, they usually aren't major. In extremely dry years, the Marias can get too low to float.

Although you won't experience all the wildlife Lewis and Clark did (they saw wolves, grizzlies, buffalo, and elk) many species still roam the hills and bottoms of the Marias. Both mule and white-tailed deer are fairly common. Large numbers of waterfowl typically congregate on the river in spring and fall. Eagles often winter along the Marias, and coyotes can be seen almost any time. One friend reported he saw over fifty of the much-maligned song-dogs on one trip. You'll find, however, that the number of coyotes seen is inversely related to the current price of coyote pelts.

Hunters should be aware of the Brinkman Game Preserve, a state wildlife refuge that extends from the Highway 223 bridge east for about 10 river miles. It ends at the Liberty-Hill County Line. This little-known refuge, which encompasses nearly 13,000 acres of public and private land, was created by the Fish and Game Commission in 1926. Its boundaries are poorly marked. Hunting is not permitted along this section of river except for deer hunting (by permit only).

Marias River

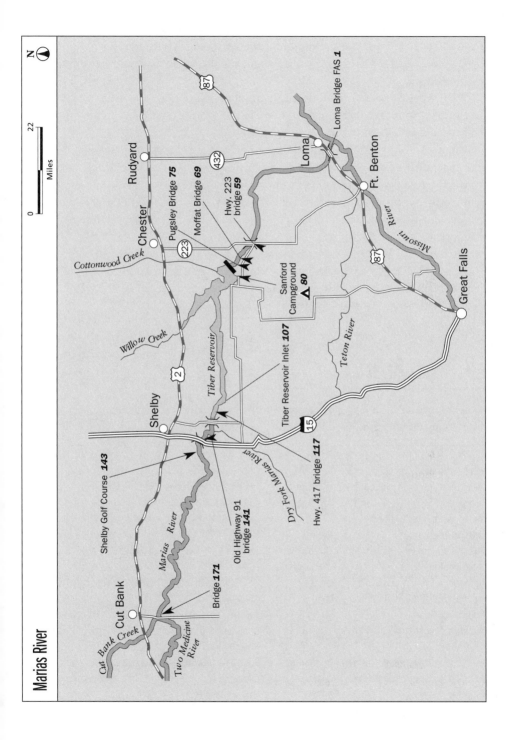

N

0   22
Miles

Rudyard

Chester

Cottonwood Creek

Willow Creek

Shelby

Cut Bank

Cut Bank Creek

Two Medicine River

Marias River

Shelby Golf Course **143**

Bridge **171**

Old Highway 91 bridge **141**

Dry Fork Marias River

Hwy. 417 bridge **117**

Tiber Reservoir

Tiber Reservoir Inlet **107**

Sanford Campground △ **80**

Teton River

Hwy. 223 bridge **59**

Moffat Bridge **69**

Pugsley Bridge **75**

Loma

Ft. Benton

Loma Bridge FAS **1**

Missouri River

Great Falls

87

432

223

2

15

87

Beavers occasionally can be spotted along the Marias, but they aren't as numerous as they once were. In 1831 James Kipp thought it was such good beaver country that he built Fort Piegan at the mouth of the Marias. He reportedly acquired over 2,400 "plews" in his first ten days of business, but the trade didn't last and the fort was abandoned.

Warmwater fish such as walleye, sauger, northern pike, catfish, and goldeye inhabit the lower sections of the river, and the experienced worm-dunker can do quite well. Goldeye usually bite on artificial lures as well as bait.

Summers along the Marias are generally short, but they can be devilishly hot. This area experiences extreme temperature fluctuations, and water temperatures in the river can get very warm in summer. Natural siltation, along with irrigation returns, accounts for the poor water quality found in most of the river. The soil in this area is the famed Missouri River gumbo—rock-hard when dry and stickier than tarpaper when wet.

Because of the impermeability of this soil, small pools of water form when it rains. These provide excellent breeding grounds for a particularly voracious race of mosquitoes. Numerous and quite large, they're sometimes mistaken for small ducks. Take plenty of repellent, and wear long pants and long sleeves.

20 Milk River

Named for its whitish color, the lengthy Milk River winds through remote prairies and seldom-visited cottonwood bottoms alive with wildlife.

Vital statistics: 437 miles in Montana (21 reservoir miles) from the confluence of the Middle and South Forks north of Browning to the Missouri River near Fort Peck.

Level of difficulty: Class I its entire length. Suitable for beginners except at high flows.

Flow: Annual mean flow: 656 cfs near Nashua. Floatable all year, except in its uppermost reaches. A 200 cfs minimum is needed below Dodson.

Hazards: Diversion dams, barbed-wire fences, mosquitoes.

Where the crowd goes: Nowhere. Dodson to Vandalia is popular with walleye anglers.

Avoiding the scene: The Milk's origin to the Highway 213 bridge (just before it enters Canada) is quite remote, with clearer water.

Inside tip: An excellent choice for a long-distance float trip.

Maps: BLM: #17 (Saint Mary), #27 (Cut Bank), #47 (Chester), #56 (Havre), #65 (Harlem), #74 (Whitewater), #75 (Malta), #84 (Glasgow)

USGS: Cut Bank, MT; Shelby, MT; Havre, MT; Glasgow, MT

River rules: Tribal fishing licenses required for Blackfeet, Fort Belknap, and Fort Peck Indian Reservations.

For more information: Bureau of Land Management, Havre; Montana Fish, Wildlife and Parks, Glasgow.

The Paddling

While not a classic beauty, the Milk River contains some of the least-explored water in Montana. At first glance, the sluggish and turbid Milk might not seem as appealing as famous rivers like the Blackfoot or Madison. But those who seek solitude, wide-open spaces, and excellent wildlife viewing opportunities won't be disappointed.

The Milk River country is a land of varied landscapes, ranging from rolling hills and badlands to low buttes and shallow valleys. It has a rough, primitive beauty composed of windswept plains once covered by glaciers.

Captain Meriwether Lewis noted the most salient characteristic of this major river while traveling up the Missouri in 1805. He wrote, "The water of this river possesses a peculiar whiteness, being about the colour of a cup of tea with the admixture of a tablespoonfull of milk." Always the astute observer, Lewis named it the Milk River.

While most people think of the Milk as a cloudy river, it flows out of the undisturbed slopes of Glacier National Park as a clear mountain stream. It then enters Canada north of Cut Bank. After a 100-mile loop, the Milk returns to Montana a changed stream. The Canadians aren't to blame, however, as most of the siltation is natural. While it was once thought the Milk's bluish-white color resulted from glacial till, it's now thought the color originates from fine sand picked up in a deep gorge near Writing-on-Stone Provincial Park in Alberta.

The Milk does carry a heavy sediment load in spring. Some say it's so muddy you can see the deer and raccoon tracks float by. Others claim you can walk across it during runoff. Despite all the jokes about the Milk, it winds through beautiful prairie country that's teeming with wildlife. The river occupies a broad floodplain, which geologists speculate was created by the Missouri River in preglacial times. The Milk doesn't have the rugged breaks of nearby rivers such as the Missouri and Marias. Tall cottonwoods and thick brush envelop the river, creating excellent habitat for deer, beaver, mink, and great blue herons. Sandhill cranes stalk the shallows, and white pelicans reside nearby. Heron and cormorant rookeries can be found along the more isolated sections. The Milk often hosts large concentrations of waterfowl during migration. It also replenishes the wetlands and prairies of Bowdoin National Wildlife Refuge, which boasts over 250 bird species.

Other once-abundant species are now represented only by their ghosts. Lewis and Clark reported seeing buffalo, wolves, and grizzlies, but they all flickered out of existence around the turn of the twentieth century, as did the plains elk. The Milk River country was renowned for its thundering buffalo herds and the Blackfeet Indians who hunted them. Today the river provides essential spawning for migratory birds and native fish.

Most people who float the Milk are anglers. The Milk sustains at least forty-two species of fish, including walleye, sauger, catfish, and northern pike. Limited trout fishing is available a few miles below Fresno Dam. Anglers often have good luck where tributaries such as Whitewater, Frenchman, and Beaver Creeks enter. Probably the

Milk River

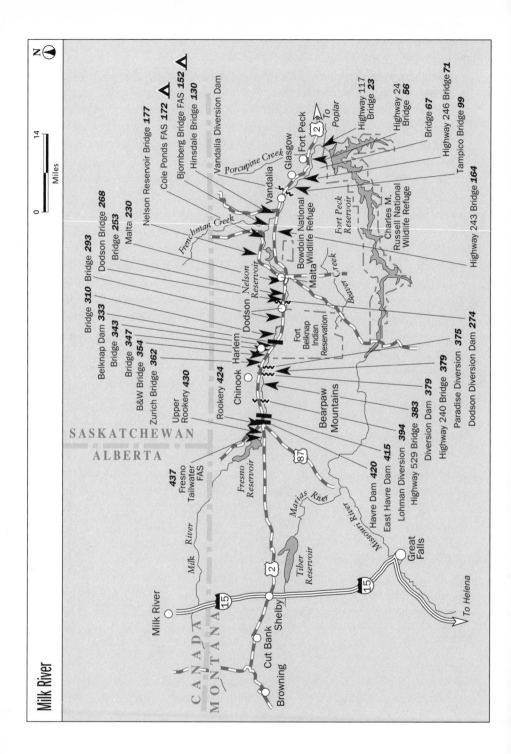

most popular section lies between Dodson and Vandalia, which biologists from Montana Fish, Wildlife and Parks rate among the best walleye stream-fishing in the state, frequently producing walleyes over ten pounds.

The Milk is Montana's longest tributary to the Missouri, coursing eastward before meeting "Old Misery" near Fort Peck. For almost 200 miles, the river parallels both the tracks of the old Great Northern Railroad (Montana's "High Line" Railroad, often spelled "Hi-Line"), and U.S. Highway 2.

Because the river meanders so repeatedly, the actual river distance is over 500 miles. While the Milk never strays far from US 2, it's usually distant enough that the highway can't be seen or the motors heard. It's an ideal river for floaters seeking an extended trip away from people.

Floating on the Milk in Montana begins below Fresno Dam and continues to where the Milk meets the Missouri. It's all suitable for beginners. The only hazards on this meandering stream are occasional diversion dams and barbed wire across the stream. Watch for major diversions at Vandalia and Dodson. The Milk can get very high during runoff, which typically peaks in early May. Mosquitoes can be fierce along the Milk in June and July.

Designated access to the Milk is almost nonexistent. Montana Fish, Wildlife and Parks has one site west of Havre (Fresno Tailwater Fishing Access Site) and one west of Hinsdale (Bjornberg Bridge Fishing Access Site), and there are public parks at Hinsdale and Malta.

Key Access Points along the Milk River

Access Point (River Mile)	Next Access Point	Access Point (River Mile)	Next Access Point
Fresno Tailwater FAS (437)	7 miles	Bridge (253)	23 miles
Upper Rookery (430)	6 miles	Malta (230)	53 miles
Rookery (424)	41 miles	Nelson Reservoir Bridge (177)	5 miles
Highway 529 bridge (383)	4 miles	Cole Ponds FAS (172)	8 miles
Highway 240 bridge (379)	17 miles	Highway 243 bridge (164)	12 miles
Zurich Bridge (362)	8 miles	Bjornberg Bridge FAS (152)	22 miles
Bridge (354)	7 miles	Hinsdale Bridge (130)	31 miles
Bridge (347)	4 miles	Tampico Bridge (99)	28 miles
Bridge (343)	33 miles	Highway 246 bridge (71)	4 miles
Bridge (310)	17 miles	Bridge (67)	11 miles
Bridge (293)	25 miles	Highway 24 bridge (56)	33 miles
Dodson Bridge (268)	15 miles	Highway 117 bridge (23)	none

21 Missouri River

The river that carried Lewis and Clark across much of Montana is a trout-filled mountainous stream in its upper reaches and a broad, scenic prairie river in its lower two-thirds. This is a trip through history.

Vital statistics: 734 miles (including 223 reservoir miles) from Three Forks to the Montana–North Dakota border. America's longest river, nearly 2,500 miles.

Level of difficulty: Class I, suitable for beginners its entire length, except below Morony Dam in Great Falls (4 miles of Class III rapids).

Flow: Annual mean flow: 7,696 cfs at Fort Benton. Plenty of water all year in this big river.

Hazards: Strong winds, sudden storms, mosquitoes, and plenty of rattlesnakes.

Where the crowd goes: The 149-mile Wild and Scenic section, especially between Coal Banks and Judith Landings. Holter Dam to Pelican Point receives heavy fishing pressure.

Avoiding the scene: Fred Robinson Bridge to Turkey Joe. For a long trip, Fort Peck Dam to the North Dakota border.

Inside tip: Float from Fred Robinson to Fort Peck Reservoir in September to see and hear one of the last remaining prairie elk herds in the nation.

Maps: BLM: #39 (Great Falls North), #40 (Great Falls South), #41 (Canyon Ferry Dam), #42 (Townsend), #43 (Bozeman), #48 (Lonesome Lake), #49 (Fort Benton), #58 (Winifred), RAG-16, RAG-17, #84 (Glasgow), #85 (Fort Peck Lake East), #93 (Wolf Point), #102 (Culbertson); Upper Missouri National Wild & Scenic River (maps 1&2, 3&4)

USFS: Helena

USGS: Bozeman, MT; White Sulphur, MT; Great Falls, MT; Shelby, MT; Lewistown, MT; Jordan, MT; Wolf Point, MT

Montana Afloat: #16 (Missouri River)

River rules: Check with Montana Fish, Wildlife and Parks regarding ever-changing trout-fishing regulations. Registration required for floating Wild and Scenic section of the Missouri (at Fort Benton, Coal Banks Landing, and Judith Landing).

For more information: Bureau of Land Management, Lewistown or Fort Benton; Montana River Outfitters, Great Falls or Fort Benton; Lewis and Clark Trail Adventures, Missoula.

The Paddling

Known as "Old Misery" to early explorers and fur trappers who fought its tricky currents and fickle moods, the Missouri River has carried boatloads of Montana history-makers on its waters. Pathway for the expansion of the West, the Missouri provided the major water route to the Rocky Mountains from the time of Lewis and Clark until the coming of the railroads in the late 1800s.

Although the river once bustled with activity, it now offers solitude and a deep sense of the past. Nearly every bend has a story to tell, and despite all the mishaps that have occurred on this historic river, even beginning floaters can handle the Missouri for its entire length in Montana.

The Blackfeet, Assiniboine, Gros Ventre, and Cree Indians ruled the lands along the Missouri before settlers arrived. In 1805 and 1806 Lewis and Clark traversed

The Missouri is still as wild as it ever was.

the entire length of the Missouri River and its tributaries in Montana. Fur trappers invaded soon after. Steamboats came next, proceeding as far up the Missouri as Fort Benton. The ships brought gold-seekers, sodbusters, homesteaders, shopkeepers, and other opportunists. Livestock came to Montana in the 1880s, and cattlemen still dominate the Missouri River area today.

Colorfully named landmarks reflect the Missouri's rich and romantic past. Places like Gates of the Mountains, Citadel Rock, Hole-in-the-Wall, Slaughter River, Bullwhacker Creek, Drowned Man's Rapids, Steamboat Rock, and Woodhawk Creek all played a role in Montana history. Floaters looking for Lewis and Clark information will find a treasure trove, but two books stand out. First is Bernard DeVoto's classic book, *The Journals of Lewis and Clark*. It's an excellent distillation of the journals, with explanatory footnotes. The other is Stephen Ambrose's more recent book, *Undaunted Courage*.

Pioneers weren't able to deal with the river's wandering ways and set out to harness it. Dams now check the Missouri for most of its 2,500-mile flow. In Montana nearly a third of the Missouri lies stilled behind concrete and earth. First come Canyon Ferry, Hauser, and Holter Dams, three dams in succession that lie east of Helena and impound the river for nearly 70 miles. Then near downtown Great Falls lie five run-of-the-river dams that check the famous falls where Lewis and Clark made an

Missouri River (Upper)

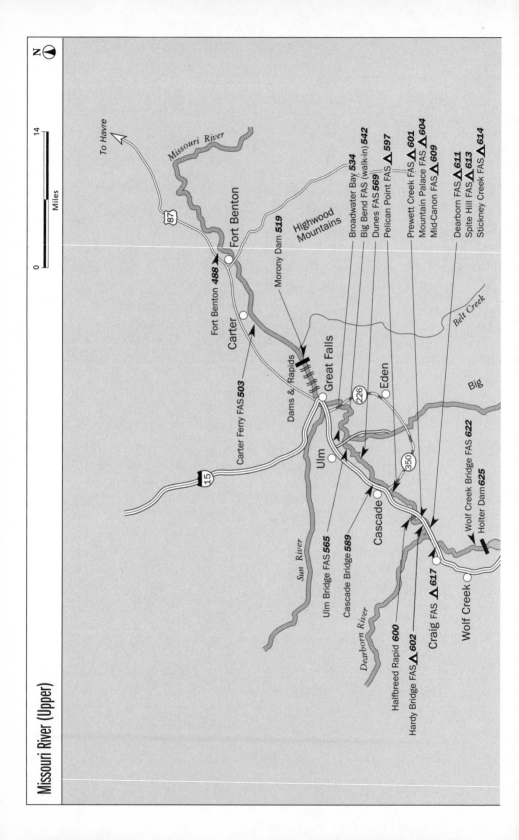

N

0   14

Miles

To Havre

Missouri River

Fort Benton

87

Fort Benton **488**

Carter

Morony Dam **519**

Highwood
Mountains

Carter Ferry FAS **503**

Dams & Rapids

Great Falls

Belt Creek

Sun River

15

Ulm

226

Eden

Big

Ulm Bridge FAS **565**

Cascade Bridge **589**

Cascade

350

Wolf Creek Bridge FAS **622**

Holter Dam **625**

Dearborn River

Halfbreed Rapid **600**

Hardy Bridge FAS ▲ **602**

Craig ▲ **617**

Wolf Creek

Broadwater Bay **534**
Big Bend FAS (walk-in) **542**
Dunes FAS **569**
Pelican Point FAS ▲ **597**

Prewett Creek FAS ▲ **601**
Mountain Palace FAS ▲ **604**
Mid-Canon FAS▲ **609**

Dearborn FAS ▲ **611**
Spite Hill FAS ▲ **613**
Stickney Creek FAS ▲ **614**

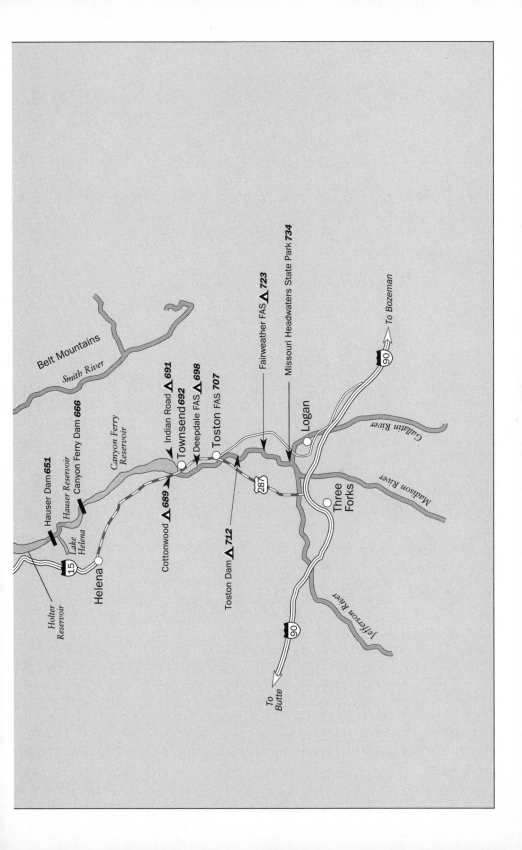

Missouri River (Wild and Scenic)

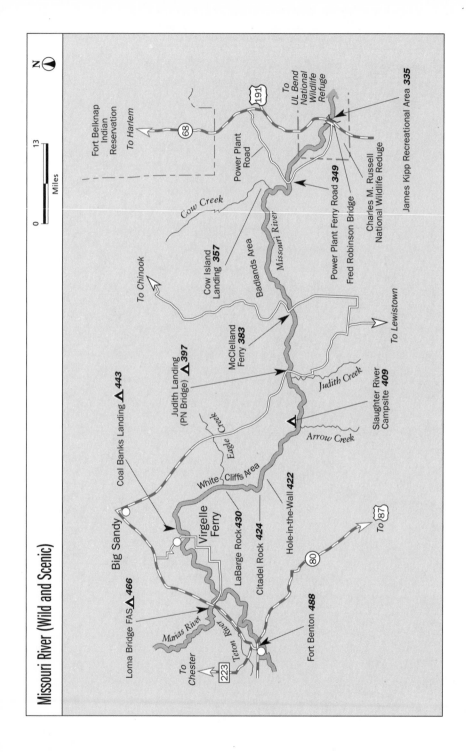

N

0   13
Miles

Fort Belknap Indian Reservation

To Harlem

68

191

To UL Bend National Wildlife Refuge

Power Plant Road

Cow Creek

Missouri River

Cow Island Landing **357**

Badlands Area

To Chinook

McClelland Ferry **383**

Judith Landing (PN Bridge) △ **397**

Coal Banks Landing △ **443**

Eagle Creek

Judith Creek

To Lewistown

Power Plant Ferry Road **349**

Fred Robinson Bridge

Charles M. Russell National Wildlife Refuge

James Kipp Recreational Area **335**

Slaughter River Campsite **409**

Arrow Creek

White Cliffs Area

Big Sandy

Virgelle Ferry

LaBarge Rock **430**

Citadel Rock **424**

Hole-in-the-Wall **422**

87

To 87

80

Loma Bridge FAS △ **466**

Marias River

Teton River

To Chester

223

Fort Benton **488**

Key Access Points along the Missouri River

Access Point (River Mile)	Next Access Point	Access Point (River Mile)	Next Access Point
Missouri Headwaters State Park (734)	11 miles	Broadwater Bay (534)	15 miles
Fairweather FAS (723)	11 miles	Morony Dam (519)	16 miles
Toston Dam (712)	5 miles	Carter Ferry FAS (503)	15 miles
Toston FAS (707)	9 miles	Fort Benton (488)	22 miles
Deepdale FAS (698)	7 miles	Loma Bridge FAS (466)	23 miles
Indian Road (691)	2 miles	Coal Banks Landing (443)	46 miles
Cottonwood (689) (reservoir)	64 miles	Judith Landing (397)	14 miles
		McClelland Ferry (383)	34 miles
Holter Dam (625)	3 miles	Power Plant Ferry Road (349) (south side)	14 miles
Wolf Creek Bridge FAS (622)	5 miles		
Craig FAS (617)	3 miles	James Kipp Recreation Area (335)	8 miles
Stickney Creek FAS (614)	1 mile	Slippery Ann (327)	7 miles
Spite Hill FAS (613)	2 miles	Rock Creek (320)	10 miles
Dearborn FAS (611)	2 miles	Turkey Joe (310) (reservoir)	125 miles
Mid-Canon FAS (609)	5 miles		
Mountain Palace FAS (604)	2 miles	Fort Peck Dredge Cuts FAS (185)	10 miles
Hardy Bridge FAS (602)	1 mile	School Trust FAS (175)	60 miles
Prewett Creek FAS (601)	4 miles	Lewis and Clark FAS (115)	38 miles
Pelican Point FAS (597)	8 miles	Bridge (77)	13 miles
Cascade Bridge (589)	20 miles	Brockton (64)	30 miles
Dunes FAS (569)	4 miles	Culbertson Bridge FAS (34)	31 miles
Ulm Bridge FAS (565)	23 miles	Snowden Bridge FAS (3)	4 miles
Big Bend FAS (542) (walk-in)	8 miles	Highway 58 bridge, ND	none

arduous 17-mile portage. Finally—and most significantly—the huge Fort Peck Dam in eastern Montana drowns nearly 100 miles of river and creates the fourth-largest reservoir in the world.

The 149-mile segment of the Missouri between Fort Benton and the Fred Robinson Bridge endures as the only major portion of the 2,500-mile-long Mighty Mo that has been protected and preserved in a free-flowing and natural state. After a hard-fought battle, it became a part of the National Wild and Scenic Rivers System in 1976. It's very popular, attracting river rats and history buffs from all over the country.

Like a great fallen tree with its branches ensnarled in the mountains, the Missouri starts near Three Forks at the confluence of the Jefferson, Madison, and Gallatin Rivers. The river flows freely for about 35 miles before being impounded by the Canyon Ferry—Hauser—Holter complex of impounded lakes.

Missouri River (Lower)

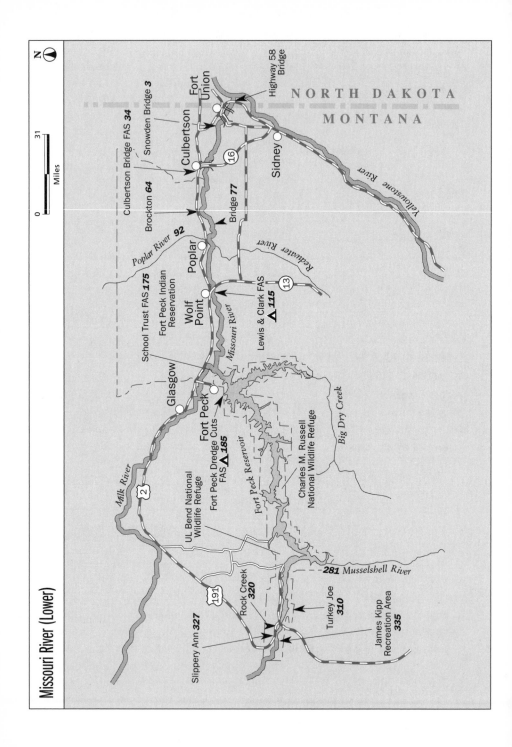

The river between Townsend and Three Forks has experienced a burst of popularity as anglers have discovered the exceptionally large trout that reside here. Fairly isolated, the area has beautiful rolling hills and wooded islands. Water quality isn't always the best here, and hot summer days can raise water temperatures. Toston Dam, which lies about halfway between Three Forks and Canyon Ferry and creates a few miles of slack water, blocks upstream movements of trout. The Toston-to-Townsend float is popular in fall, when the brown trout are spawning and the fish are concentrated below the dam.

Except for a short float from Hauser Dam to Holter Reservoir, the next floating opportunity starts below Holter Dam near Wolf Creek, where the river flows through a narrow canyon. Lewis and Clark watched mountain goats and bighorn sheep prance along the cliffs here. Although Interstate 15 is close to the river and subdivisions sometimes mar the scenery, the Missouri between Helena and Great Falls remains magical. The water flows clear, and the fishing is excellent. Access is easy with the Missouri River Recreation Road paralleling the river for 35 miles.

According to state fisheries studies, the Missouri between Wolf Creek and Craig ranks with the Beaverhead and Big Hole Rivers for trophy trout production. This section contains about 3,000 fish 10 inches or longer per mile, with about 300 per mile that are 18 inches or over. Whirling disease is present in the Missouri but has had little effect, so far, on trout populations. It's easy floating all the way to Great Falls except for some difficult water about 1.5 miles below Hardy Bridge.

The well-known falls of the Missouri preclude floating through Great Falls, but expert kayakers can try surfing the waves just downstream from Black Eagle Dam. Other floaters may want to put in right below Morony Dam and try the short section of whitewater (about 2.5 miles) that lasts until about 1 mile beyond Belt Creek. Less-skilled paddlers can launch at Carter Ferry to avoid the whitewater. After Carter Ferry, the river is easy for the rest of its way across Montana. The biggest danger is the wind that can create waves and make maneuvering a boat nearly impossible. Although old maps may show rapids, they're only dangerous if you're piloting a steamboat.

The Missouri begins to change character once it cuts into the plains near Great Falls, picking up sediment and getting more turbid. The Sun River pushes the first mud into the Missouri, and the Marias River completes the job. At runoff times, it justly earns its nickname, "Big Muddy." Some farmers claim to fill pipes with Missouri River water and then saw them into disks to use as grindstones.

The "wild" Missouri starts at Fort Benton, a historic Montana town with a great museum. For the first 40 miles below Fort Benton, canyon walls slope obliquely toward the river as the Missouri slowly sheds itself of civilization. Most of the land along this section is privately owned. After passing Virgelle and Coal Banks Landing, the river becomes completely isolated as the sloping canyons turn into sheer white cliffs that rise directly from the river's edge. Wind and rain have shaped the soft rock into peculiar formations, guaranteed to mesmerize river explorers.

This bizarre but attractive country enchanted Captain Lewis. Always the person for detail, his 1805 description of the river and its scenery is hard to top:

"The hills and river Clifts which we passed today exhibit a most romantic appearance. . . . The water in the course of time in decending from those hills and plains on either side of the river has trickled down the soft sand clifts and woarn it into a thousand grotesque figures. . . . As we passed on it seemed as if those seens of visionary inchantment would never have an end. . . ."

After nearly 35 miles of white cliffs, the scenery changes to rugged badlands. A maze of coulees and ravines, this legendary Missouri River breaks country invites exploration. Below Cow Island the valley broadens and the bluffs are lower and more distant. Dense cottonwood stands dominate the river bottom for most of the remaining distance to the Fred Robinson Bridge.

The Bureau of Land Management has developed an excellent map of the Wild and Scenic portion of the river. These water-resistant maps provide a mile-by-mile guide to the river as well as other important logistical considerations. They may be purchased at most BLM offices in Montana.

Those looking for a one-day trip on the "wild" Missouri usually float between Fort Benton and Loma. Depending on how fast one paddles (and whether there's wind), Coal Banks Landing to Judith Landing takes two or three days, as does the section from Judith Landing to the Fred Robinson Bridge. Most people allow five to seven days to float the entire 149 miles. While the widely spaced access points preserve the primitive nature of the river, they make shuttling vehicles difficult. Shuttles take several hours or can be arranged in Fort Benton. (Check with the BLM office in Fort Benton for names of individuals who offer shuttle services.)

The Wild and Scenic portion of the Missouri grows more popular every year, and high national interest in the Lewis and Clark Expedition could lead to levels of use that compromise solitude. Floaters traveling between Fort Benton and the Fred Robinson Bridge between Memorial Day and the weekend after Labor Day must register with BLM (it's free). Self-registration is available at Fort Benton, Coal Banks Landing, and Judith Landing.

While you may encounter large numbers of people at major put-in points, this is a big river and people seem to spread out during the day. Unfortunately, campsites on public land are limited, as is shade. Mature cottonwoods are dying, and there is little new growth, mainly due to cattle grazing along the banks. Measures need to be taken by the BLM to protect existing trees and provide for regeneration of new trees. BLM may limit cows on the south side of the river from Cabin Rapids to Woodhawk Creek (about 17 miles) during the float season. It's a start.

BLM estimates that at least 8,000 people float the "wild" Missouri each year. Floaters should be prepared for an irritant you wouldn't expect on a Wild and Scenic

River: motorboats. The droning of motors off the canyon walls diminishes the primitive experience that is a key part of this trip. Motorboats also make the river seem smaller and more crowded. BLM says the river has a tradition of motorboat use and contends the decision to allow motors was made after extensive public participation. There is a no-wake restriction (about 5 miles per hour), and only downstream travel is allowed for motorboats on the Wild and Scenic sections from the weekend before Memorial Day to the weekend after Labor Day. Nevertheless, the time seems right to reexamine the issue of motorized use.

Although beginners can handle the Missouri, hazards exist. Thunderstorms can be severe and can occur suddenly. The Missouri's strong winds are legendary. Stay close to shore if the winds get brisk, and stop if they worsen. But if the wind is steady and in your favor, take advantage of it. Rig a poncho or ground cloth (be creative!) between your canoe paddles for a sail. The person in the bow holds the sail between his legs (to drop or adjust depending on the wind), while the person in the stern uses another paddle as a rudder. You will fly!

Be sure to take along drinking water. The river water is unsafe to drink unless boiled or filtered. There is potable water at Coal Banks Landing, Hole-in-the-Wall, and Judith Landing. When camping overnight, take along gas stoves for cooking; firewood is scarce. Beware of camping in cottonwood groves when winds are strong, as the trees snap easily. Be sure to camp and hike on public land unless you have permission to access private land. Vault toilets have been installed at most campsites. Rattlesnakes are common along the river and have been encountered at every campsite. Consider carrying a snakebite kit.

If you're looking for wildlife, head for the prairie dog towns—they're usually a center of activity. More than thirty different species of Great Plains wildlife use the dog towns. Floaters also have an excellent opportunity to see Rocky Mountain bighorn sheep. These animals were reintroduced into the Missouri Breaks country in the 1960s to replace the Audubon sheep that had been wiped out after the settlement of the white man. Today there are large populations on both sides of the river below Judith Landing.

Bird-watchers will enjoy the river. Kingbirds perch along the river and grab insects, while many warblers sing from the brush. Pheasants use the thick vegetation often found on islands, and great blue herons and Canada geese appear along the shores. Look for white pelicans either floating on the river or circling overhead.

The spiny softshell turtle, uncommon in Montana, can sometimes be spotted sunning on a beach. Don't pick them up—they may bite. The Missouri has excellent populations of warmwater fish species, including catfish, sauger, and northern pike. Night fishing for catfish is a pleasant way to spend a warm summer evening. Or leave a baited hook out overnight and have fish for breakfast.

While most people head for the "wild" Missouri, the 25 miles of river below Fred Robinson Bridge (James Kipp Recreation Area) is equally primitive and spectacular.

Bounded on each side by the Charles M. Russell National Wildlife Refuge (CMR), an incredibly productive prairie elk herd roams the bottoms and sometimes can be seen swimming the river or grazing on the islands. Deer, sage grouse, and coyotes are also common. Floating ends where the river backs up to form Fort Peck Reservoir at Turkey Joe.

The prehistoric paddlefish is also a denizen of this section of the Missouri. Spring triggers a spawning run of these strange fish up the Missouri from Fort Peck Reservoir. Fish as heavy as 141 pounds have been caught near the Fred Robinson Bridge. Paddlefish, however, aren't taken by conventional fishing methods. Heavily weighted treble hooks are used to snag these fish, which may live thirty years or more. They feed on plankton, which are rarely larger than the period at the end of this sentence.

The public owns much of the land adjacent to the "wild" Missouri, and this is one of the few places in the United States to experience prairie wilderness. Although the Bureau of Land Management has studied six areas adjacent to the river, Congress has taken no action, and no real constituency has formed yet to push for a designation. If you want to help, contact the Montana Wilderness Association at the address in appendix B.

Below Fort Peck Reservoir, the Missouri remains primitive and the rough breaks country gently merges with woodlands as the river approaches North Dakota. Although U.S. Highway 2 is never far away, this section of the river is quite isolated for its entire 185-mile course. If you don't like the crowds on the "wild" Missouri, this section will please the crustiest of river hermits. Count on seeing plenty of wildlife, and for those seeking the unusual, this is probably the best spot in Montana to see a whooping crane. They migrate through this part of Montana in spring and fall.

22 Powder River

A remote eastern Montana river, described by pioneers as "a mile wide and an inch deep," that flows through some of Montana's most uninhabited, desolate badlands and prairies.

Vital statistics: 218 miles long from the Wyoming border to its juncture with the Yellowstone near Terry.

Level of difficulty: All Class I, suitable for beginners, except for 200 yards of Class II+ rapids beginning at Mile 8.

Flow: Annual mean flow: 584 cfs near the U.S. Highway 12 bridge. Can get too low by late summer. At least 750 cfs is needed for floating.

Hazards: Fences, mud and quicksand, rattlesnakes, hard-to-see sandbars.

Where the crowd goes: It just isn't done. Most accessible is the 30-mile stretch from the US 12 bridge at Locate to the Yellowstone.

Avoiding the scene: The higher in the drainage you go, the more remote it gets. It's downright lonely at the top.

Inside tip: Take a spring float to look for turkeys. Beware of high water in May.

Maps: BLM: #96 (Terry), #97 (Miles City), #98 (Powderville), #99 (Broadus)
USFS: Custer (Ashland Division)
USGS: Ekalaka, MT; Miles City, MT

River rules: Mostly private land; camp within the high-water marks.

For more information: BLM, Miles City; FWP, Miles City.

The Paddling

The Powder River may well be Montana's most remote nonwilderness river. Although there are a few isolated ranches or abandoned homesteads nearby, you'll rarely see a light at night or hear a motor. The river enters Montana not far from Kaycee, Wyoming, and flows north for 218 miles before meeting the Yellowstone River not far from Terry. The Powder channels and braids through cottonwood bottoms for most of its course. Noted for its shifting channels and hidden sandbars, the Powder carries more sediment than probably any other Montana river. "Too thin to plow and too thick to drink" is a favorite local description.

But the Powder is quite scenic and extremely isolated. The uppermost parts in Montana flow through rugged badlands, which then give way to cottonwood bottoms. In the last 14 miles, downstream from the Coal Creek Bridge, the river stops braiding, the cottonwoods disappear, and the Powder turns into an arid, wide-open river that's quite unique. At one place, about 8 miles above where the Powder hits the Yellowstone, exposed bedrock juts up in the river and creates rapids that last for about 200 yards. Intermediate rafters or canoeists can handle this hazard (known locally as Ed's Rapids) or walk around it.

Since the Powder is quite shallow, the floating season is short. In a typical year, flows will be too low by late July. River trips in the fall are rarely possible, which is

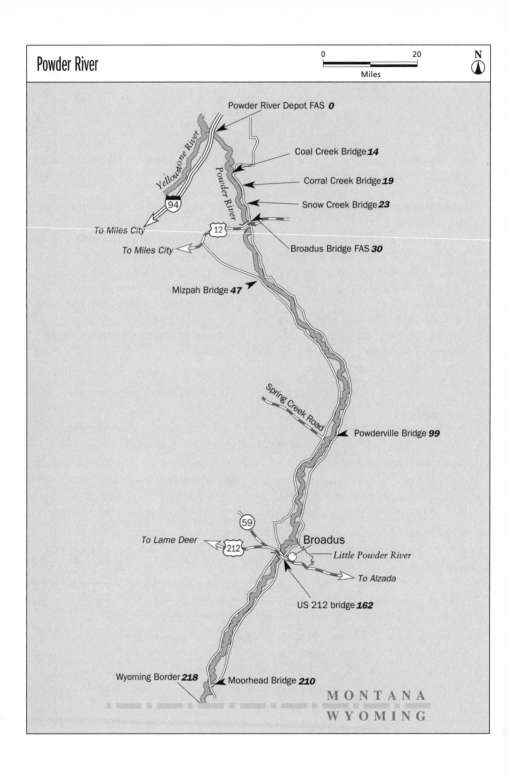

Powder River

Miles
0   20

N

Powder River Depot FAS **0**

Yellowstone River

Powder River

Coal Creek Bridge **14**

Corral Creek Bridge **19**

Snow Creek Bridge **23**

To Miles City

94

12

To Miles City

Broadus Bridge FAS **30**

Mizpah Bridge **47**

Spring Creek Road

Powderville Bridge **99**

59

To Lame Deer

212

Broadus

Little Powder River

To Alzada

US 212 bridge **162**

Wyoming Border **218**   Moorhead Bridge **210**

MONTANA

WYOMING

Key Access Points along the Powder River

Access Point (River Mile)	Next Access Point	Access Point (River Mile)	Next Access Point
Moorhead Bridge (210)	48 miles	Snow Creek Bridge (23)	4 miles
U.S. Highway 212 bridge (162)	63 miles	Corral Creek Bridge (19)	5 miles
Powderville Bridge (99)	52miles	Coal Creek Bridge (14)	14 miles
Mizpah Bridge (47)	17 miles	Powder River Depot FAS (0)	none
Broadus Bridge FAS (30)	7 miles		

really too bad given the hunting opportunities that abound. Turkeys and mule deer are plentiful, as are sharp-tailed grouse, sage grouse, and antelope. The Powder River basin was one of the last areas in the nation that had free-roaming bison herds, and it's still possible to find bones and teeth in the riverbank. This is also a great area for fossils; several dinosaur finds have been made nearby.

The best floating is below where the Little Powder River enters near Broadus. A local biologist who has done fish surveys on the Powder tells us his favorite stretch is from Mizpah to Locate (the US 12 bridge). At high flows it took him less than eight hours to cover this 17-mile section. This same biologist reports that the Powder is one of Montana's very best spawning streams for shovelnose sturgeon and catfish. Their spawning runs coincide with spring runoff and the floating season.

The floating is easy on the Powder, suitable for practiced beginners in rafts or canoes. There really aren't many hazards except for an occasional downed tree and the occasional barbed-wire fence. But the fences aren't even much of a problem—they get washed out during the season when you'd want to be floating.

The Powder has great appeal for those who like long, isolated trips. We heard of one canoeist who floated the entire river by himself (218 miles in Montana and 185 miles in Wyoming) in thirty-two days. Public land along the river is quite limited; access points are very far apart and consist mainly of county road bridges. You'll be treated like an explorer if anyone encounters you on this river.

23 Red Rock River

Small, windy, and remote, the Red Rock River originates in one of Montana's most scenic high-altitude valleys.

Vital statistics: 113 miles (27 miles of lakes and reservoir) from Lillian Lake to where it enters Clark Canyon Reservoir.

Level of difficulty: Class I its entire length. Sharp turns, fast current, and logjams below Lima Reservoir require at least intermediate skill.

Flow: Annual mean flow: 143 cfs near Monida. Usually too low by midsummer.

Hazards: Logjams, swift current, sharp bends, barbed wire, and diversion dams below Lima Reservoir. Above the reservoir, beware of remoteness and bad weather.

Where the crowd goes: Nowhere. The "wilderness" section between Upper and Lower Red Rock Lakes is the most popular.

Avoiding the scene: Not an issue.

Inside tip: Good wildlife viewing for trumpeter swans, which regularly use the river between Lower Red Rock Lake and Brundage Lane.

Maps: BLM: #35 (Lima), #45 (Hebgen Lake) USFS: Beaverhead Interagency Travel Plan (East and West) USGS: Ashton, ID; Dubois, WY USFWS: Red Rock Lakes Recreation Guide

River rules: The river between Upper and Lower Red Rock Lakes is open to floating between September 1 and freeze-up (typically late October). Above the Upper Lake, floating is open July 15 to freeze-up. No motors on Red Rock Lakes National Wildlife Refuge. Check with refuge for updated regulations.

For more information: Red Rock Lakes National Wildlife Refuge, Lima; Montana Fish, Wildlife and Parks, Bozeman.

The Paddling

If you're bothered by the heavy traffic on the upper Beaverhead, try driving a little farther south to the Red Rock River. This little-known stream, which empties into Clark Canyon Reservoir, receives only modest floating pressure.

Between Lima and Clark Canyon, the Red Rock closely resembles the Beaverhead, both in scenery and fishing. It's a little smaller, but it turns and twists in the same distinctive fashion and has similar outstanding trout habitat. In its upper reaches in the isolated Centennial Valley, the river flows through Red Rock Lakes National Wildlife Refuge, a unique high-altitude marsh that teems with birdlife. Much of the 32,000-acre refuge is designated wilderness, one of the largest roadless wetlands in the United States.

The Red Rock River gets its start amidst the towering peaks of the Centennial Mountains, just west of Yellowstone National Park. Herds of cattle were driven into the valley in 1876, a hundred years after the Revolutionary War, giving the area its name. Cattle remain the predominant sign of man's pressure.

Most people know the Red Rock Lakes National Wildlife Refuge as the place where trumpeter swans were rescued from extinction. In the 1930s these majestic white birds numbered less than seventy, and many ornithologists predicted their

Red Rock Lakes National Wildlife Refuge was created to save the trumpeter swan.

demise. Stringent protection brought them back to where they now number close to 2,500 and are expanding their range. These large birds, which may weigh as much as thirty-five pounds and have a wingspan of 8 feet, have a distinct, low-pitched bugling call that seems to resound across the entire valley.

Floating on the Red Rock begins within the refuge after a short paddle across Upper Red Rock Lake. A canoe is the craft of choice. The river snakes its way through a maze of marshy islands before emptying into Lower Red Rock Lake. Since there is little current, it's possible to lose your way while picking a path through the marsh. A detailed map of the refuge and the 7-mile trip between the lakes is available at the refuge headquarters.

Wildlife viewers have spotted over 200 species of birds on the refuge, and at least 18 species of waterfowl nest there. Shorebirds including long-billed curlews, avocets, and willets frequent the mudflats bordering the marshes, while gulls, terns, and pelicans wheel overhead. Sandhill cranes are common, particularly in the meadows bordering the upper lake.

Allow a full day for the trip between the lakes, as the slack water requires more paddling than on a normal river. To protect nesting waterfowl, no boats are allowed on this section before September 1. Check at the refuge headquarters for information on boating regulations.

Between the refuge boundary and Lima Reservoir, the thick marsh gradually gives way to open range. The river is quite isolated and can only be reached by a few county roads. The only time of year this section sees any traffic is during waterfowl season. It's an excellent float to see waterfowl almost any time, and trumpeter swans use the river extensively.

Red Rock River

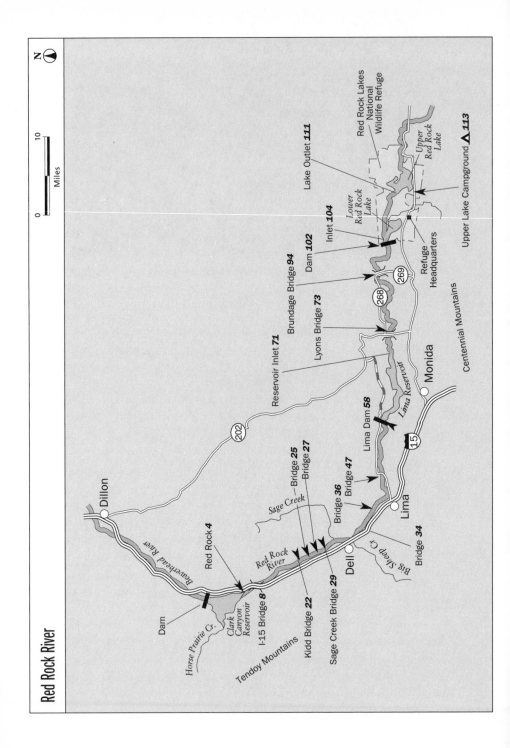

0   10
Miles

Dillon

Beaverhead River

Dam

Horse Prairie Cr.

Clark Canyon Reservoir

Red Rock 4

I-15 Bridge 8

Tendoy Mountains

Kidd Bridge 22

Sage Creek Bridge 29

Red Rock River

Sage Creek

Bridge 25

Bridge 27

Dell

Bridge 36

Bridge 47

202

Reservoir Inlet 71

Brundage Bridge 94

Lyons Bridge 73

Lima Dam 58

Lima Reservoir

Big Sheep Cr.

Lima

Bridge 34

15

Monida

Dam 102

Inlet 104

Lake Outlet 111

Red Rock Lakes National Wildlife Refuge

Lower Red Rock Lake

268

269

Refuge Headquarters

Centennial Mountains

Upper Red Rock Lake

Upper Lake Campground ▲ 113

Key Access Points along the Red Rock River

Access Point (River Mile)	Next Access Point	Access Point (River Mile)	Next Access Point
Upper Lake Campground (113)	11 miles	Bridge (36)	7 miles
Dam (102)	8 miles	Sage Creek Bridge (29)	2 miles
Brundage Bridge (94)	21 miles	Bridge (27)	2 miles
Lyons Bridge (73)	15 miles	Bridge (25)	3 miles
Lima Dam (58)	11 miles	Kidd Bridge (22)	18 miles
Bridge (47)	11 miles	Red Rock (4) (Clark Canyon Reservoir)	none

Don't be surprised to hear a motor on the river between Lima Reservoir and Lower Red Rock Lake. Hunters occasionally bring motorboats upstream from the lake. No motorboats are permitted on the refuge.

The water between the refuge and the reservoir is slightly turbid, and fishing is erratic. Reports indicate some trout are present (cutthroat and grayling), as well as ling. The water in this section is slow and flat, suitable for beginners. Beware of bad weather, however, as storms are quite unpredictable in this 6,000-foot-elevation valley.

Floating the Red Rock from Lima Dam to Kidd is possible, but it's strictly for the adventuresome. Be on the lookout for blind corners with barbed-wire fences, downed trees, and low bridges. It's only recommended for experienced boaters who don't mind occasional portages. The sharp turns, fast currents, and occasional logjams found below Lima Dam require intermediate skill. It's best floated in a canoe, as the river is rather small and winding for rafts. Moreover, hitting barbed wire can be a deflating experience. Low flows in dry years may preclude floating by midsummer.

The river grows increasingly larger as it approaches Clark Canyon Reservoir. Below Kidd, the river is much less hazardous. This section has great fishing, but the only access other than floating is by paying the landowner. If you float this section, be sure to stay within the high-water marks.

Access to the Red Rock downstream from Lima is exclusively by county bridges, and most are overgrown with brush or blocked by barbed wire. Although the State of Montana has affirmed that county bridges provide legal access for floaters and anglers, some landowners disagree and have filed lawsuits. Be aware that the size of the county right-of-way can vary significantly. Be sure you know the law (see appendix D) when floating sections with difficult or controversial access.

24 Rock Creek

This well-graveled, clean-flowing mountain stream gushes past spectacular palisades and through thick pine forests, providing some of the best fishing in western Montana.

Vital statistics: 51 miles from the confluence of its two forks above Gilles Bridge to its juncture with the Clark Fork.

Level of difficulty: All Class I, except for a short Class II whitewater section through the Dalles. All suitable for intermediates in rafts.

Flow: Annual mean flow: 513 cfs near the mouth. Usually too low for floating by mid-July. Minimum flow is 650 cfs; 2,800 cfs is maximum. Flows between 1,000 and 1,500 cfs are optimum.

Hazards: Dangerous logjams, swift currents, narrow channels, standing waves.

Where the crowd goes: Windlass to the White Bridge (and just about everywhere else) during the salmon fly hatch.

Avoiding the scene: Float downstream from Elkhorn on weekdays and below Welcome Creek on weekends to avoid outfitter traffic.

Inside tip: During a high-moisture year, try a fall overnight trip on the upper river.

Maps: BLM: #21 (Missoula East), #22 (Philipsburg), #23 (Wisdom)
USFS: Lolo, Deerlodge
USGS: Butte, MT
Montana Afloat: #3 (Rock Creek)

River rules: No float-fishing from July 1 to November 30. Outfitters not allowed from Elkhorn Landing to Valley of the Moon and from Harry's Flat to Welcome Creek. Outfitters cannot float on weekends or on Memorial Day from Welcome Creek to Elkhorn. Check fishing regulations with Montana Fish, Wildlife and Parks.

For more information: Montana Fish, Wildlife and Parks, Missoula; Grizzly Hackle, Missoula; Missoulian Angler, Missoula; Rock Creek Mercantile, Rock Creek.

The Paddling

What is the difference between a creek and a river? Only the name. Rock Creek, which starts west of Philipsburg and flows for more than 51 miles before hitting the Clark Fork about 20 miles east of Missoula, has the attributes and flow of many small Montana rivers. This world-class trout stream courses through a largely undeveloped valley, flowing past thick forests and stunning rock formations. Many of the heavily timbered hillsides give way to grassy meadows near their crests. Like many other Montana streams, Rock Creek has experienced problems with whirling disease, an infection that affects all salmonids but seems to hit rainbow trout the hardest.

The creek gets its name from the rockslides that stretch down the mountainsides and occasionally into the stream. It's one of the best rivers in the state for seeing bighorn sheep, especially on the hills near Solomon Creek at the lower end of the river and near Windlass Bridge on the upper river. Moose and black bear are common along the river, as are western tanagers and ruffed grouse.

Rock Creek is one of only a few Montana streams where agencies have restricted fishing from boats. Because it's a small stream that receives heavy use from anglers on

Rock Creek has a short floating season in the spring.

foot, conflict between floaters and waders increases as water levels decrease. All fishing from boats is prohibited between July 1 and November 30. While state law guarantees the right to float navigable rivers like Rock Creek at any time, agencies can restrict the ability to float and fish. People who float Rock Creek in summer should expect to encounter a steady stream of anglers who may have to move out of the stream channel to avoid you. They won't be happy. Since the creek is usually too low for floating anyway, we suggest you avoid it during the summer fishing season.

Almost all Rock Creek floating takes place from May 15 to July 1, coincidental with the salmon fly hatch. For nonfishing people, this is the hatch of giant stoneflies that brings large trout to the surface. Rock Creek can become extremely crowded during this time, especially on the upper river.

Floating can begin where the West and Middle Forks come together. The river is always swift and flows over a cobbled bottom. Logjams and snags pose the biggest hazards, and there are occasional big waves. Although Rock Creek contains only Class I water except for a short section through the Dalles, it's too difficult for beginners in canoes or rafts at the higher flows typically encountered in May and June. The Dalles are mostly Class II and III water that intermediate rafters can handle. A road parallels the river for its entire length, but it's usually unnoticeable.

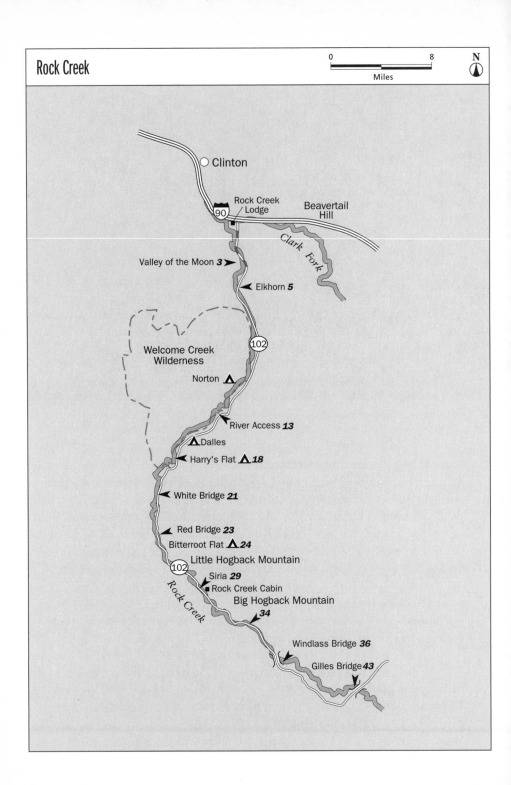

Rock Creek

0   8
Miles

N

Clinton

Rock Creek Lodge

90

Beavertail Hill

Clark Fork

Valley of the Moon *3*

Elkhorn *5*

102

Welcome Creek Wilderness

Norton

River Access *13*

Dalles

Harry's Flat *18*

White Bridge *21*

Red Bridge *23*

Bitterroot Flat *24*

Little Hogback Mountain

102

Siria *29*

Rock Creek Cabin

Big Hogback Mountain

Rock Creek

34

Windlass Bridge *36*

Gilles Bridge *43*

Key Access Points along Rock Creek

Access Point (River Mile)	Next Access Point	Access Point (River Mile)	Next Access Point
Gilles Bridge (43)	7 miles	White Bridge (21)	3 miles
Windlass (Concrete) Bridge (36)	2 miles	Harry's Flat (18)	5 miles
River Access (34)	5 miles	River Access (13)	8 miles
Siria (29)	6 miles	Elkhorn (5)	2 miles
Red Bridge (23)	2 miles	Valley of the Moon (3)	none

The upper river has some exceptional scenery as it winds past brightly colored rock outcroppings. Sunsets are spectacular. Public land adjoins much of the river. A popular float at high flows is the 22-mile section between Gilles Bridge and the White Bridge. At high flows, it takes about six hours.

A 4-mile section of whitewater known as the Dalles lies between Harry's Flat and Welcome Creek. The stream constricts into a narrow channel that contains many large boulders. The rapids are not particularly difficult, mostly Class II or easier. The Welcome Creek Wilderness lies immediately adjacent to the river and has excellent hiking.

Logjam problems can be acute on the lower river, particularly in the vicinity of the Valley of the Moon. In some years large jams completely block the river. Check with local sources, including the Rock Creek Mercantile and the Missoula fly shops listed in appendix A, for current information. Depending upon logjams, a good early season float starts at Valley of the Moon and ends at the Schwartz Creek Bridge on the Clark Fork.

25 Ruby River

This small, sinuous stream snakes its way through the historic Ruby Valley, providing excellent fishing along its way.

Vital statistics: 103 miles (including 3 miles of reservoir) from its headwaters south of Alder to its confluence with the Beaverhead River.

Level of difficulty: Class I all the way. Practiced beginners can handle this river at low flows.

Flow: Annual mean flow: 210 cfs below Ruby Reservoir. Frequently too low for floating by late July, especially above Ruby Reservoir.

Hazards: Extremely sharp bends, brushy banks, narrow channels, protruding trees, barbed-wire fences, diversion dams, and cranky landowners. Contentious access.

Where the crowd goes: Nowhere in particular. Silver Springs to Twin Bridges is most popular.

Avoiding the scene: Upstream from Ruby Reservoir is isolated and difficult to reach. Perfect for explorers.

Inside tip: Floating can get you to some great, otherwise inaccessible fishing.

Maps: BLM: #33 (Butte South), #34 (Dillon)
USFS: Beaverhead Interagency Travel Plan (East)
USGS: Dillon, MT; Bozeman, MT; Ashton, ID; Dubois, ID

River rules: Check with Montana Fish, Wildlife and Parks concerning floater access. Spillway area below dam closed to fishing.

For more information: Montana Fish, Wildlife and Parks, Bozeman; Four Rivers Fishing Company, Twin Bridges; Harmon's Fly Shop, Sheridan.

The Paddling

With its well-developed curves and bends, the Ruby River makes an excellent little sister to the Beaverhead, the river it flows into near Twin Bridges. The river slinks and turns through the picturesque Ruby Valley, former home of outlaws and gold miners. Piles of gravel that line the banks of many of the Ruby's tributaries are remnants of the area's gold rush legacy. Robber's Roost, a famous roadhouse located between Sheridan and Laurin, was once a favorite hangout for outlaws and bandits who preyed upon gold miners.

Key Access Points along the Ruby River

Access Point (River Mile)	Next Access Point	Access Point (River Mile)	Next Access Point
Cow Camp (92)	6 miles	Vigilante FAS (46)	2 miles
Cottonwood Camp (86)	4 miles	Coy Brown Bridge FAS (44)	4 miles
Vigilante Ranger Station Bridge (82)	2 miles	Alder Bridge FAS (40)	1 mile
Bridge (80)	11 miles	Ruby Island FAS (39)	19 miles
Ledford Creek Bridge (69)	11 miles	Silver Springs Bridge FAS (20)	22 miles
Sweetwater Creek Bridge (58) (reservoir)	10 miles	Jesen Park, Twin Bridges (Beaverhead River)	none
Ruby Dam FAS (48)	2 miles		

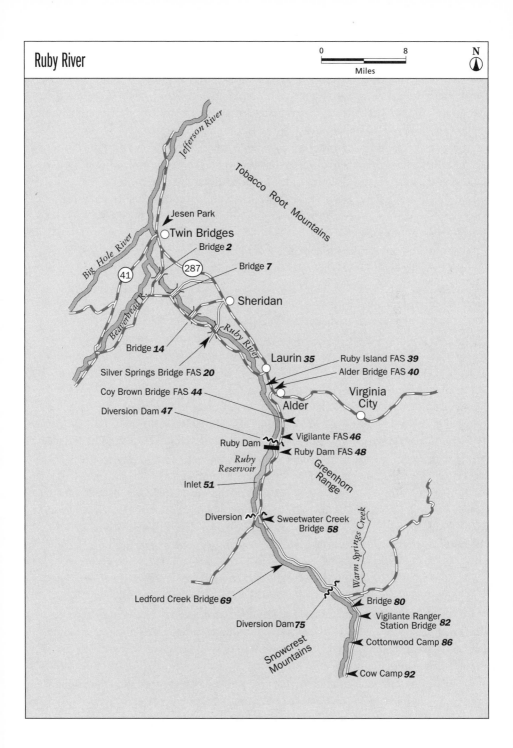

Ruby River

0   8
Miles

N

Jefferson River

Tobacco Root Mountains

Jesen Park

Twin Bridges

Bridge **2**

Big Hole River

41   287   Bridge **7**

Sheridan

Beaverhead R.

Ruby River

Bridge **14**

Laurin **35**   Ruby Island FAS **39**
                 Alder Bridge FAS **40**

Silver Springs Bridge FAS **20**

Coy Brown Bridge FAS **44**   Virginia
                               City
Alder

Diversion Dam **47**

Vigilante FAS **46**

Ruby Dam   Ruby Dam FAS **48**

Ruby
Reservoir   Greenhorn
             Range

Inlet **51**

Diversion   Sweetwater Creek
             Bridge **58**

Warm Springs Creek

Ledford Creek Bridge **69**   Bridge **80**

Vigilante Ranger
Station Bridge **82**

Diversion Dam **75**

Cottonwood Camp **86**

Snowcrest
Mountains

Cow Camp **92**

The Shoshone Indians called this river Passamari, meaning "water of the cottonwood groves." When Lewis and Clark passed through, Captain Lewis named it Philanthropy, for what he considered one of Thomas Jefferson's three cardinal virtues (he named the Big Hole River "Wisdom" and the Jefferson River, "Philosophy").

Pioneers later downgraded the name to Stinkingwater River after a large number of buffalo carcasses befouled the water one spring. Now it's called the Ruby for the garnets that sharp-eyed people still pick out of the stream's gravel.

This small river originates in the Snowcrest Mountains and flows north for about 40 miles before reaching Ruby Reservoir. Below the reservoir it flows another 25 miles before meeting the Beaverhead. The river above the reservoir is small with sharp bends, barbed wire, and occasional obstructions. It requires small crafts and large patience; it's often too low to float by August. Almost all floating on the Ruby takes place below the reservoir.

Then there's the access problem. Most land along the Ruby is private, and landowners are quite sensitive about trespassers. The Ruby has excellent fishing, and some landowners charge hefty fees to access the river. The problem? People floating the river can fish for free, and landowners resent it (as do their paying clients). Fortunately, Montana law says that all navigable rivers are property of the state. Landowners may charge fees for crossing their private property, but they cannot interfere with recreation within the high-water marks. If you plan to float this river, know your stream access rights (see appendix D).

While the Ruby is smaller than the Beaverhead, it has the same brushy banks and excellent trout habitat. It's predominately a brown trout fishery below the dam and mostly cutthroats and rainbows above. While it's difficult to fish from a boat on the Ruby, a canoe can be useful for reaching inaccessible portions of the river. The Ruby's brushy habitat and frequent backwater sloughs also generate outstanding birdlife. It's a great area for sandhill cranes.

Because of limited access, the small size of the river, and long float distances between access points, the Ruby gets very little floating pressure. This river has so many bends that you should plan on traveling about 3 river miles for every air mile. Access is strictly by fishing access sites. Most floating occurs between Silver Springs access and Twin Bridges. A small canoe is the best craft; it can handle sharp turns and narrow channels and can be portaged easily. Moreover, barbed wire and sharp willows will puncture all but the sturdiest rafts.

While the Ruby isn't difficult, it takes considerable skill to negotiate the repeated sharp bends, narrow channels, diversion dams, and protruding trees. Beginners should stay away when the river is high. But beware of flows getting too low. In 1985 parts of the Ruby went completely dry.

While Lewis and Clark called the Ruby "mild and placid," they didn't encounter present-day hazards such as barbed wire around blind corners, water diverted from the river, and landowners who feel they own the river. It makes one pine for the old days.

26 Smith River

One of Montana's premier floating streams, the Smith River cuts a narrow swath through a spectacular canyon. Its colorful cliffs, abundant wildflowers, outstanding wildlife, and excellent fishing bring people back year after year.

Vital statistics: 125 miles from the confluence of its two forks to its juncture with the Missouri River near Ulm.

Level of difficulty: At normal flows, Class I, except for two Class II rapids. Suitable for practiced beginners in rafts, intermediates in canoes. Requires continuous maneuvering.

Flow: Annual mean flow: 148 cfs near Fort Logan. Usually floatable until early July. In a drift boat don't try it below 400 cfs. In a raft you need at least 250 cfs. If you read water well, you can get by with as little as 150 cfs in a non-aluminum canoe.

Hazards: Sharp bends with currents flowing into cliff walls, snags, narrow channels, and float-through fences; sudden, intense lightning or windstorms. Rattlesnakes, bears, and raccoons may cause problems if you fail to keep a clean camp.

Where the crowd goes: Camp Baker to Eden Bridge.

Avoiding the scene: Go in spring or fall.

Inside tip: After the river drops below floatable levels, summer rainstorms sometimes raise flows enough for spur-of-the-moment canoeists.

Maps: BLM: #40 (Great Falls South), #41 (Canyon Ferry Dam)
USFS: Lewis and Clark (Jefferson Division), Helena
USGS: White Sulphur, MT; Great Falls, MT
Montana Afloat: #9 (The Smith River)

River rules: Float fee and permit required. No motors. Camping in designated sites only. Campers must declare their campsites prior to departure at Camp Baker. Maximum group size 15. No more than 4 nights of camping from June 10 to July 10. Check on special fishing regulations.

For more information: Montana Fish, Wildlife and Parks, Great Falls or Camp Baker; Think Wild Enterprises shuttle service, White Sulphur Springs; Montana River Outfitters, Great Falls; U.S. Weather Service, Great Falls.

The Paddling

Henry David Thoreau once wrote, "He who hears the rippling of rivers will never despair of anything." The bubbling waters of the Smith River have that magical ability to soothe one's soul. Squadrons of floaters seek a special kind of spiritual salvation along the Smith's shores each year.

Located south of Great Falls, the Smith rises out of the Castle Mountains, crooks by White Sulphur Springs, and then courses between the Big Belt and Little Belt Mountains before meeting the Missouri River. Lewis and Clark named the river in 1805 in honor of Robert Smith, President Thomas Jefferson's Secretary of the Navy. The river winds by Fort Logan (first known as Camp Baker), a military outpost established in 1869 to protect ranchers and miners from Indians.

Although the Smith is small in comparison to many other Montana rivers—and frequently is too low for floating in late July and August—it's a high-quality stream

The Smith is the only Montana river where private parties need a permit.

cast in a primitive setting. The heart of the river, and the highlight of all float trips, is a deep limestone canyon that envelops the river. Long riffles alternate with deep pools on this emerald-colored stream, creating excellent trout habitat. Towering rock formations and thick forests alive with wildlife complete the scene.

Given these alluring qualities, it's only natural that many people want to float the Smith. To protect and maintain this river's natural qualities, Montana Fish, Wildlife and Parks manages the river under a permit system. Competition for permits is stiff during the prime floating months of May, June, and July. Applications are taken beginning January 1, and permits are issued after February 15. It costs $30 for a Montana resident to apply for a permit and $55 for nonresidents. In addition to the permit fee, the following floater fees are also required at Camp Baker: five years and younger, free; six to twelve, $15; thirteen and over, $25 ($50 for nonresidents). If you don't get a permit, call Montana Fish, Wildlife and Parks in Great Falls to check for cancellations. Maximum group size per permit is fifteen.

Most Smith River floats start at Camp Baker and end at Eden Bridge, 60 miles downstream. Although it's possible to start as high in the drainage as where the two major forks of the river join, not many do. For those who try, it's an early-season proposition; heavy irrigation usually precludes floating by mid-July. Only intermediates or better should try the Smith above the Fort Logan Bridge. Beware of a short, rocky canyon with some difficult rapids not far below the Buckingham Bridge.

The Smith also receives modest pressure near its mouth, below Eden Bridge. It's a flat, lazy river that flows mostly through open farmland before meeting the Missouri about 20 miles downstream from Ulm. Although the scenery isn't spectacular, it can have good brown trout fishing in the fall as far downstream as the Truly Bridge.

The popular float from Camp Baker to Eden Bridge takes a minimum of two nights and three full days at normal water levels. The average trip lasts four days, but many people take five days. While most think a slow trip is best, two canoeists hold the speed record: Camp Baker to Eden Bridge twice in one day! The trips took place at peak flows and maximum daylight.

The shuttle between Camp Baker and Eden Bridge is roundabout, so allow yourself several hours each way if you do it yourself. There are two options: The shorter route is a dirt road that's dusty when dry and nearly impassable when wet. The longer but more comfortable route is via U.S. Highway 89. The other possibility is to use one of the commercial shuttle services listed above. They generally cost about $75 per car. Wild Enterprises in White Sulphur Springs has done shuttles for us for almost twenty years and has always done a great job. For a complete list of shuttle services, contact the Great Falls office of Montana Fish, Wildlife and Parks.

About 60 percent of floaters use rafts, and about 30 percent use canoes; the rest use inflatable kayaks, rowboats, and drift boats. Drift boats are a poor choice during low-water conditions. Canoes, however, shine when the river gets scratchy, particularly ones made of synthetic materials that slide over rocks without damage. Canoes have good maneuverability and better speed, and they handle headwinds more effectively. They provide a better feeling of being part of the river than most other crafts. Rafts offer stability and lots of cargo space. They're a good choice for beginners, families, serious fishermen, and party animals.

After leaving Camp Baker, grassy hillsides eventually give way to rock outcroppings and sheer walls as the river approaches the canyon. By the time floaters reach Tenderfoot Creek, cliffs rise sharply on both sides of the river. Colorful lichens adorn stone walls, as do swallow's nests and occasional Indian pictographs.

Wildlife viewing can be outstanding, especially in the early morning or late evening. Mule deer can be seen bouncing up hillsides, and beaver, mink, and muskrat are common streamside denizens. Birds to look for include kingfishers, spotted sandpipers, golden eagles, dippers, great horned owls, and an assortment of warblers. On a recent trip we counted eighty-two bird species.

Floaters today may even see an animal Lewis and Clark never saw in Montana— the raccoon. This masked mammal has extended its range west during the last century. One may invade your campsite looking for unsecured food. Careful wildlife observers may also glimpse river otters and black bears.

Fishing can be excellent on the Smith, although it ebbs and flows based on water

Weather can be unpredictable on the Smith.

levels and wintertime ice scouring episodes. Above the canyon the river supports mainly rainbow trout with occasional browns. In the canyon expect a mixture of browns and rainbows. Browns predominate below the canyon. Native cutthroats can be caught throughout. Conscientious fishermen release them. Check regulations for special restrictions.

Montana Fish, Wildlife and Parks requires floaters to declare their boat campsites before they leave Camp Baker. There's competition for the best campsites, and they are issued on a first-come, first-served basis.

May 15 to July 1 is the prime Smith River floating period, so those seeking solitude go in April and September. Peak flows usually occur in late May and early June, and the floating season typically is over by mid-July. When irrigation ceases in September, flows may pick up enough for a fall float. The minimum flow for a raft is about 250 cfs; for a canoe, about 150 cfs. Check flow conditions on the Internet by searching "Montana current streamflow" and select the USGS Web site(it's updated every four hours). Or you can do it the old way by calling Montana Fish, Wildlife and Parks in Great Falls.

The Smith is a fairly easy river to float. Practiced beginners in rafts will do fine except at high flows. Canoeists require more experience to negotiate the repeated sharp turns and the occasional small rapids. The most significant rapids occur near Mile 35, just before and after the Rattlesnake Bend campsite. Other hazards include frequent rocks (many just under the surface and difficult for the uninitiated to detect), sharp bends into cliff walls, rocky shallows, and occasional snags. While fences may cross the river in low periods, they almost always have float gates that permit easy passage.

The biggest hazard with the Smith is its remoteness. If you hit a spell of bad weather, there's no choice but to stick it out. Be prepared for rain or cold weather. All floaters—especially canoeists—should avoid overloading their craft with equipment or people. An overladen boat does not handle properly. Don't carry three people in a canoe unless the boat is designed for it.

Montana Fish, Wildlife and Parks highly discourages floaters from bringing their dogs along on the Smith River. Even though a leash law is in place, FWP reports that too many dogs are running free, causing problems with landowners, chasing wildlife, and disrupting the aesthetic beauty of the river. If you do bring your dog, obey the leash law and pick up its waste.

Despite the Smith's outstanding attributes, every silver lining has a cloud. Those who have floated the Smith for a long time have noted the ever-growing number of cabins and houses along the river. These subdivisions threaten the Smith's natural qualities. Another serious Smith River problem is the proliferation of leafy spurge—a

Key Access Points along the Smith River

Access Point (River Mile)	Next Access Point	Access Point (River Mile)	Next Access Point
Smith River FAS (92)	8 miles	Trout Creek (52)	2 miles
Camp Baker FAS (84) car access	6 miles	Crow's Foot (50)	1 mile
Spring Creek (78)	1 mile	Table Rock (49)	2 miles
In-lieu (77)	0.4 mile	Fraunhofer (47)	2 miles
Indian Springs (77)	1 mile	Upper Parker Flat (45)	1 mile
Rock Creek (76)	2 miles	Parker Flat (44)	2 miles
Mouth of Rock Creek (74)	3 miles	Paradise Bend (42)	4 miles
Scotty Allen's Black Canyon (71)	4 miles	Staigmiller (38)	0.5 mile
Syringa Camp (67)	1 mile	Merganser Bend (38)	0.3 mile
Canyon Depth (66)	1 mile	Black Butte (37)	0.2 mile
Two Creek (65)	0.6 mile	Ridge Top (37)	2 miles
Sheep Wagon (65)	5 miles	Givens Gulch (35)	0.2 mile
Cow Coulee (60)	1 mile	Rattlesnake (35)	12 miles
Sunset Cliff (59)	2 miles	Eden Bridge (23) car access	14 miles
County Line (57)	4 miles	Truly FAS (9) car access	5 miles
Bear Gulch (53)	1 mile	Highway 330 bridge (4) car access	none

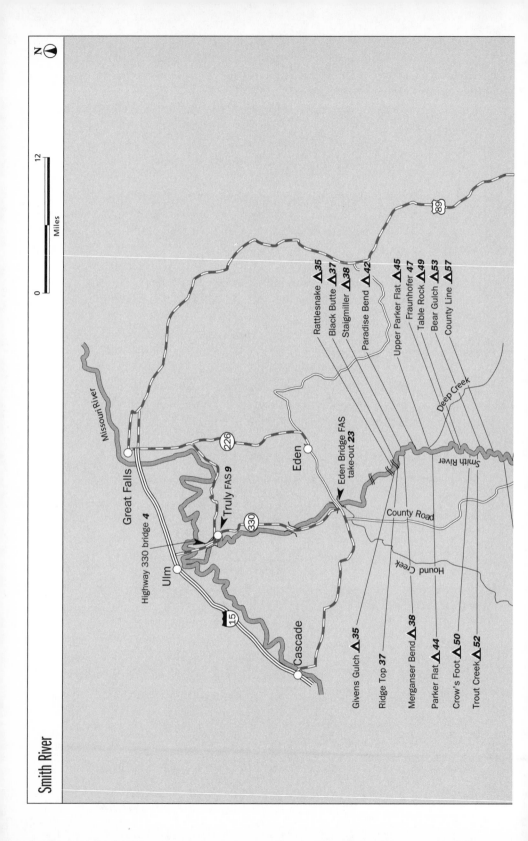

Smith River

N

0   12
Miles

Missouri River

Great Falls

Highway 330 bridge 4

Ulm

Truly FAS 9

226

330

Eden

Eden Bridge FAS take-out 23

Cascade

15

County Road

Hound Creek

Deep Creek

Smith River

Hound Creek

89

Rattlesnake △35
Black Butte △37
Staigmiller △38
Paradise Bend △42

Upper Parker Flat △45
Fraunhofer 47
Table Rock △49
Bear Gulch △53
County Line △57

Givens Gulch △35
Ridge Top 37
Merganser Bend △38
Parker Flat △44
Crow's Foot △50
Trout Creek △52

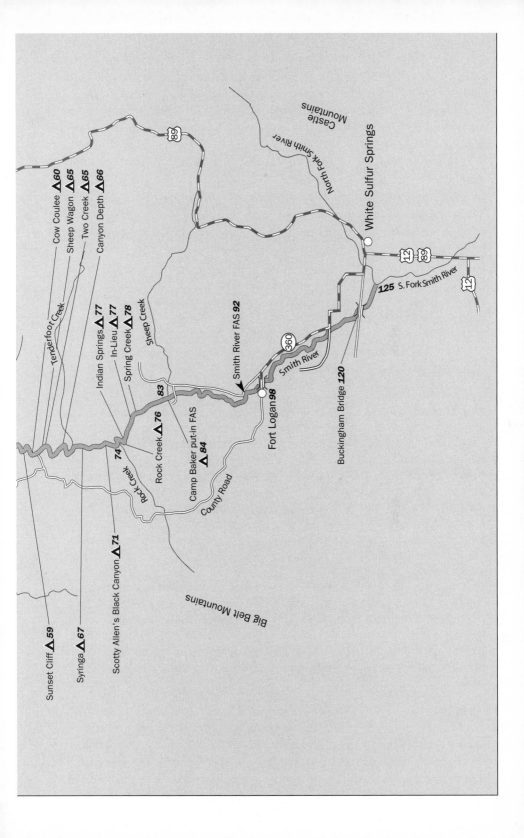

Sunset Cliff △**59**

Syringa △**67**

Scotty Allen's Black Canyon △**71**

Cow Coulee △**60**
Sheep Wagon △**65**
Two Creek △**65**
Canyon Depth △**66**

Tenderfoot Creek

Indian Springs△**77**
In-Lieu △**77**
Spring Creek△**78**

Sheep Creek

Rock Creek

Rock Creek △**76**

83

74

Camp Baker put-in FAS
△ **84**

County Road

Smith River FAS **92**

Fort Logan **98**

Smith River

360

Big Belt Mountains

Castle
Mountains

North Fork Smith River

White Sulfur Springs

12 **89**

125 S. Fork Smith River

12

Buckingham Bridge **120**

89

noxious weed that chokes out native plants and reduces forage for wildlife. This plant, which has a bright yellow flower that blooms in July, has taken over much of the river bottom and most large meadows. Montana Fish, Wildlife and Parks, the USDA Forest Service, and Meagher and Cascade Counties are working cooperatively to battle this invader with biological and chemical control, as well as landowner and floater education.

While the Smith is an obvious candidate for the National Wild and Scenic Rivers System, most local landowners oppose the concept of federal management. Nevertheless, many landowners want to preserve the river corridor and might support a locally developed cooperative management plan similar to the one that now protects a sizable part of the Blackfoot River. Such an effort could be the best prescription for protecting the Smith from inappropriate development.

27 Stillwater River

The Stillwater is a fast, rocky mountain river that flows through timbered bottomlands and past large ranches with the spectacular Beartooth Mountains as a backdrop.

Vital statistics: 68 miles from its headwaters in the Beartooth Mountains southwest of Absarokee to its confluence with the Yellowstone River near Columbus.

Level of difficulty: A challenging whitewater river. Class IV and V rapids in its upper reaches, Class II and III from Cliff Swallow downstream.

Flow: Annual mean flow: 947 cfs near Absarokee. Often too low by August above Absarokee. Usually has adequate flows all year below Absaroka Fishing Access Site. Float the river with at least 300 cfs (about 1.5 feet), and don't go when it is over 2,000 cfs (about 3 feet).

Hazards: Logjams, snags, boulders, diversion dams. Extremely dangerous low bridges at high flows.

Where the crowd goes: Absaroka FAS to Fireman's Point.

Avoiding the scene: Cliff Swallow Fishing Access Site to Absaroka FAS.

Inside tip: Great milk shakes and burgers at the Dew Drop Inn in Absarokee.

Maps: BLM: #62 (Big Timber), #63 (Red Lodge)
USFS: Custer (Beartooth), Gallatin-East
USGS: Billings, MT

River rules: None

For more information: Absaroka River Adventures, Absarokee; Adventure Whitewater, Red Lodge; Beartooth Whitewater, Red Lodge; Montana Fish, Wildlife and Parks, Billings; Custer National Forest (Beartooth Division), Red Lodge.

The Paddling

Mention the Stillwater River and somewhere a kayaker's heart pounds a little faster, for the Stillwater is anything but still. Named by Captain Clark, who must have stumbled onto one of this river's few quiet spots, this picturesque stream dashes madly

There's fun whitewater on the Stillwater.

from the Beartooth Mountains, cascades through sizable boulder fields, and only slows down in its lower reaches before meeting the Yellowstone River near Columbus. It's one of the top whitewater streams in the state.

While the Corps of Discovery never tested the Stillwater's rapids, Captain Clark camped at the mouth of the river for a week and built two canoes for the trip down the Yellowstone. The dugouts were 28 feet long, 16 or 18 inches deep, about 16 to 24 inches wide, ax-hewn, and hollowed by fire. They proved excellent boats to carry the intrepid explorers down the Yellowstone—Clark's group averaged more than 30 miles per day.

Thanks to Congress's 1978 designation of the Absaroka-Beartooth Wilderness, the headwaters of the Stillwater are protected. It's possible for kayakers to float about 5 miles of the river within the wilderness, but the only access is via foot or horse. The upper river has a distinct alpine flavor, with heavy timber running to the edge of the river. Downed trees—a result of forest fires—have made floating the upper stream extremely difficult

Just downstream from Woodbine Rapids are Chrome Mine Rapids. Located adjacent to the Mouat Mine, they are also extremely challenging. Both rapids require careful scouting and top-quality equipment, including wet suits, helmets, and high-flotation life jackets. From Mouat Mine to Cliff Swallow, the river remains tumultuous but not quite as dangerous.

Stillwater River

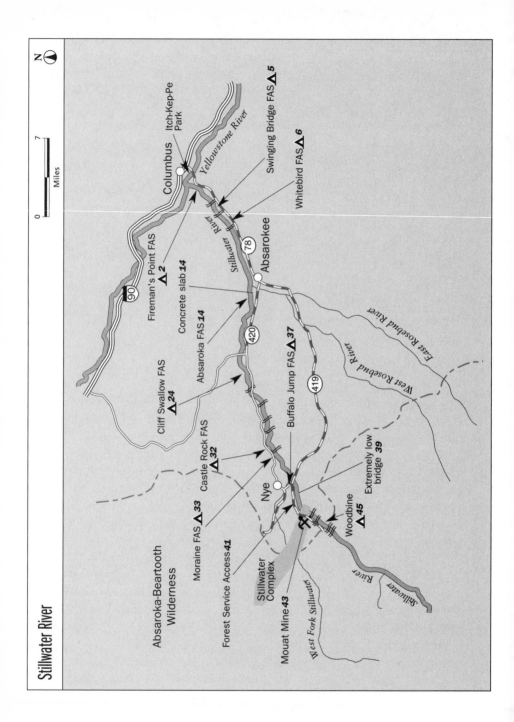

N

0   7
Miles

Columbus   Itch-Kep-Pe Park

Yellowstone River

Swinging Bridge FAS△5

Fireman's Point FAS △2

Whitebird FAS △6

Concrete slab 14

Absarokee

Stillwater River

78

Cliff Swallow FAS △24

Absaroka FAS 14

420

Castle Rock FAS △32

Buffalo Jump FAS△37

419

Moraine FAS △33

Absaroka-Beartooth Wilderness

East Rosebud River

West Rosebud River

Nye

Extremely low bridge 39

Forest Service Access41

Woodbine △45

Stillwater Complex

Mouat Mine 43

West Fork Stillwater

Stillwater River

Key Access Points along the Stillwater River

Access Point (River Mile)	Next Access Point	Access Point (River Mile)	Next Access Point
Woodbine (45)	4 miles	Absaroka FAS (14)	8 miles
Forest Service Access (41)	4 miles	Whitebird FAS (6)	1 mile
Buffalo Jump FAS (37)	4 miles	Swinging Bridge FAS (5)	3 miles
Moraine FAS (33)	1 mile	Fireman's Point FAS (2)	2 miles
Castle Rock FAS (32)	8 miles	Itch-Kep-Pe Park (Yellowstone River)	none
Cliff Swallow FAS (24)	10 miles		

In an average year, the Stillwater above Absarokee usually gets too low for floating by mid-July. Below Absarokee the river typically holds up throughout the summer.

While the Stillwater sees plenty of kayakers, more rafters and canoeists have discovered it in recent years. For those interested in boating the Stillwater, the Beartooth Paddler's Society extends an open invitation for people to show up at the Moraine or Cliff Swallow access points on nearly any Saturday or Sunday during the peak floating season (usually about mid-May to mid-July). It's a good opportunity to go down the river with experienced people.

For inexperienced people who want to try out the Stillwater, contact the guiding services listed above and in appendix A. Call these experts if you have any questions about flows or where to float. They're happy to help out.

With its broad, gravel bottom and large cottonwood groves, some people compare the Stillwater to western Montana's Bitterroot. The Stillwater has extraordinary water quality for a river so far east. Like the Bitterroot, the Stillwater has many new houses popping up along its shores, and floating pressure on the river has escalated markedly in the last decade.

Although the Stillwater now flows clean and pure, its future is cloudy. Directly adjacent to the main river and the West Fork of the Stillwater lies a mineralized zone known as the Stillwater Complex. This area, which is about 15 miles long and 2 or 3 miles wide, contains one of the country's richest supplies of minerals, including copper, chrome, nickel, and platinum.

Because most of the ore in this complex is low grade, fluctuating metal prices have dictated the level of mining, which has been ongoing for nearly a century. Mining has taken off again recently. While the federal Mining Law of 1872 grants the miner his discovery, Montana state law clearly speaks to preserving natural ecosystems. Is it possible to balance a free-flowing, unpolluted stream with mines, mills, and tailing dumps? The questions are difficult, but one thing is certain: If those who care about rivers aren't involved, there won't be any balance.

STILL WATERS RUN STEEP
Whitewater action on the Stillwater starts at the end of the road near the Woodbine campground, where the rapids are extremely formidable. The Woodbine Rapids last for about a mile and at high flows contain some Class IV water as well as one Class V drop. At peak flows, even experts consider these rapids unrunnable. Below Woodbine there's near-continuous whitewater for the next 1.5 miles before hitting Chrome Mine Rapids, opposite the old Mouat Mine. This extremely difficult spot lasts about 300 yards and is a bona fide Class V. Few people run this rapid. Those who do should scout it carefully and wear top-quality equipment, including wet suits, helmets, and high-flotation life jackets. At peak flows it's Class VI—unrunnable.

Chrome Mine Rapids start out with an 8-foot waterfall and then dash through a plethora of rocks. An upset spells extreme punishment and possible death. This entire 3-mile section is only for the best of the kayak experts. It is probably the toughest 3 miles of whitewater in Montana.

After the Chrome Mine Rapids, the river calms down for the next 10 miles before reaching the Moraine access. This stretch is almost all Class I and II water. The next 9-mile stretch between Moraine and Cliff Swallow is a popular whitewater run that's mostly Class III, with some Class IV at higher flows. Sharp turns and abrupt drops characterize this section. The biggest rapids are named for nearby access points: First comes the Moraine Rapids, then Castle Rock, then finally Roscoe Rapids about 2 miles upstream from Cliff Swallow. You'll want to stop and scout all of these spots. This section of river is suited for advanced intermediate and expert kayakers and rafters.

Boaters should be aware of a number of low bridges that span the river between Woodbine and Cliff Swallow; there's a particularly bad one at Mile 39. At high flows these bridges can be too low for rafts to pass under. They are very dangerous, so be sure to watch ahead. Boaters on all sections should be aware of logs and other debris that tend to build up around bridge pilings during high water.

After Cliff Swallow the serious rapids subside, and skilled intermediate to expert canoeists can try their skills. It's about a 10-mile run from Cliff Swallow to Absaroka, with mostly strong Class II water. It's the same story from Absaroka to Whitebird: solid Class II whitewater, nothing outrageous. Immediately downstream from Absaroka Fishing Access Site, take the right channel to avoid a dangerous concrete slab in the river. Also look out for a decent drop with a big wave about 1 mile upstream from Whitebird. At low to moderate flows, this rapid douses many boaters. At high water it gets washed out.

Finally there's the 4-mile trip between Whitebird and Fireman's Point. Just above Swinging Bridge Fishing Access Site start the Swinging Bridge Rapids, solid Class II rapids that are usually fun for all. Watch out for a big hole less than 1 mile downstream from Swinging Bridge fishing access. This hole, Mad Max, is just past the private Beartooth Ranch Bridge on river left and is big enough to swamp the best. When flows are up it is a Class IV; at normal flows it's a solid Class III. Avoid it by taking the right channel.

28 Sun River

The Sun River starts in a deep canyon, runs through prairie grasslands, and finally meanders past cottonwood bottoms on its way to the Missouri. In the upper river, horizontal upthrusts create ledges of rock that cross the river and create challenging rapids.

Vital statistics: 101 miles long from Gibson Dam to the Missouri River at Great Falls.
Level of difficulty: Class I and Class II at normal flows with occasional harder spots. Very difficult water (Class V) for 2.5 miles immediately below Gibson Dam. Excellent canoeing stream for solid intermediate paddlers.
Flow: Annual mean flow: 696 cfs near Vaughn. Gibson Dam has erratic flows. Flows may be low during spring runoff and high in the fall. Minimum floating level is 400 cfs. Anything over 3,000 cfs is for experts only.
Hazards: Rock gardens, ledges, standing waves, diversion dams, snags; big winds.
Where the crowd goes: Access below diversion dam to U.S. Highway 287 bridge.

Avoiding the scene: Between US 287 and Vaughn, where you'll find only an occasional fisherman or ranch hand cooling off.
Inside tip: When many other streams are high and muddy with spring runoff, the Sun may be perfect.
Maps: BLM: #29 (Choteau), #39 (Great Falls North)
USFS: Lewis and Clark (Rocky Mountain Division), Bob Marshall Complex
USGS: Choteau, MT; Great Falls, MT
River rules: Mostly private land; camp within high-water marks. If you camp or hike on state land, a recreational-use permit is required.
For more information: Montana Fish, Wildlife and Parks, Great Falls; Medicine River Canoe Club, Great Falls.

The Paddling

The Sun River cuts a handsome swath through a narrow canyon, unlike any other in Montana, as it wends its way out of the remote Bob Marshall Wilderness. Many historians have remarked on the beauty of this stream as it plunges out of the mountains. Its towering sandstone formations, multicolored rocks, occasional waterfalls, and parched surroundings make it look like a river of the southwestern United States. The canyon between the diversion dam access and US 287 is a geologist's delight of thrusts, folds, uplifts, and layers of sedimentary rock. They tell a story of how this land was formed. The area surrounding the river has special significance to the Blackfeet Indians, who defended it fiercely.

The scenery of the Rocky Mountain Front will make you wish for a rearview mirror.

The Blackfeet knew the Sun as the Medicine River, reportedly because of unusual mineral deposits along its banks that possessed remarkable medicinal properties. One can only speculate on how the river came to be known as the Sun. The river flows directly east, causing it to reflect the sun in the morning and evening hours. Viewed from afar, it often appears as a ribbon of light.

What must once have been a bronco of a river has since been tamed and bridled. Gibson Dam, built in 1913, blocks the river's flow. Two miles below Gibson there's a large diversion dam. Approximately 97 miles of the Sun remain free flowing, but they, too, have felt the hand of man.

The river remains strikingly beautiful as it leaves the sheer walls of the majestic Rocky Mountain Front. Sawtooth Ridge rises prominently from the south side of

Key Access Points along the Sun River

Access Point (River Mile)	Next Access Point	Access Point (River Mile)	Next Access Point
Access below diversion dam (97)	25 miles	Sun River Old Railroad Bridge (30)	13 miles
US 287 bridge (72)	22 miles	Vaughn Bridge (17)	5 miles
Lowry Bridge FAS (50)	5 miles	Manchester Bridge (12)	12 miles
Simms Bridge (45)	8 miles	Missouri River at Great Falls (0)	none
Fort Shaw Bridge FAS (37)	7 miles		

Sun River

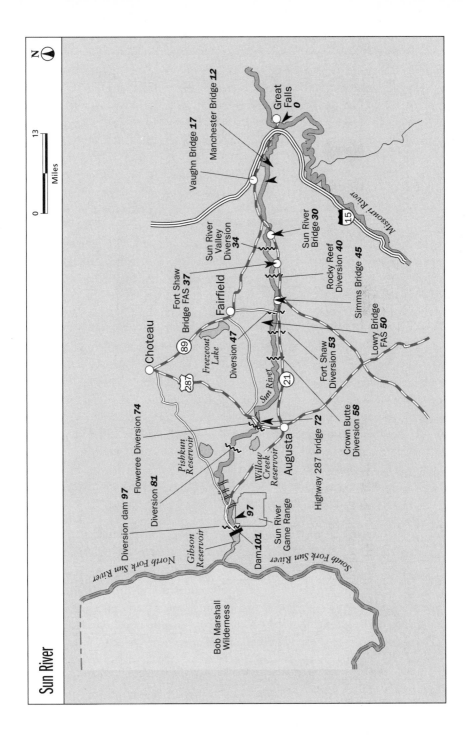

the river, and Castle Reef juts just as spectacularly to the north. If the river weren't so tricky, there would be a real temptation to float down the river backward.

Along parts of the upper river, the stream bottom is solid bedrock and smooth as a pool table. In other places, reefs of rock cross the river, creating ledges and sharp drops. Experienced hands can maneuver around most of the ledges, but some drop several feet and require caution, especially for canoeists. Rocky riffles alternate with large, extremely deep pools that are excellent swimming holes in the heat of summer. Surrounding cliffs make good jumping platforms. The water is deep, emerald green, and usually quite clear.

The canyon section of the Sun starts immediately below the diversion dam (a short distance above an old bridge) and continues for about 25 river miles to the bridge over US 287. When water flows are low, it's a long two-day trip, as the river meanders a great deal. The constant maneuvering will wear you down. When the water is high, it's a rip-roaring whitewater trip that can be done in six to eight hours. Be aware of two diversions, one at Mile 81 and Floweree Diversion at Mile 74. The first can be run with caution, but Floweree may have to be portaged on river right.

The narrow canyon of the upper river eventually gives way to open agricultural land after the US 287 bridge. Rolling, grass-covered hillsides dominate the landscape, and deer, antelope, and coyotes can often be seen from the river. While the river generally gets easier, several difficult rapids can be found about 4 or 5 miles below the US 287 bridge.

About halfway between the US 287 bridge and Simms, cottonwood groves become denser and willows thicken, creating excellent fish and wildlife habitat that lasts all the way to Vaughn. Fishing for brown trout can be good when the river isn't seriously dewatered. The river bottom between the US 287 bridge and Vaughn is isolated and largely undeveloped, even though civilization isn't far away. Most of the land along the river is privately owned, and access comes via county bridges. Be careful of the Fort Shaw Diversion, 3.5 miles above Lowry Bridge. Portage on river left.

Below the town of Sun River, the water slows and becomes heavily silted at Vaughn with the entry of Muddy Creek. It's not really very scenic after this—the river more closely resembles a big ditch. Rocky Reef, a major diversion 2.5 miles above Fort Shaw, needs to be portaged on river right.

The entire Sun River receives only moderate floating pressure. Access is limited, and the scarcity of public land limits the amount of overnight camping (although stream access law permits camping within the high-water marks of major rivers provided you aren't within sight, or within 500 yards, of an occupied dwelling).

The Sun's difficulty is directly proportional to its flows, which can be irregular. Although the Sun is a sizable river, it has frequent agricultural diversions, and the releases from Gibson Dam are unpredictable. In some years even spring flows may be too low for floating. In other years the river may be bank-full and very challenging. Check flows before you go by calling the numbers or checking the Web sites listed in appendix A. Minimum floating level is 400 cfs. If you prefer, use low-tech and take a look at the river gauge on the northwest side of the US 287 bridge near the old bridge abutments. If the gauge reads below 2 feet, forget it. At 2 feet it's marginal but possible if you read water well.

While intermediate canoeists and rafters will find the rock gardens and ledges of the upper Sun great fun, these hazards will eat up beginners. Much of the upper river calls for quick maneuvering and excellent boat control. Some of the runs should be scouted. When the river is very high, large standing waves can spell trouble for open canoes. Below the US 287 bridge, the rapids and ledges gradually give way to occasional cottonwood snags and numerous diversion dams. It's easier, but still too much for beginners. Anyone can handle the river below the town of Sun River.

Much of the land surrounding the Sun is used intensively for irrigation. The frequent diversion dams take large gulps of water out of the river, sometimes leaving it almost completely dry. Erratic flows not only limit recreation, but they hurt wildlife as well. Fluctuating flows from the dam may keep a healthy riparian zone from establishing and may hurt aquatic insect populations, to the detriment of species further up the food chain like beaver, mink, waterfowl, and trout. This river sorely needs consistent flows as well as regulations that retain a minimum amount of water in stream.

29 Swan River

The sparkling Swan flows through pine forests and cottonwood bottoms, providing occasional views of spectacular mountain ranges on both sides of the river.

Vital statistics: 93 miles long (including 15 miles of lakes and reservoirs) from its headwaters above Lindbergh Lake to Flathead Lake.
Level of difficulty: Mostly Class I water except for a very difficult 1-mile Class V section immediately below Bigfork Dam. Wicked logjams limit most of the Swan to intermediates, but practiced beginners can handle specific sections. Very dangerous at high flows.
Flow: Annual mean flow: 1,155 cfs near Bigfork. Above Point Pleasant it can get too low by mid-August. A gauge at Piper Creek Bridge should read at least 2.25 feet to float the river above Point Pleasant.
Hazards: Numerous logjams and sharp bends.
Where the crowd goes: Fatty Creek Road bridge to Point Pleasant.

Avoiding the scene: Lindbergh Lake to Condon.
Inside tip: Include huckleberry picking in the nearby woods with an August float.
Maps: BLM: #10 (Kalispell), #18 (Hungry Horse Reservoir), #19 (Swan Peak)
USFS: Flathead
USGS: Choteau, MT; Cut Bank, MT; Kalispell, MT
River rules: Piper Creek to Swan Lake, catch-and-release for cutthroat and rainbows with artificial lures only.
For more information: Bigfork Chamber of Commerce; Montana Fish, Wildlife and Parks, Kalispell.

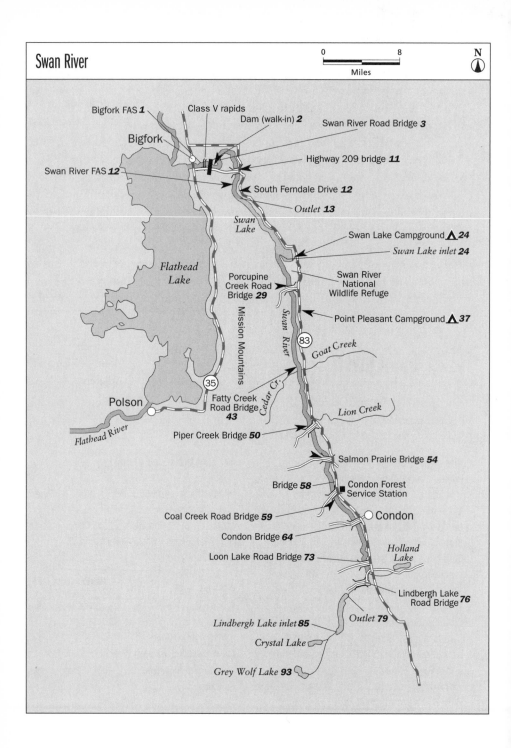

Swan River

0 — 8
Miles

N

Bigfork FAS *1*

Class V rapids

Dam (walk-in) *2*

Swan River Road Bridge *3*

Bigfork

Highway 209 bridge *11*

Swan River FAS *12*

South Ferndale Drive *12*

Outlet 13

Swan Lake

Swan Lake Campground *24*

Swan Lake inlet 24

Flathead Lake

Porcupine Creek Road Bridge *29*

Swan River National Wildlife Refuge

Point Pleasant Campground *37*

Mission Mountains

Swan River

83

Goat Creek

35

Cedar Cr.

Fatty Creek Road Bridge *43*

Lion Creek

Polson

Piper Creek Bridge *50*

Flathead River

Salmon Prairie Bridge *54*

Bridge *58*

Condon Forest Service Station

Coal Creek Road Bridge *59*

Condon

Condon Bridge *64*

Holland Lake

Loon Lake Road Bridge *73*

Lindbergh Lake Road Bridge *76*

Lindbergh Lake inlet 85

Outlet 79

Crystal Lake

Grey Wolf Lake 93

The Paddling

Any mountains as spectacular as the Missions would have to spawn a beautiful stream, and the Swan River is that gem. The Swan springs out of Crystal and Grey Wolf Lakes and then dashes wildly down the mountains until it reaches Lindbergh Lake on the valley floor. Then it flows more placidly for about 80 river miles northward before entering Swan Lake. After Swan Lake it meanders slowly for about 13 miles before entering Flathead Lake near Bigfork.

Thick timber and abundant vegetation characterize the Swan Valley, which generally ranges from about 4 to 16 miles wide. This valley receives nearly 25 inches of precipitation per year, significantly more than most other western Montana valleys. The moisture creates a thick mantle of pines that frequently extend right to the river's edge. Nearly every coniferous tree native to Montana can be found close to the Swan River.

Early logging companies tried to use the river to float logs, but it was too small. Above Condon it's barely large enough to float a canoe. The abundant trees make continual contributions to the river; numerous logjams and downed trees are the Swan's claim to fame. This creates difficult and hazardous floating. You might consider taking along an ax to make the trip easier for the next floater.

At peak flows Swan River float trips can be hair-raising and dangerous. Sharp bends in the river hide impenetrable logjams, and the river frequently braids into small, ever-changing channels. Expect to encounter jams that completely block the river. This river's many blind corners require excellent boat control.

About 2 or 3 miles above Swan Lake, the river slows down and begins to flow in wide, easy meanders. Beginners can handle this section if they start at the first county bridge upstream from the lake—Porcupine Creek Road Bridge. This section includes part of the Swan River National Wildlife Refuge, which supports large populations of waterfowl and shorebirds, as well as deer, mink, and muskrat. This area receives heavy hunting pressure in the fall.

Those floating the last few miles of the upper river above Swan Lake have to

Key Access Points along the Swan River

Access Point (River Mile)	Next Access Point	Access Point (River Mile)	Next Access Point
Coal Creek Road Bridge (59)	5 miles	South Ferndale Drive (12)	0.5 mile
Salmon Prairie Bridge (54)	4 miles	Swan River FAS (12)	1 mile
Piper Creek Bridge (50)	7 miles	Highway 209 bridge (11)	8 miles
Fatty Creek Road Bridge (43)	6 miles	Swan River Road bridge (3)	1 mile
Point Pleasant Campground (37)	8 miles	Bigfork Dam (2) (walk-in)	1 mile
Porcupine Creek Road Bridge (29)	5 miles	Bigfork FAS (1)	none
Swan Lake Campground (24)	12 miles		

Thick forests often result in logjams on the Swan.

paddle across the lake for about a mile to reach the take-out point at Swan Lake Campground. Stick close to the shore when strong winds are blowing.

Except for the last few miles, the entire river above Swan Lake requires at least intermediate canoe skill. The logjams make it perilous for rafts, too. The upper Swan gobbles up boats every year and occasionally claims lives, so note water conditions carefully. Peak runoff usually occurs around the first week in June. Since the area receives heavy snowfall, high flows may continue into July. When the runoff subsides, the river is safer. Spills that might be catastrophic in June will likely mean only wet feet in August.

Floaters can expect to encounter anglers on foot. The Swan retains one of the nation's best populations of bull trout, an imperiled fish species. There are also good populations of rainbows (about 800 per mile) and whitefish.

Except for ever-increasing subdivisions, much of the upper Swan River bottom remains undeveloped. It's a great place to see wildlife such as white-tailed deer and black bear. A few grizzlies prowl the valley, but they're rarely seen. While the Swan has great birdlife, this river's namesake is not common.

There's also floating downstream from Swan Lake. For the first several miles below the lake, the river flows briskly and has some tricky rapids. Beginners should steer clear.

A float popular with Bigfork residents is the 8-mile trip beginning at the Highway 209 bridge east of Ferndale. From here the river takes a giant loop, and floaters end this tranquil trip at the Swan River Road Bridge. This section of river is a popular spring and fall float-fishing section, suitable for beginners.

The Bigfork Dam blocks the river a couple of miles above where the Swan empties into Flathead Lake. Right below the dam flows an unbroken stretch of extremely difficult whitewater. Every spring the Swan River is host to the Bigfork Whitewater Festival, where experienced kayakers try their luck at the "Mad Mile." The river plummets 100 feet in 1 mile. This section is for expert boaters, and scouting is essential. It's very difficult to catch an eddy to size up the next rapid. Additionally, many rocks along this stretch have sharp edges. In sum, wear a good life jacket and helmet, use quality equipment, and be careful.

Since white people settled the Swan Valley in the late 1800s, towering trees have attracted timber cutters. The Forest Service approved the first timber sale in the Swan in 1907, and the cutting continues both on public and private lands. Scars on the land bear testimony to past abuses. Many of the last big trees remain along scenic Highway 83. They line the road like a Hollywood set, hiding the hatchet job behind.

30 Tongue River

A true prairie river, the Tongue River winds through narrow canyons and cottonwood bottoms, the only moist spot in a parched landscape.

Vital statistics: 207 miles long (including 8 reservoir miles) from Tongue River Reservoir to the Yellowstone River near Miles City.
Level of difficulty: Class I all the way. Suitable for beginners.
Flow: Annual mean flow: 389 cfs near Birney. Usually floatable all year, although irrigation diversions may dewater river in dry years, especially in the lower 20 miles. A minimum of 150 cfs is needed (Miles City gauge).
Hazards: Diversion dams, irrigation jetties, cables, barbed wire, rattlesnakes.
Where the crowd goes: Nowhere. Between the dam and Birney gets the most traffic.

Avoiding the scene: Not to worry. Try downstream from the Highway 332 bridge.
Inside tip: A good early-season float (April and May) in an area that tends to be hotter and drier than most of Montana. If you hit it just right, the river may even be clear.
Maps: BLM: #88 (Forsyth), #89 (Lame Deer), #90 (Birney), #97 (Miles City)
USFS: Custer (Ashland Division)
USGS: Hardin, MT; Forsyth, MT; Miles City, MT
River rules: Mostly private land. Respect private landowner rights.
For more information: Custer National Forest, Ashland; Montana Fish, Wildlife and Parks, Miles City.

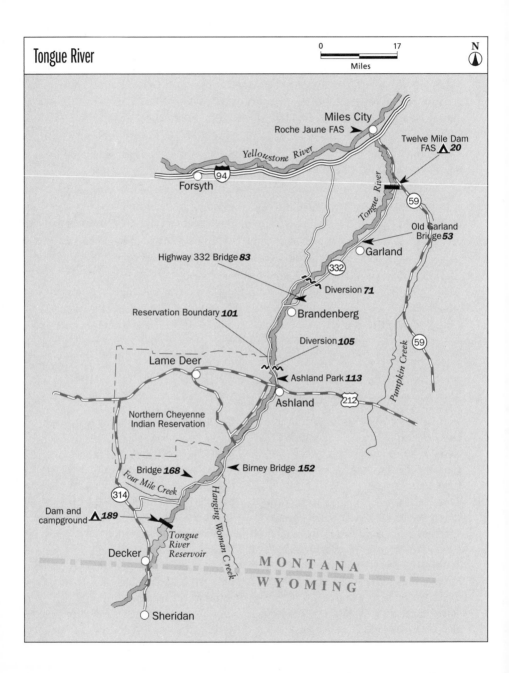

Tongue River

0 — 17
Miles

N

Miles City
Roche Jaune FAS

Twelve Mile Dam
FAS △ **20**

Yellowstone River

94

Forsyth

Tongue River

59

Old Garland
Bridge **53**

Highway 332 Bridge **83**

Garland

332

Diversion **71**

Reservation Boundary **101**

Brandenberg

Diversion **105**

Lame Deer

Pumpkin Creek

59

Ashland Park **113**

Northern Cheyenne
Indian Reservation

Ashland

212

Bridge **168**

Birney Bridge **152**

Four Mile Creek

314

Hanging Woman Creek

Dam and
campground △ **189**

Decker

*Tongue
River
Reservoir*

MONTANA

WYOMING

Sheridan

The Paddling

The Tongue River may be Montana's most overlooked float stream. It provides easy paddling, excellent fishing, fine scenery, and almost unexcelled solitude. This prairie stream flows from Wyoming into Montana and provides a unique perspective for observing eastern Montana's quiet beauty. The Tongue offers more than 100 miles of quality floating before joining the Yellowstone River near Miles City.

Scholars argue about how the Tongue got its name. Some say the river was named for the prominent buttes on the upper sections of the river, which resemble a tongue. Others say the Indians named the meandering river the Tongue because it goes in every direction. Still others say the river derived its name from Indians who thought it looked like a protruding tongue when viewed from the Bighorn Mountains, the river's birthplace.

Floating on the Tongue starts right below the Tongue River Dam at the Montana-Wyoming border. For the first 10 miles below the dam, the river winds through a narrow canyon that some consider the most scenic section of the river. Persistent fishermen might even catch a few trout here. After exiting the canyon, the river winds through lush cottonwood bottoms. These big trees stand in marked contrast to their sparsely vegetated, parched surroundings. Sometimes visible along the riverbanks are thick seams of coal, which may someday spell trouble for this beautiful stream.

Wildlife thrives in the cottonwood bottoms. Whitetails are plentiful, as are ducks and beavers. The river has some exceptionally large turtles. Birdlife includes double-crested cormorants, vultures, white pelicans, and sandhill cranes.

The Tongue River contains one of Montana's few smallmouth bass fisheries. The river also provides habitat for northern pike (some as large as fifteen pounds!), walleyes, sauger, and catfish. It is the only river in the state with rock bass. In the lower river near Miles City, anglers pursue such oddities as the paddlefish and shovelnose sturgeon, two ancient fish species. Sturgeon in the fifteen-pound class have been netted by fisheries workers. Paddlefish may exceed one hundred pounds. A diversion dam 12 miles above Miles City blocks the migration runs of these species.

Although the Tongue is frequently turbid, it often clears in August, especially in the upper reaches. But the sunshine in the water can result in thick algae growth, which can impede fishing. The algae usually diminish after a couple of hard freezes, and fishing usually reaches its peak around mid-September and remains good until

Key Access Points along the Tongue River

Access Point (River Mile)	Next Access Point	Access Point (River Mile)	Next Access Point
Tongue River Dam (189)	21 miles	Highway 332 bridge (83)	30 miles
Bridge (168)	16 miles	Old Garland Bridge (53)	33 miles
Birney Bridge (152)	39 miles	Twelve Mile Dam FAS (20)	20 miles
Ashland Park (113)	30 miles	Roche Jaune FAS (0) Yellowstone River	none

The Tongue River is a hidden treasure in eastern Montana.

freeze-up. Fishermen can sometimes find clear water in late April and early May, before spring runoff.

The Tongue provides easy floating even for beginners, but beware of cables, barbed wire, and occasional diversion dams. Access is extremely limited, consisting mostly of county road bridges.

Because of the massive coal reserves that lie nearby, the Tongue is one of the most endangered rivers in Montana. Major corporations would like to open two new major strip mines near the towns of Ashland and Birney. They would also like to build 80 miles of railroad along the river. Such development threatens both water quality and water quantity.

Although relatively undeveloped right now, the Tongue's water is in demand. Developers of irrigation projects, coal gasification and liquefaction plants, and coal slurry pipelines all would like to remove water from the river.

One firm has suggested that the best way to make more water available to industries wanting to use this coal-rich area would be to construct another dam near Four Mile Creek in Rosebud County.

31 Whitefish River

The slow-moving Whitefish River meanders past grassy meadows and willow-lined banks, providing a quiet escape close to town.

Vital statistics: 26 miles from Whitefish Lake to its juncture with the Stillwater River near Kalispell.

Level of difficulty: A Class I river, suitable for beginners.

Flow: Annual mean flow: 190 cfs near Kalispell. Sufficient water for floating all year except in driest years.

Hazards: Fences, irrigation jetties, numerous logjams, and debris.

Where the crowd goes: Not a busy river. Whitefish Lake to the Highway 40 bridge is the most popular section.

Avoiding the scene: Bowdish Road to Kalispell.

Inside tip: Perfect spot to take nervous-Nellie relatives. No dunking danger.

Maps: BLM: #10 (Kalispell)
USFS: Flathead
USGS: Kalispell, MT

River rules: None

For more information: Sportsman and Ski Haus, Kalispell; Montana Fish, Wildlife and Parks, Kalispell.

The Paddling

The Whitefish River begins at Whitefish Lake and flows for nearly 26 miles before joining the Stillwater River about a mile north of Kalispell (near where U.S. Highway 2 crosses the Stillwater). The Stillwater's juncture with the Flathead River lies another 3 miles downstream.

The Whitefish flows through agricultural land that's gradually being converted to homesites and golf courses. It's a deep river with a sandy streambed that frequently has thick vegetation along its shoreline. Occasional pine groves alternate with willows and marsh grasses. The water moves slowly and the banks are undercut, creating excellent beaver habitat. The Whitefish River is an excellent spot for a quiet, after-work float. The thick vegetation effectively screens the not-too-distant city life. The fishing isn't much, but the birdlife is excellent. Access is good, as county bridges cross the river at regular intervals. This river is almost all flatwater and can be handled by beginners. Because there's minimal current, a canoe is the craft of choice.

The Whitefish's claim to fame is its annual lake-to-lake (Whitefish Lake to Flathead Lake) canoe race. In past years the race started at Whitefish Lake, proceeded for the length of the Whitefish River, went for a short distance on the Stillwater River, continued down the main-stem Flathead River to Flathead Lake, and ended with a short paddle across the lake to Bigfork, a distance of almost 53 miles. In recent years the race has been abbreviated and comprises only 12 miles of the Whitefish River.

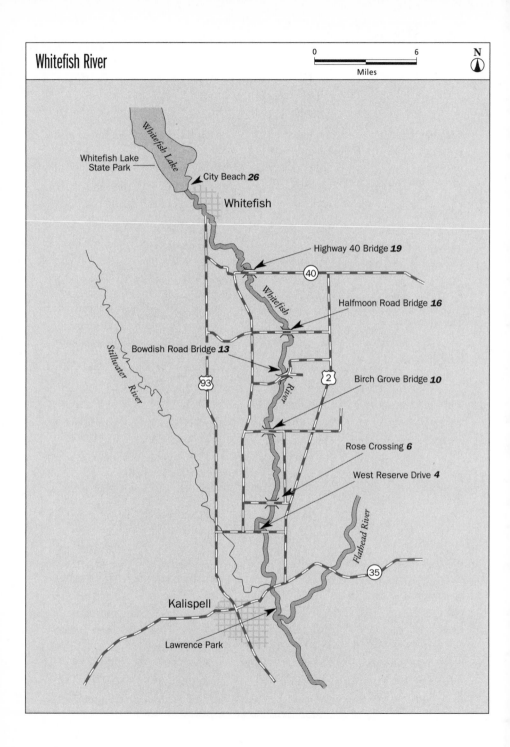

Whitefish River

0   6
Miles

N

Whitefish Lake
State Park
City Beach *26*
Whitefish

Highway 40 Bridge *19*
40

Halfmoon Road Bridge *16*

Bowdish Road Bridge *13*

93

Birch Grove Bridge *10*
2

Rose Crossing *6*

West Reserve Drive *4*

Flathead River

35

Kalispell

Lawrence Park

Stillwater River

Whitefish River

Key Access Points along the Whitefish River

Access Point (River Mile)	Next Access Point	Access Point (River Mile)	Next Access Point
City Beach (26)	7 miles	Birch Grove Bridge (10)	4 miles
Highway 40 bridge (19)	3 miles	Rose Crossing (6)	2 miles
Halfmoon Road Bridge (16)	3 miles	West Reserve Drive (4)	4 miles
Bowdish Road Bridge (13)	3 miles	Lawrence Park (Stillwater River)	none

This river is a popular stopping place for ducks and geese during migration, providing both viewing and hunting opportunities. Floating pressure on the entire river is minimal.

32 Yellowstone River

The longest free-flowing river in the lower forty-eight states, the Yellowstone tumbles down a mountain valley, traverses prairie grasslands, and meanders through cottonwood groves on its way to meeting the Missouri River. The only physical evidence of the Lewis and Clark Expedition in Montana—Captain Clark's name carved on a rock—can still be seen near the Yellowstone east of Billings.

Vital statistics: 554 miles long from the Wyoming boundary to the North Dakota boundary.
Level of difficulty: The river is Class I at normal flows except for the first 20 miles below Gardiner, where it is Class II and Class III (Class IV at peak flows).
Flow: Annual mean flow: 6,947 cfs at Billings. A big river with strong flows all year. Exercise extreme caution in Yankee Jim Canyon with flows over 15,000 cfs (Corwin Springs gauge).
Hazards: Logjams, tricky currents, diversion dams.
Where the crowd goes: Mill Creek to Carters Bridge in the Paradise Valley.
Avoiding the scene: Terry to Glendive.
Inside tip: Spend a month and take a Lewis and Clark trip from Billings to the North Dakota border.
Maps: BLM: RAG-36, #53 (Livingston), #54 (Gardiner), #62 (Big Timber), #71 (Billings),
79 (Hysham), #80 (Hardin), #88 (Forsyth), #96 (Terry), #97 (Miles City), #103 (Sidney), #104 (Glendive), #105 (Wibaux) USFS: Custer (Beartooth)
USGS: Bozeman, MT; Billings, MT; Forsyth, MT; Miles City, MT; Glendive, MT
FWP: Treasure of Gold (Billings to Missouri River)
Montana Afloat: #12 (The Yellowstone River from Gardiner to Big Timber), #13 (The Yellowstone River from Big Timber to Huntley)
River rules: 10 horsepower limit above U.S. Highway 89 Bridge near Livingston.
For more information: Dan Bailey's Fly Shop, Livingston; Parks' Fly Shop, Gardiner; Sweet Cast Angler, Big Timber; Yellowstone Raft Company, Gardiner; Montana Fish, Wildlife and Parks, Billings.

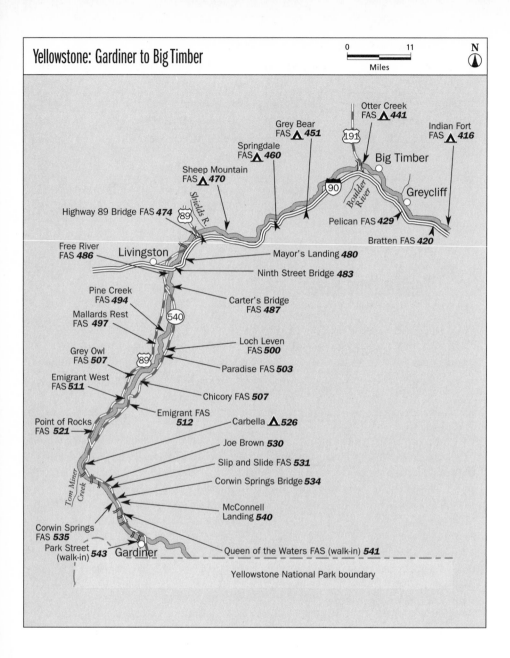

Yellowstone: Gardiner to Big Timber

0   11

Miles

N

Otter Creek FAS ▲ *441*

Grey Bear FAS ▲ *451*

191

Indian Fort FAS ▲ *416*

Springdale FAS ▲ *460*

Sheep Mountain FAS ▲ *470*

Big Timber

90

Boulder River

Greycliff

Highway 89 Bridge FAS *474*

89

Shields R.

Pelican FAS *429*

Bratten FAS *420*

Free River FAS *486*

Livingston

Mayor's Landing *480*

Ninth Street Bridge *483*

Pine Creek FAS *494*

Carter's Bridge FAS *487*

Mallards Rest FAS *497*

540

Grey Owl FAS *507*

89

Loch Leven FAS *500*

Paradise FAS *503*

Emigrant West FAS *511*

Chicory FAS *507*

Point of Rocks FAS *521*

Emigrant FAS *512*

Carbella ▲ *526*

Joe Brown *530*

Slip and Slide FAS *531*

Tom Miner Creek

Corwin Springs Bridge *534*

McConnell Landing *540*

Corwin Springs FAS *535*

Park Street (walk-in) *543*

Gardiner

Queen of the Waters FAS (walk-in) *541*

Yellowstone National Park boundary

Key Access Points along the Yellowstone River

Access Point (River Mile)	Next Access Point	Access Point (River Mile)	Next Access Point
Park Street (543) (walk-in)	2 miles	Billings Big Ditch Diversion (391)	18 miles
Queen of the Waters (541) (walk-in)	1 mile	Buffalo Mirage FAS (373)	6 miles
McConnell Landing (540)	5 miles	Laurel Riverside Park (367)	16 miles
Corwin Springs FAS (535)	1 mile	Billings Riverfront Park (351)	1 mile
Corwin Springs Bridge (534)	3 miles	South Hills (350)	4 miles
Slip and Slide FAS (531)	1 mile	Coulson Park (346)	1 mile
Joe Brown (530)	4 miles	East Bridge FAS (345)	23 miles
Carbella (526)	5 miles	Gritty Stone FAS (322)	3 miles
Point of Rocks FAS (521)	9 miles	Voyagers Rest FAS (319)	5 miles
Emigrant FAS (512)	1 mile	Pompeys Pillar (314)	18 miles
Emigrant West FAS (511)	4 miles	Captain Clark FAS (296)	15 miles
Grey Owl FAS (507)	0 miles	Manuel Lisa (281)	12 miles
Chicory FAS (507)	4 miles	Howrey Island (269)	9 miles
Paradise FAS (503)	3 miles	Amelia Island FAS (260)	36 miles
Loch Leven FAS (500)	3 miles	Rosebud West FAS (224)	1 mile
Mallards Rest FAS (497)	3 miles	Rosebud East FAS (223)	13 miles
Pine Creek FAS (494)	7 miles	Far West FAS (210)	26 miles
Carter's Bridge FAS (487)	1 mile	Moon Creek (184)	15 miles
Free River FAS (486)	3 miles	Roche Jaune FAS (169)	12 miles
Ninth Street Bridge (483)	3 miles	Kinsey Bridge FAS (157)	11 miles
Mayor's Landing FAS (480)	6 miles	Bonfield FAS (146)	11 miles
Highway 89 bridge FAS(474)	4 miles	Powder River Depot FAS (135)	12 miles
Sheep Mountain FAS (470)	10 miles	Terry Bridge (123)	11 miles
Springdale FAS (460)	9 miles	Fallon Bridge FAS (112)	36 miles
Grey Bear FAS (451)	10 miles	Glendive (76)	20 miles
Otter Creek FAS (441)	12 miles	Intake FAS (56)	20 miles
Pelican FAS (429)	9 miles	Elk Island FAS (36)	12 miles
Bratten FAS (420)	4 miles	Seven Sisters FAS (24)	9 miles
Indian Fort FAS (416)	8 miles	Highway 23 bridge (15)	14 miles
Access (408)	12 miles	Diamond Willow FAS (1)	none
Itch-Kep-Pe Park (396)	5 miles		

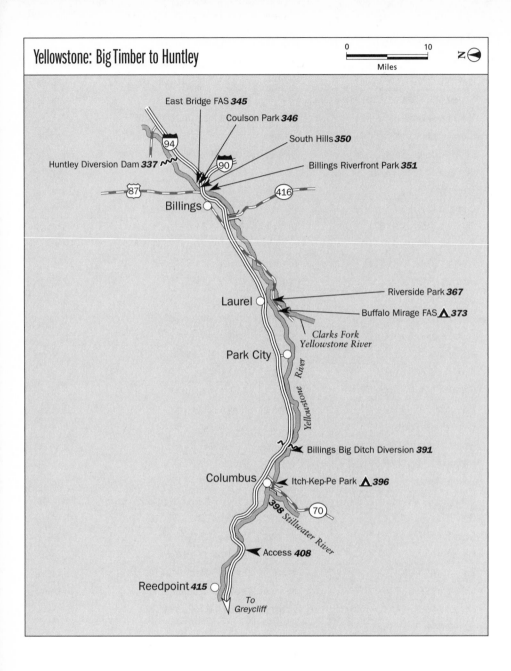

Yellowstone: Big Timber to Huntley

0   10

Miles

N

East Bridge FAS **345**

Coulson Park **346**

South Hills **350**

Huntley Diversion Dam **337**

Billings Riverfront Park **351**

94

90

87

416

Billings

Riverside Park **367**

Laurel

Buffalo Mirage FAS **373**

Clarks Fork
Yellowstone River

Park City

Yellowstone River

Billings Big Ditch Diversion **391**

Columbus

Itch-Kep-Pe Park **396**

398 Stillwater River

70

Access **408**

Reedpoint **415**

To
Greycliff

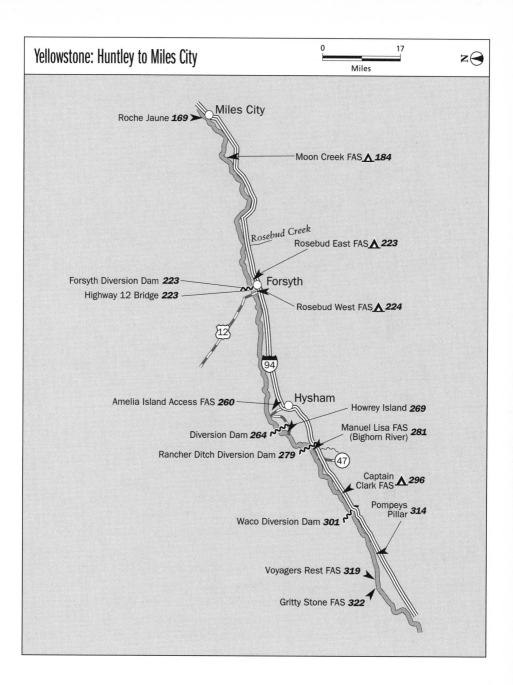

0   17
Miles

N

Roche Jaune **169** ➤ ◯ **Miles City**

Moon Creek FAS △ **184**

Rosebud Creek
Rosebud East FAS △ **223**

Forsyth Diversion Dam **223**
Highway 12 Bridge **223**
◯ **Forsyth**

Rosebud West FAS △ **224**

12

94

Amelia Island Access FAS **260**
◯ **Hysham**

Howrey Island **269**

Diversion Dam **264**
Manuel Lisa FAS **281**
(Bighorn River)

Rancher Ditch Diversion Dam **279**

47

Captain △ **296**
Clark FAS

Pompeys **314**
Pillar

Waco Diversion Dam **301**

Voyagers Rest FAS **319**

Gritty Stone FAS **322**

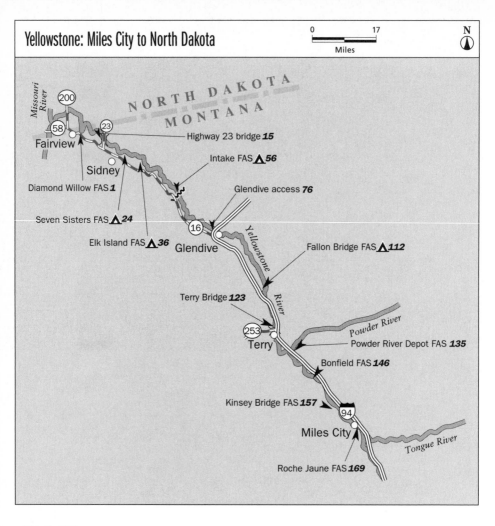

0   17
Miles

N

North Dakota
Montana

Missouri River

200

58   23   Highway 23 bridge **15**

Fairview

Intake FAS ▲ **56**

Sidney

Diamond Willow FAS **1**   Glendive access **76**

Seven Sisters FAS ▲ **24**

16

Elk Island FAS ▲ **36**   **Glendive**   Fallon Bridge FAS ▲ **112**

Yellowstone River

Terry Bridge **123**

253   Powder River

Terry   Powder River Depot FAS **135**

Bonfield FAS **146**

Kinsey Bridge FAS **157**

94

Miles City

Tongue River

Roche Jaune FAS **169**

The Paddling

King of Montana rivers, the Yellowstone flows clean and free for over 678 miles, making it the nation's longest free-flowing river outside Alaska. This meandering ribbon of water, which the Indians knew as the Elk River, originates high in the mountains of Wyoming and flows for about 100 miles through Yellowstone National Park, forming such landmarks as Yellowstone Lake and the Grand Canyon of the Yellowstone. It then flows across central and eastern Montana before meeting the Missouri River just over the Montana–North Dakota border.

Few rivers have spawned so rich a history as the Yellowstone. Early explorers and fur trappers—including Lewis and Clark, John Colter, Jim Bridger, and Jed Smith—all used this pathway to the wilderness. With their bullboats, pirogues, and hollowed-out logs, they explored the river's most remote points. Barges and even steamboats later

The aptly named Paradise Valley lies along the Yellowstone River.

arrived on the Yellowstone, providing passage for miners, cowboys, soldiers, home-steaders, and other pioneers intent on opening the West.

Since no floating is allowed on this river in Yellowstone National Park, the first access point is near Gardiner, the start of the 100-mile "mountain" section of the river, which extends to Big Timber. This part of the Yellowstone is nationally renowned for its trout fishery. Biologists estimate fish populations as high as 500 fish per 1,000 feet of stream. In the 50-mile stretch between Gardiner and Livingston, this translates into more than fifty tons of trout! Those who want to see how big the fish can get should visit the "Wall of Fame" in Dan Bailey's Fly Shop in Livingston. The wall displays outlines of hundreds of Yellowstone trout over four pounds, all taken on flies. Conservation-minded fishermen release large fish, which account for most of the reproduction. It's key to maintaining healthy populations.

The appropriately named Paradise Valley lies between Gardiner and Livings-ton. Cold, clear water and cobbled bottoms characterize the river, which alternates between long riffles and deep pools. The Yellowstone is shaded by the saw-toothed Absaroka Mountains to the east and the Gallatin Range to the west. Locals joke that these mountains cast shadows bigger than many eastern states. Canada geese nest along the river bottom, golden and bald eagles patrol the skies, and deer haunt the willow thickets and aspen stands.

Don't expect to stay dry on a float through Yankee Jim Canyon.

The upper river flows north from the park until it reaches Livingston, where it turns east at the point the Lewis and Clark Expedition termed "the Great Bend." Just upstream is the narrow spot in the Allenspur Canyon that for two decades marked the location of the proposed Allenspur Dam, which would have flooded 31 miles of the Paradise Valley. Fortunately, sanity prevailed.

The Yellowstone's only whitewater lies in the first 20 miles of river below Gardiner.

"YANKEE JIM" GEORGE Yankee Jim Canyon deserves special mention for its colorful history. The area was named for an enterprising pioneer named "Yankee Jim" George, who built a cabin at the mouth of the canyon in 1872. Yankee Jim charged a toll to anyone wanting to use the narrow road through the canyon. Since this was the main route to Yellowstone National Park, the ex-miner had constructed a veritable "gold mine." Like St. Peter guarding the pearly gates, Yankee Jim became known as the guardian of Yellowstone National Park. He was such a character that famous people (including Teddy Roosevelt and Rudyard Kipling) often stopped to visit him. Kipling respectfully called the yarn-spinning Yankee Jim "the biggest liar I ever met."

Between Tom Miner Bridge and Livingston, practiced beginners can handle the Yellowstone at low flows. Beware of downed trees and snags. Canoeists should watch for big standing waves.

Numerous access points contribute to the upper Yellowstone's popularity, and they help distribute use. All sections of river in the Paradise Valley receive heavy floating pressure in summer. One method for avoiding summer crowds: Go very early in the morning—at sunrise—on a long section of river that doesn't have intermediate access points. You will have solitude, because most of the boat traffic will be behind you.

Between Livingston and Big Timber, the fishing remains good and boat traffic decreases. Floating gets a little more hazardous, however, as the river frequently braids and creates tricky currents where the channels rejoin. Side channels may be blocked by trees, so be careful when you wander off the main channel. Practiced beginners can handle this section at low flows if they remain alert.

YELLOWSTONE WHITEWATER
While the Yellowstone is best known for its fishing and wildlife, both the 8-mile stretch between Gardiner and Corwin Springs and the 4-mile section through Yankee Jim Canyon offer good whitewater excitement.

Gardiner to Corwin Springs has become increasingly popular with intermediate rafters and canoeists. Access is excellent, and much of the land along the river is publicly owned. A standard access point is an undeveloped site in the town of Gardiner. Take Park Street east off U.S. Highway 89 in town. Go 2 blocks to a dead-end turnaround. Carry 100 yards down to the river. The best whitewater lies in the first 3 or 4 miles below town. Not overwhelmingly difficult, this run contains solid Class II water that becomes Class III at peak flows. Look for a steep gradient, many rocks, and numerous sharp turns. This stretch has more rapids than Yankee Jim Canyon, but they aren't as big.

Yankee Jim Canyon starts about 13 miles below Gardiner and lasts only 4 miles. Most runs start near Corwin Springs. Although it's flatwater for the first 4 or 5 miles, the scenery is exceptional. Those interested in whitewater only should launch at Joe Brown access, which lies immediately upstream from Yankee Jim Canyon. The standard take-out point is about 4 miles downstream at Tom Miner Bridge. The Tom Miner access is private, so be especially considerate. There's a public access only 0.25 mile below Tom Miner Bridge at Carbella.

Yankee Jim offers exciting but not particularly difficult water at normal summer flows (Class II and easy Class III). Intermediate rafters and kayakers can handle it then with little trouble, and beginners will have fun if they go with outfitters. Canoeists in open boats should stay clear unless they are experts.

At peak flows (over 15,000 cfs at Corwin Springs gauge), a large volume of water gets squeezed into a very narrow canyon. The waves get big and the holes get deep, and at least two of the rapids become Class IV. Two anglers drowned in the canyon in 1998.

Yankee Jim Canyon consists of three major rapids. This first is known as either Yankee Jim's Revenge or Boateater. Outfitters say it flips more boats than any other rapid. At high flows Revenge consists of a long tongue of water that leads directly into a huge standing wave. If boaters aren't set up right for the wave, it's swim time. This rapid has a reputation for taking the unwary by surprise.

The second major rapid is the easily identified Big Rock Rapid. You can guess what to look for. While not technically difficult, a dangerous hole forms behind the rock at high flows. At peak flows the river goes over the rock and forms a huge standing wave. Under normal conditions it's a straight shot past the rock that makes you wonder what all the fuss is about.

The final major whitewater in the canyon is known as Boxcar Rapids. At high water it's generally considered the toughest, and some outfitters say it's unrunnable at peak flows. The river constricts considerably at this point, and huge standing waves develop. The higher the water, the higher the waves—and the higher the likelihood of an upset.

The lesson of Yankee Jim is the same as for other free-flowing rivers: Conditions change dramatically with spring runoff. In August the river may move at a placid 3 miles per hour and hit temperatures as high as 60 degrees. In June the river may roar by at 7 miles per hour with temperatures in the upper 30s. Don't forget that it's hard to define an "average" year. High water may extend until late July, or it may not happen at all.

Those interested in up-to-date water conditions can call the Yellowstone Raft Company in Gardiner, a local outfitting company that works the river regularly. The company's number is in appendix A.

The 165-mile-long "transition" section of the river runs from Big Timber to the Yellowstone's confluence with the Bighorn River near Custer. Here the river changes from a mountain stream to a prairie river. The water gets warmer, the river valley opens up, and yellowish bluffs (the river's namesake) and rocky cliffs flank the stream. On a rock outcropping east of Billings, one can find the only physical evidence of Lewis and Clark's journey through Montana—the words "Wm Clark, July 25, 1806," scrawled on the rock. Clark named this particular rock formation Pompeys Pillar in honor of the infant son of the party's guide, Sacagawea.

The river in this section frequently braids and changes its channel, as free-flowing rivers typically do. Peak flows in spring create islands, bars, backwaters, and the kind of riparian diversity that makes ideal wildlife habitat. This is still the excellent beaver country that early fur trappers told tall tales about and risked their own hides for. Furbearers such as mink, muskrat, and a few otter lurk in the cottonwood and willow bottoms that border the river. Geese and ducks raise their young on the islands, and great blue heron rookeries can be found in isolated pockets. Whistling swans and sandhill cranes use the river heavily during migration.

It was on this section of the Yellowstone that Captain Clark finally was struck silent by the incredible numbers of wildlife the Corps of Discovery observed. He wrote in his journal in 1806, ". . . for me to mention or give an estimate of the different Species of wild animals on this particularly Buffalow, Elk Antelopes & Wolves would be increditable. I shall therefore be silent on the subject further. So it is we have a great abundance of the best of meat."

Although the trout fishing is not quite as good below Big Timber, scenery remains superb. The Montana Department of Fish, Wildlife and Parks access points provide good river entry. Although Interstate 90 and Interstate 94 parallel the Yellowstone for its entire run across Montana, they're usually unnoticeable.

Each July a Livingston-to-Billings float trip attracts hundreds of participants, and the overloaded beer coolers give a literal twist to the notion of getting "Yellowstoned." Beginners can handle this section if they are cautious and don't drink too much. Watch for occasional weirs and diversions.

The "prairie" section of the Yellowstone flows for about 350 miles from the mouth of the Bighorn River to the North Dakota border, where the Yellowstone joins the Missouri. It provides one of Montana's most exceptional floating opportunities, following the same route Captain Clark and his men followed when crossing Montana on their return to St. Louis in 1806. Winding through wooded bottomlands shaded by rocky bluffs, a lower Yellowstone trip offers solitude and easy floating. It's an excellent choice for an extended boat trip.

Despite its aridity, the prairie section of the Yellowstone contains a greater diversity and abundance of wildlife than any other part of the river. The river itself supports at least forty-five species of fish, including two ancient rarities (the paddlefish and the shovelnose sturgeon) and a freshwater cod (the burbot, or ling). Walleye, sauger, northern pike, and channel catfish add to the fisherman's smorgasbord. Fishing can be quite good, particularly where tributaries enter the river.

The lower river often sustains unexpected avian species, including white pelicans, eared grebes, and double-crested cormorants. The endangered whooping cranes occasionally visit the river during migration, and sandhill cranes and whistling swans are common. Antelope can often be seen from the river. Turkeys are abundant.

Although a few organized float trips are conducted each year between Forsyth and Miles City, the lower river is usually devoid of people. While access isn't as good as on the upper river, highway bridges and occasional Montana Fish, Wildlife and Parks access sites suffice. Beginners can handle the lower river except during runoff. The only real hazards are occasional weirs and diversions. The five most dangerous diversions are at Huntley, Waco, Rancher Ditch, Forsyth, and Intake. Be prepared for difficult, unmarked portages at Forsyth and Intake; portage river right (south bank) for both. There are channels around the diversions at Huntley and Waco, but no signs marking them.

The most serious environmental threat to the Yellowstone is clearly visible along the banks of the lower river: thick, black-banded layers of coal. Captain Clark observed these "straters" of coal, as did an 1876 journalist by the name of Finerty. He predicted, "Someday, I think, when the Sioux are all in the happy hunting ground, this valley will rival the Lehigh of Pennsylvania." Industrial forces that want the Yellowstone's limited water have tried their best to make Finerty's woeful forecast come true.

They suffered a strong setback in 1978 when the Montana Board of Natural Resources and Conservation decided that substantial amounts of water must remain in the Yellowstone for the benefit of fish and wildlife and water quality. Unless the legislature changes this decision, it means Montana has rejected massive industrial development of the Yellowstone. Instead the state has chosen to emphasize natural values of the river while maintaining present agricultural uses. If trout could cheer or beaver could applaud, their clamor would be heard for the length of the river.

The Yellowstone River has consistently been mentioned as a prime candidate for the National Wild and Scenic Rivers System. Such designation would protect the river from inappropriate shoreline development and from dams. Those who would like to help write the final chapter on Yellowstone River conservation should stay alert for new developments in the long battle to keep the river free.

Who Will Speak for the Rivers?

"The rivers are our brothers. They quench our thirst. They carry our canoes and feed our children . . . and you must henceforth give the rivers the kindness you would give any brother."
—Chief Seattle of the Duwamish Indians

Montana is blessed to have so many free-flowing and undisturbed rivers. The forces that have killed many of America's spectacular waterways have been slow to reach the Treasure State. Now, however, threats to Montana's rivers are building. Energy development, mining, streamside subdivision, water depletion, and pollution hang like dark clouds over these sparkling streams.

Most Montana streams do not face problems with overuse. So why write a floater's guide and risk promoting more use? If floating in Montana gets too popular, it could lead to use restrictions and limitations, just as it has in many other western states.

The answer is simple. Limiting the number of boats going down a river is easy compared to preventing impoundment, channelization, depletion, or pollution of wild waterways. It takes overwhelming public pressure to deny such tragedies. Rivers have no voice of their own, so people who value rivers must speak for them. Time and again, the people who use these streams and appreciate their natural qualities arise as the rivers' defenders.

There are several important aspects of river protection. First and foremost is keeping sufficient water in streams, not only for floating but also to protect fish and wildlife and maintain water quality. Several of Montana's most outstanding rivers—including the Big Hole, Jefferson, Bitterroot, Sun, and Beaverhead—suffer from serious dewatering problems.

State law does permit state agencies to file for in-stream flows to protect fish and wildlife, recreation, and water quality. The Montana Board of Natural Resources decides if the amount of water requested for in-stream uses is necessary to protect the resource. To this point, only the Yellowstone River and its tributaries have gone through this exhaustive water-allocation process. Who gets the water in many of Montana's rivers may be decided in the near future. When this process begins, citizens must become involved so that industrial and agricultural interests don't predominate. Watch for notices of public hearings.

In addition to maintaining adequate in-stream flows, the habitat and shorelines adjacent to rivers need protection from inappropriate development. Streamside subdivisions not only destroy a river's naturalness, they provide the impetus for riprapping, channelization, and levees. These problems can be attacked on a local level by regulating building activities in the floodplain. Contact your county commissioners.

A tactic that has been used successfully on the Blackfoot River is cooperative management. Landowners, concerned citizens, and appropriate state agencies get together and work out agreements whereby the river corridor is preserved and opened to

Angling regulations focus on maintaining sustainable populations of fish.

carefully managed recreation. In areas where local landowners are strongly concerned about protecting natural attributes, this system has real potential.

Montana has no state Wild and Scenic Rivers program. While state law does afford moderate protection for the streambed itself, the state has no means of protecting segments of rivers that have outstanding natural attributes. This is where the National Wild and Scenic Rivers System comes in. Montana currently has four federally designated Wild and Scenic Rivers: the three forks of the Flathead and a 149-mile section of the Missouri River. While many Montana rivers have been proposed for designation by citizens (the Madison and Yellowstone Rivers were even temporarily part of a congressional study bill in 1978), this concept has met staunch resistance from Montana landowners who worry that such designations may unduly impact both private and public lands. Those concerned about Montana's rivers—who live both in state and out of state—should let their congressional representatives know these rivers are a national resource that merit protection.

Those concerned about the future of Montana's rivers should help support the efforts of citizens' organizations working to protect them. These include the Clark

Fork Coalition, the Montana Council of Trout Unlimited, the Montana Environmental Information Center, the Montana Audubon Council, the Montana Wilderness Association, and the Montana Wildlife Federation. National organizations such as Trout Unlimited, Defenders of Wildlife, Sierra Club, National Audubon Society, American Rivers Conservation Council, American League of Anglers, River Network, and the National Wildlife Federation have also been involved and deserve support.

Most often, however, the work is done by local groups and individual citizens, who seem to pop up like mushrooms when they learn their river is threatened. These organizations always need help, both physical and financial. Lend a hand so that future generations have the same opportunities to enjoy clean and free rivers that you've enjoyed.

Appendix A: For More Information

Flow information for these rivers is available from the United States Geological Survey (USGS) by calling the Helena office at (406) 457-5900 or visiting the Web site at http://waterdata.usgs.gov/MT/nwis/current/?type=flow. Additional sources for flow information are listed in entries below.

1. Beaverhead River
Frontier Anglers, Dillon; (800) 228-5263
Four Rivers Fishing Company, Twin Bridges; (888) 4-RIVERS
FWP, Bozeman; (406) 994-4042
Flow information: Bureau of Reclamation, Billings; (406)247-7318

2. Big Hole River
Montana Fish, Wildlife and Parks, Bozeman; (406) 994-4042
Four Rivers Fishing Company, Twin Bridges; (888) 4-RIVERS
Big Hole River Outfitters, Wise River; (406) 832-3252

3. Bighorn River
Bighorn Trout Shop, Fort Smith; (406) 666-2375
Bighorn Angler, Fort Smith; (406) 666-2233
Quill Gordon Fly Fishers, Fort Smith; (406) 666-2253
Montana Fish, Wildlife and Parks, Billings; (406) 247-2940
National Park Service, Fort Smith; (406) 666-2412
Flow information: BOR, Billings; (406) 247-7318

4. Bitterroot River
Grizzly Hackle, Missoula; (406) 721-8996; www.grizzlyhackle.com
Missoulian Angler, Missoula; (406) 728-7766; www.missoulianangler.com
Montana Fish, Wildlife and Parks, Missoula; (406) 542-5500

5. Blackfoot River
Grizzly Hackle, Missoula; (406) 721-8996; www.grizzlyhackle.com
Missoulian Angler, Missoula; (406) 728-7766; www.missoulianangler.com
Montana Fish, Wildlife and Parks, Missoula; (406) 542-5500

6. Clark Fork River
Montana Fish, Wildlife and Parks, Missoula; (406) 542-5500
Grizzly Hackle, Missoula; (406) 721-8996; www.grizzlyhackle.com
Missoulian Angler, Missoula; (406) 728-7766; www.missoulianangler.com
Lewis & Clark Trail Adventures, Missoula; (800) 366-6246; www.trailadventures.com
10,000 Waves-Raft & Kayak Adventures, Missoula; (800) 537-8315
Montana River Guides, Missoula; (800) 381-RAFT; www.montanariverguides.com
Western Waters, Missoula: (877) 822-8282

University of Montana Campus Recreation Outdoor Program, Missoula; (406) 243-2802

7. Clarks Fork of the Yellowstone River
Montana Fish, Wildlife and Parks, Billings; (406) 247-2940

8. Clearwater River
Lolo National Forest, Seeley Lake; (406) 677-2233
Montana Fish, Wildlife and Parks, Missoula; (406) 542-5500

9. Dearborn River
Montana Fly Goods, Helena; (800) 466-9589
The Trout Shop, Craig; (406) 235-4474
Montana Fish, Wildlife and Parks, Great Falls; (406) 454-5840

10. Flathead River, Main Stem
Confederated Salish and Kootenai Tribes, Pablo; (406) 675-2700
Montana Fish, Wildlife and Parks, Kalispell; (406) 752-5501
Flathead Raft Company, Polson; (800) 654-4359
Ronan Sports and Western, Ronan; (406) 676-3701
Kerr Dam, Polson; (406) 883-4450

11. North Fork Flathead River
Montana Raft Company, West Glacier; (800) 521-RAFT; www.glacierguides.com
Glacier Raft Company, West Glacier; (800) 235-6781; www.glacierraftco.com
Montana Fish, Wildlife and Parks, Kalispell; (406) 752-5501
Flathead National Forest, Hungry Horse; (406) 387-5243
(flow information also available from this number)

12. Middle Fork Flathead River
Montana Raft Company, West Glacier; (800) 521-RAFT; www.glacierguides.com
Glacier Raft Company, West Glacier; (800) 235-6781; www.glacierraftco.com
Great Northern, West Glacier; (800) 735-7897; www.gnwhitewater.com
Flathead National Forest, Hungry Horse; (406) 387-5243
(flow information also available from this number)

13. South Fork Flathead River
Spotted Bear Ranger Station; (406) 758-5376 (summer only)
Flathead National Forest, Hungry Horse; (406) 387-5243
(flow information also available from this number)

14. Gallatin River
Montana Whitewater, Bozeman; (800) 799-4465
Northern Lights Trading Company, Bozeman; (406) 586-2338
Montana Fish, Wildlife and Parks, Bozeman; (406) 994-4042

15. Jefferson River
Four Rivers Fishing Company, Twin Bridges; (800) 4-RIVERS
Frontier Anglers, Dillon; (800) 228-5263
Montana Fish, Wildlife and Parks, Bozeman; (406) 994-4042

16. Judith River
Bureau of Land Management, Lewistown; (406) 538-7461

17. Kootenai River
Montana Fish, Wildlife and Parks, Kalispell; (406) 752-5501
Kootenai National Forest, Libby; (406) 293-6211
Army Corp of Engineers, Libby Dam; (406) 293-5577
Kootenai Angler, Libby; (406) 293-7578

18. Madison River
Madison River Fishing Company, Ennis; (800) 227-7127
The Tackle Shop, Ennis; (800) 808-2832
Montana Fish, Wildlife and Parks, Bozeman; (406) 994-4042
Bureau of Land Management, Dillon; (406) 683-2337

19. Marias River
Bureau of Land Management, Havre; (406) 265-5891
Montana Fish, Wildlife and Parks, Great Falls; (406) 454-5840
Coyotes Den Sports, Chester; (406) 759-5305

20. Milk River
Bureau of Land Management, Havre; (406) 265-5891
Montana Fish, Wildlife and Parks, Glasgow; (406) 228-3700
Bureau of Reclamation, Billings; (406) 247-7318

21. Missouri River
Bureau of Land Management, Lewistown; (406) 538-7461 or Fort Benton;
(406) 622-5185
Montana River Outfitters, Great Falls; (406) 761-1677
Missouri River Outfitters, Fort Benton; (406) 622-3295
Lewis and Clark Trail Adventures, Missoula; (800) 366-6246

22. Powder River
Bureau of Land Management, Miles City; (406) 233-2800
Montana Fish, Wildlife and Parks, Miles City; (406) 232-0900

23. Red Rock River
Red Rock Lakes National Wildlife Refuge, Lima; (406) 276-3536
Montana Fish, Wildlife and Parks, Bozeman; (406) 994-4042
Flow information: Bureau of Reclamation, Billings; (406) 247-7318

24. Rock Creek

Montana Fish, Wildlife and Parks, Missoula; (406) 542-5500

Grizzly Hackle, Missoula; (406) 721-8996; www.grizzlyhackle.com

Missoulian Angler, Missoula; (406) 728-7766; www.missoulianangler.com

Rock Creek Mercantile, Rock Creek; (406) 825-6440

25. Ruby River

Montana Fish, Wildlife and Parks, Bozeman; (406) 994-4042

Four Rivers Fishing Company, Twin Bridges; (800) 4-RIVERS

Harmon's Fly Shop, Sheridan; (406) 842-5868

26. Smith River

Montana Fish, Wildlife and Parks, Great Falls; (406) 454-5840 or Camp Baker; (406) 547-3893

Amy's Think Wild Shuttle Service, White Sulphur Springs; (406) 547-2215

Montana River Outfitters, Great Falls; (406) 761-1677

U.S. Weather Service, Great Falls; (406) 453-2081; http://nimbo.wrh.noaa.gov/greatfalls

27. Stillwater River

Absaroka River Adventures, Absarokee; (406) 328-7440

Adventure Whitewater, Red Lodge; (800) 446-3061

Beartooth Whitewater, Red Lodge; (800) 799-3142

Montana Fish, Wildlife and Parks, Billings; (406) 247-2940

Custer National Forest (Beartooth Division), Red Lodge; (406) 446-2103

28. Sun River

Montana Fish, Wildlife and Parks, Great Falls; (406) 454-5840

29. Swan River

Bigfork Chamber of Commerce; (406) 837-5888

Montana Fish, Wildlife and Parks, Kalispell; (406) 752-5501

30. Tongue River

Custer National Forest, Ashland; (406) 784-2344

Montana Fish, Wildlife and Parks, Miles City; (406) 232-0900

31. Whitefish River

Sportsman and Ski Haus, Kalispell; (406) 755-6484

Montana Fish, Wildlife and Parks, Kalispell; (406) 752-5501

32. Yellowstone River

Dan Bailey's Fly Shop, Livingston; (406) 333-4401

Parks' Fly Shop, Gardiner; (406) 848-7314

Sweet Cast Angler, Big Timber; (406) 932-4469

Yellowstone Raft Company, Gardiner; (800) 858-7781

Montana Fish, Wildlife and Parks, Billings; (406) 247-2940

Appendix B: Conservation Organizations

Local Organizations

Big Hole River Foundation
P.O. Box 3894
Butte, MT 59702
www.bhrf.org

North Fork Preservation Association
P.O. Box 4
Polebridge, MT 59928
www.gravel.org

Rock Creek Trust
P.O. Box 8953
Missoula, MT 59807
www.rockcreektrust.org

Clark Fork Coalition
P.O. Box 7593
Missoula, MT 59807
(406) 726-3247
www.clarkfork.org

State Organizations

Montana Environmental Informational
Center
P.O. Box 1184
Helena, MT 59624
(406) 443-2520
www.meic.org

Montana Wilderness Association
P.O. Box 635
Helena, MT 59624
(406) 443-7350
www.wildmontana.org

Montana Wildlife Federation
P.O. Box 1175
Helena, MT 59624
(406) 449-8946
www.montanawildlife.com

Montana Trout Unlimited
P.O. Box 7186
Missoula, MT 59870
(406) 543-0054
www.montanatu.org

Montana Audubon Council
P.O. Box 595
Helena, MT 59624
(406) 443-3949
www.mtaudubon.org

National Organizations

Trout Unlimited
1300 North Seventeenth Street,
Suite 500
Arlington, VA 22209
(703) 522-0200
www.tu.org

Defenders of Wildlife
1130 Seventeenth Street NW
Washington, DC 20036
(800) 385-9712
www.defenders.org

Sierra Club
85 Second Street, Second Floor
San Francisco, CA 94105
(415) 977-5500

National Audubon Society
700 Broadway
New York, NY 10003-9501
(212) 979-3000
www.audubon.org

American Rivers
1101 Fourteenth Street NW, Suite 1400
Washington DC 20005
(202) 347-7550
www.americanrivers.org

River Network
520 Southwest Sixth Avenue, Suite
1130
Portland, OR 97204
(503) 241-3506
www.rivernetwork.org

Clean Water Network
1200 New York Avenue NW, Suite 400
Washington, DC 20005
(202) 289-2421
www.cwn.org

National Wildlife Federation
11100 Wildlife Center Drive
Reston, VA 20190
(800) 822-9919
www.nwf.org

American Recreation Coalition
1225 New York Avenue NW, Suite 450
Washington, DC 20005
(202) 682-9530
www.funoutdoors.com

American Wildlands
40 East Main Street, Suite 2
Bozeman, MT 59771
(406) 586-8175
www.wildlands.org

The Wilderness Society
1615 M Street NW
Washington, DC 20036
(800) 843-9453
www.wilderness.org

Appendix C: Map Resources

Bureau of Land Management Maps:
5001 Southgate Drive
P.O. Box 36800
Billings, MT 59107-6800
(406) 896-5000

Forest Service's Forest Visitors Series:
USDA Forest Service
Northern Region Headquarters, Federal Building
Box 7669
Missoula, MT 59807
(406) 329-3511

Montana Recreation Map and Fishing Guide:
Montana Fish, Wildlife and Parks
1420 East Sixth Avenue
P.O. Box 200701
Helena, MT 59620-0701
(406) 444-2535
http://fwp.mt.gov/fishing/guide

USGS Topographical Maps:
U.S. Geological Survey
Branch of Information Services
Box 25286
Denver, CO 80225-0286
(800) USA-MAPS

Lewis and Clark Maps:
Portage Route Chapter
Lewis & Clark Trail Heritage Foundation Inc.
P.O. Box 2424
Great Falls, MT 59403
www.corpsofdiscovery.org

Bear Trap Canyon Wilderness Visitor's Guide:
Bureau of Land Management
1005 Selway Drive
Dillon, MT 59725

Red Rock River Map:
Red Rock Lake National Wildlife Refuge
Monida Star Route
Lima, MT 59739

Yellowstone River Map:
Montana of Fish, Wildlife and Parks
2300 Lake Elmo Drive
Billings, MT 59105

Specialty Maps

Specialty maps are available for certain rivers, including:

Bighorn River—The National Park Service produces a free map of Bighorn Canyon National Recreation Area that includes the portion of river from Afterbay to Bighorn. The map is not very detailed. It's available at the Park Service visitor center. Montana Fish, Wildlife and Parks produces a free map with river regulations and access points. It can be picked up at the FWP's Billings office.

Blackfoot River—Montana Fish, Wildlife and Parks has a small brochure on the Blackfoot River Recreation Corridor (Russell Gates to Johnsrud Park). The free brochure provides regulations and a small map that shows camping sites and day-use areas.

Flathead River—The Glacier Natural History Center (in cooperation with the Flathead National Forest and Glacier National Park) has produced an excellent map of the three forks of the Flathead. *3 Forks of the Flathead River Floating Guide* can be purchased for $4.95 at Forest Service offices or Glacier National Park.

Madison River—The Bureau of Land Management's *Bear Trap Canyon Wilderness Visitor's Guide* is available for free at the Powerhouse access or by writing to the BLM at its Dillon office. (See appendix A.)

Missouri River—The Bureau of Land Management has a special waterproof floater's map for the Wild and Scenic section of the Missouri River. It comes in two parts and provides information about making the trip as well as a mile-by-mile report. The maps are $4 for each part and are available at most BLM offices. (Maps 1 and 2 are printed back-to-back and cover Fort Benton to Slaughter River. Maps 3 and 4 cover Slaughter River to James Kipp State Park.)

Red Rock River—Red Rock Lake National Wildlife Refuge has a refuge map that shows the river between Upper and Lower Red Rock Lakes. It's free and available at the address listed in appendix A.

Yellowstone River—Montana Fish, Wildlife and Parks has an excellent publication with a map of the Yellowstone River from Billings to the Missouri confluence titled *Treasure of Gold*. This small book contains detailed maps, historical information, and biological details. It's free by writing to the FWP office in Billings. (See appendix A.) A more detailed and updated version of this guide is in the works.

To see where the Corps of Discovery camped along the Beaverhead, Jefferson, and upper Missouri Rivers, consult the maps in *Lewis and Clark in the Three Rivers Valley*, published by The Patrice Press (Tucson, Arizona). It's available from the Lewis and Clark Trail Heritage Foundation, Box 2424, Great Falls, MT 59403.

Appendix D: Stream Access

This appendix summarizes how Montana's 1985 stream access law affects the recreational use of the state's streams and rivers. Please read the following definitions carefully; they are important in determining the recreational uses that require permission. The information in this appendix is taken from the Montana Fish, Wildlife and Parks brochure titled *Stream Access in Montana*.

The law says that, in general, all surface waters capable of recreational use may be so used by the public without regard to the ownership of the land underlying the waters. It also states that recreationists can use rivers and streams up to the ordinary high-water mark. The law does not address recreational use of lakes; it applies only to rivers and streams.

The law defines surface water, recreational use, and ordinary high-water mark as follows:

Surface water means a natural river or stream, its beds, and banks up to the ordinary high-water mark.

Recreational use means fishing, hunting, swimming, floating in small craft or other flotation devices, boating in motorized craft (except where prohibited by law), boating in craft propelled by oars or paddles, other water-related pleasure activities, and related unavoidable or incidental uses. The law imposes certain restrictions on some forms of recreation. These restrictions are listed later in the appendix.

Ordinary high-water mark means the line that water impresses on land by covering it for sufficient time to cause different characteristics below the line, such as deprivation of the soil of substantially all its terrestrial vegetation and destruction of its value for agricultural vegetation. Floodplains next to streams are considered to be above the ordinary high-water mark and are not open for recreation without permission.

Water Classification

Class I waters are defined as those that are capable of recreational use and have been declared navigable or that are capable of specific kinds of commercial activity, including commercial outfitting with multiperson watercraft. Montana Fish, Wildlife and Parks has developed a preliminary list of rivers that meet at least one of the criteria listed in the law for Class I rivers. This preliminary list includes the main stems of the following waters, as described:

Kootenai River Drainage: Kootenai River—from Libby Dam to the Idaho border; Lake Creek—from the Chase cutoff road to its confluence with the Kootenai River; Yaak River—from Yaak Falls to its confluence with the Kootenai River.

Flathead River Drainage: South Fork of the Flathead—from Youngs Creek to Hungry Horse Reservoir; Middle Fork of the Flathead—from Schaffer Creek to its confluence with the main stem of the Flathead River; North Fork of the Flathead—

Sandstone cliffs frame the Marias River.

from the Canadian border to its confluence with the main stem of the Flathead River; Flathead River (main stem)—to its confluence with the Clark Fork River.

Clark Fork of the Columbia River Drainage: Clark Fork River—from Warm Springs Creek to the Idaho border; North Fork of the Blackfoot—from Highway 200 east of Ovando to its confluence with the main stem of the Blackfoot River; Blackfoot River—from the Cedar Meadow Fishing Access Site west of Helmville to its confluence with the Clark Fork; Bitterroot River—from the confluence of the East and West Forks to its confluence with the Clark Fork; Rock Creek—from the mouth of the West Fork to its confluence with the Clark Fork.

Missouri River Drainage: Missouri River—from Three Forks to the North Dakota border; Beaverhead River—from Clark Canyon Dam to its confluence with the Jefferson; Big Hole River—from Fishtrap Fishing Access Site downstream from Wisdom to its confluence with the Jefferson; Gallatin River—from Taylors Fork to its confluence with the Missouri; Jefferson River—from its confluence with the Missouri; Madison River—from Quake Lake to its confluence with the Missouri; Dearborn River—from the Highway 434 bridge to its confluence with the Missouri; Sun

River—from Gibson Dam to its confluence with the Missouri; Smith River—from Camp Baker Fishing Access Site near Fort Logan to its confluence with the Missouri; Marias River—from Tiber Dam to its confluence with the Missouri; Judith River—from the mouth of Big Spring Creek to its confluence with the Missouri.

Yellowstone River Drainage: Yellowstone River—from Yellowstone National Park to the North Dakota border; Bighorn River—from Yellowtail Dam to its confluence with the Yellowstone; Tongue River—from Tongue River Dam to its confluence with the Yellowstone.

Keep in mind that this list is preliminary and that other waters may be added to it in the future as other criteria listed in the law for determining Class I waters are addressed. Also, keep in mind that there may be times during a year when the flow and physical condition of these waters may not permit their use for certain kinds of recreation.

Class II waters are all rivers and streams capable of recreational use that are not Class I waters.

Activities Requiring Landowner Permission

What types of activities between the ordinary high-water marks require landowner permission?

On Class I streams, landowner permission is required for the following recreational activities, even if these activities take place between the high-water marks:

- Overnight camping, unless necessary for the enjoyment of the water resource AND it is done out of sight of, or more than 500 yards from, an occupied dwelling.
- Big-game hunting.
- Making recreational use of stock ponds or private impoundments fed by intermittent streams.
- Making recreational use of water diverted from a stream, such as an irrigation canal or drainage ditch.
- The placement or creation of a permanent duck blind, boat moorage, or any other permanent object.
- The placement or creation of any seasonal objects, such as a duck blind or boat moorage, unless necessary for the enjoyment of that particular water resource and they are placed out of sight of, or more than 500 yards from, any occupied dwelling.
- Using a streambed as a right-of-way for any purpose when no water is flowing.

On Class II waters no overnight camping is permitted without landowner permission.

On both Class I and Class II waters, landowner permission is required for the following recreational uses:

- Operating all-terrain vehicles or other motorized vehicles not intended for use on the water.
- Making recreational use of stock ponds or private impoundments fed by intermittent streams. Although this restriction deals specifically with only those stock ponds or impoundments fed by intermittent streams, it's recommended, as a matter of courtesy, that recreationists obtain permission from landowners before using any private ponds.
- Making recreational use of water diverted away from a stream, such as an irrigation canal or drainage ditch.
- Big-game hunting.
- Overnight camping, unless necessary for the enjoyment of the water resource AND it is done out of sight of, or more than 500 yards from, any occupied dwelling. For example, camping is allowed if you are around a river bend and out of sight of a home, but only 200 yards away. It is also allowed if you are more than 500 yards away, but still within sight of a home.
- The placement or creation of any permanent duck blind, boat moorage, or any other permanent object.
- The placement or creation of any seasonal objects, such as a duck blind or boat moorage, unless necessary for the enjoyment of that particular water resource and they are placed out of sight of, or more than 500 yards from, any occupied dwelling. Any necessary placement of seasonal objects on Class I waters within sight of or within 500 yards of an occupied dwelling (whichever is less) requires landowner permission.
- Using a streambed as a right-of-way for any purpose when no water is flowing.

In addition, on all Class II waters, the following activities require landowner permission.

- Overnight camping.
- The placement or creation of any seasonal objects, such as a duck blind or boat moorage.
- Any other pleasure activities not primarily water related.

These restrictions apply to streams flowing through privately owned land. Of course, if the landowner grants permission for any of the activities mentioned, they would be permitted. Recreation on public lands may take place in accordance with the regulations of the agencies managing these lands.

Portage

The stream-access law says that floaters using a stream may go above the ordinary high-water mark to portage around barriers but must do so in the least intrusive manner possible, avoiding damage to the landowner's property and violating his rights. A "barrier" is defined by the law as an artificial obstruction (like a fence or a bridge) that totally or effectively obstructs the recreational use of the surface water. The law does not address portage around natural barriers and does not make such a portage either legal or illegal.

If a landowner puts a fence or other structure across a stream, such as a float-over cable or a float-through gate, and it does not interfere with the recreational use of the water, the public does not have the right to go above the ordinary high-water mark to portage. In all cases, recreationists must keep portages to a minimum and should realize that landowners may place fences and other barriers across streams for purposes of land or water management or to establish land ownership, if otherwise allowed by law.

Portage Routes

The law sets out a process by which either a landowner or a member of the public may, if necessary, request that a portage route over or around a barrier be established. Montana Fish, Wildlife and Parks encourages, however, that portage problems be resolved through other means if at all possible. If establishing a portage route is deemed the only workable solution, the request would have to be submitted to the board of supervisors of the local conservation or grazing district, or to the board of county commissioners. For assistance in determining where to file a request, or for other information regarding establishment of a portage route, maintenance, and signing, contact the Montana Fish, Wildlife and Parks' Portage Coordinator at (406) 444-2449.

Liability

The legislature has limited the situations in which a landowner may be liable for injuries to people using a stream flowing through his property. This limitation on liability applies not only to the landowner but also to his agent or tenant and to supervisors who participate in a decision regarding a portage route. The law states that landowners and others covered by the restriction on liability are liable only for acts or omissions that constitute "willful or wanton misconduct."

Prescriptive Easements and Land Title

The legislature has stated that a prescriptive easement cannot be acquired through recreational use of rivers and streams, the beds and banks, portage routes, or property crossed to reach streams. It has also said that the law does not affect title to surface waters, including the beds and banks of any rivers or streams, or portage routes used by the public.

Trespass Legislation

This legislation states that a member of the public has the privilege to enter or remain on private land by the explicit permission of the landowner or his agent or by the failure of the landowner to post notice denying entry onto the land. The landowner may revoke the permission by personal communication.

The law states that notice denying entry must consist of written notice or of notice by painting a post, structure or natural object with at least 50 square inches of fluorescent orange paint. In the case of a metal fencepost, the entire post must be painted. This notice must be placed at each outer gate and all normal points of access to the property and wherever a stream crosses an outer boundary line.

Access from County Roads at Bridge Crossings

Recreationists may gain access to streams and rivers from a county road right-of-way at bridge crossings. However, recreationists should be aware that (1) access at a bridge could be restricted by a county commission for public safety and (2) access at some bridges may be restricted where the establishment of the county road right-of-way did not allow access to the stream or river.

About the Authors

Hank Fischer has been floating Montana rivers for over thirty years and has written about them in publications like *Canoe, Backpacker, Sierra,* and *Montana Outdoors.* He received a master's degree from the University of Montana in environmental studies and worked for Defenders of Wildlife as their Northern Rockies field representative for twenty-five years. He now works for the National Wildlife Federation in Missoula, Montana.

He is author of *Wolf Wars: The Remarkable Inside Story of the Restoration of Wolves to Yellowstone* (Fischer Outdoor Discoveries, 2003) and coauthor of the *Montana Wildlife Viewing Guide* (Falcon, 1995)

Carol Fischer holds a Master of Science degree in forestry from the University of Montana with an emphasis in recreation resource management. She is coauthor of the *Montana Wildlife Viewing Guide.* Carol is an avid floater, angler, hiker, golfer, skier, and fisherwoman. She has worked as a fishing guide and was co-owner of an international wildlife travel company. Carol lives with her husband Hank in Missoula, Montana.

Kit Fischer has been floating Montana rivers for nearly all of his twenty-five years. He is an American Canoe Association certified kayak instructor and an avid fisherman and hunter. Kit has a B.A. in English from Colorado College and has worked for the Peace Corps in Zambia promoting aquaculture and as a fishing guide in Mongolia.